THE WOMEN'S AWAKENING IN EGYPT

THE WOMEN'S
AWAKENING IN EGYPT

Culture, Society, and the Press

BETH BARON

Yale University Press ❧ New Haven & London

Published with assistance from the Simon H. Rifkind Center for
the Humanities at the City College of New York.

Designed by Jill Breitbarth and set in Berkeley Book type by
Tseng Information Systems, Inc., Durham, North Carolina.
Printed in the United States of America by BookCrafters, Inc.,
Chelsea, Michigan.

Library of Congress Cataloging-in-Publication Data
Baron, Beth.
The women's awakening in Egypt : culture, society, and the press /
Beth Baron.
p. cm.
Includes bibliographical references and index.
ISBN 0-300-05563-3 (cloth: alk. paper)
0-300-07271-6 (pbk.: alk. paper)
1. Women—Egypt—Social conditions.   2. Women—Egypt—
Intellectual life.   3. Women's periodicals, Arabic—Egypt—
History—19th century.   4. Women's periodicals, Arabic—Egypt
—History—20th century.   5. Egypt—Intellectual life—19th
century.   6. Egypt—Intellectual life—20th century.
I. Title.
HQ1793   1994
059' 927'082—dc20   93-27067   CIP

A catalogue record for this book is available from the
British Library.

The paper in this book meets the guidelines for permanence and
durability of the Committee on Production Guidelines for Book
Longevity of the Council on Library Resources.

10 9 8 7 6 5 4 3 2

To my parents
and to T. and N.

CONTENTS

ACKNOWLEDGMENTS

When I first began research on women and the family in turn-of-the-century Egypt, I set aside two weeks for reading Arabic women's periodicals housed in Dar al-Kutub (the Egyptian National Library). As I began to read the journals, one led to another and weeks turned into months. The focus of my inquiry changed to a study of the intellectuals behind the early women's press. This seemed a necessary step before tapping the periodicals as a source for Egyptian cultural and social history. It is my hope that more scholars will be persuaded by this study to peruse the pages of Arabic women's periodicals.

A book about literary culture is particularly indebted to the librarians and archivists who have contributed to the preservation of that culture. I would like to thank the staffs at Dar al-Kutub and Dar al-Watha'iq al-Qawmiyya (the Egyptian National Archives). Many Egyptians assisted me during my stay, which the Fulbright Commission of Egypt facilitated. The friendships of Soha Abdel Kader and of Fifi Mandour made it a much richer experience.

This book has evolved over a period of years. Amos Funkenstein, Afaf Marsot, Georges Sabagh, and Kathryn Kish Sklar steered me in the early stages in framing the appropriate questions. Kamal Abdel-Malek, Leila Ahmed, Muhammad Amin, Annette Aronowicz, Ami Ayalon, Nathan Brown, Israel Gershoni, Albert Hourani, Thomas Philipp, Sasson

Somekh, and Gabriel Warburg gave perceptive comments and useful suggestions. Gene Garthwaite, Mary Kelley, P. J. Vatikiotis, and Malcolm Yapp have inspired me to persist on the path of historical inquiry. And Nikki Keddie has been a reader, adviser, co-editor, and friend whose guidance has been highly valued.

My colleagues in the history department at City College have encouraged me in my work. Dean Paul Sherwin has been especially kind, giving both moral and financial support. Funding for this project has come from a Fulbright-Hays Fellowship, the Woodrow Wilson Foundation, the National Endowment of the Humanities, the American Council of Learned Societies, the Professional Staff Congress of the City University of New York, and the Simon H. Rifkind Center for the Humanities at the City College of the City University of New York.

It has been my great pleasure to work with the staff at Yale University Press once again. Charles Grench's enthusiasm and Eliza Childs's empathy helped me over the last hurdles.

Itzik Nakash read the manuscript more times than he cared to, sharing his vision of history. I thank him for his insights and assistance at critical moments. And I thank my parents for the gift of education, a treasure that transcends borders and time.

INTRODUCTION

When the monthly journal *al-Fatah* (The young woman) appeared in
Alexandria, Egypt, in November 1892, its editor Hind Nawfal called it
the "first of its kind under the Eastern sky" and promised to "adorn its
pages with pearls from the pens of women." Hind explained that she had
established *al-Fatah* to defend women's rights and express their views,
and she called on women to send in their literary contributions. "Do not
imagine that a woman who writes in a journal is compromising her modesty or violating her purity and good behavior," she assured her readers.[1]
Al-Fatah was the first in a series of Arabic periodicals by, for, and about
women that came to be known as *al-majallat al-nisa'iyya* (women's journals). By the eve of the 1919 revolution, close to thirty such periodicals
had been produced for circulation inside and outside of Egypt.[2]

These Arabic women's journals present us with a unique historical
source and give us an opportunity to recover the voices of women so
that we can balance other accounts of their lives with their own descriptions. Collectively the journals are one of the earliest troves of material
of this sort, for this was the first generation of women in the Arab world
to write in numbers and to produce and publish their works as printed
texts. Editors and chroniclers of the press who noted the appearance
of women's journals at the time were not unaware of the significance
of women's entry onto the literary stage. Martin Hartmann, a German

scholar who collected copies of Arabic periodicals in Egypt, remarked as early as 1899, "The 'Ladies' Journal,' written by women is quite a conspicuous feature in the press, and bids fair to be a lasting one."[3]

The Arabic press flourished in Egypt from the late 1870s for a variety of reasons. The government had relinquished its monopoly on publishing and from the time of the British occupation in 1882 had limited its censorship of the press. The middle and upper classes had the funds to invest in literature, the number of printing presses increased, and printed texts multiplied. Journals and newspapers quickly became important media for communication. The women's press developed from the early 1890s, almost from the start of the private press, in response to increasing interest in women's affairs and a growing female readership. Women's journals explored new markets, providing a forum to debate such issues as marriage and divorce, veiling and seclusion, and education and work. At the same time, they offered domestic instruction and entertainment.

The dawn of the Arabic women's press led to the rise of a new female literary culture in Egypt. As literacy opened a new world to a growing number of young women, literary expression became a way to advance their cause. Almost anything seemed possible in a world of expanding horizons, and the enthusiasm of these years was palpable and infectious. The sense of progress and possibility was summed up by a phrase that recurred throughout the women's press: *al-nahda al-nisa'iyya* (the women's awakening). Female intellectuals used this term to describe the literary movement that they led, yet it also took on a broader cultural and social resonance. It referred to, among other developments, expansion in education, the rise of associations, and greater mobility for women. The phrase captured the mood of the period—the sense of momentous beginnings—marking the origins of the women's movement in Egypt.

Newspapers and periodicals proved key instruments for transmitting ideas in Egypt. Many books first appeared serialized in the press, speeches were reprinted there, and new forms, styles, and language emerged from its pages.[4] The Arabic press has proven a rich source for the views of intellectuals and has been mined for expressions of public opinion. However, the means by which the press was produced and consumed, the mechanism by which it disseminated ideas, and its impact on society remain elusive. The connection between ideas and social change therefore becomes a leap of faith. A study of the Egyptian women's press and the intellectuals behind it allows us to trace the transmission of culture within a society in an effort to span that leap of faith.

The Women's Awakening in Egypt examines the connections between literary culture and social transformation. It explores the nexus between the production of a group of writers—who formed the vanguard of a female intellectual elite—and change in the lives of women. The degree of this change, its direction, and its timing have all been subjects of contention. With respect to the period 1800 to 1914, Gabriel Baer wrote, "Evidently the traditional structure of the family and the status of women did not undergo any change at all."[5] Although she concurs that there was no radical transformation in family structure, Judith Tucker disagrees with the notion that women's status did not undergo a transition in that period. In her view, the restructuring of Egyptian agriculture toward production of a cash crop (cotton) under a centralizing state weakened the peasant family as a unit of production, to women's disadvantage. Egypt's entry into the world market further undermined domestic crafts and small businesses and hurt the family economy and cottage industries upon which many women depended. These processes, as well as the policies of the colonial state, constricted the activities of peasant and urban lower-class women, eroding women's position in the family and society.[6]

This book shifts focus from peasants and lower-class women to middle- and upper-class women in Egypt, attempting to show that significant changes occurred in their lives in the decades before the 1919 revolution. The study ends in 1919 when the narrative of Egyptian women's history and the story of the women's movement often begins.[7] Yet women's participation in the 1919 revolution must be seen as a continuation of actions undertaken in earlier decades. Moreover, the seeds that bore fruit in the 1920s and 1930s—notably the formation of women's organizations, educational and legislative reform, and greater integration in society—were planted from the 1890s. The Egyptian women's press stood at the center of this process, documenting and defending a widening range of activities in certain urban circles.

The existence of a body of Arabic women's journals pioneered by female intellectuals in Egypt from the late nineteenth century calls for a rethinking of the intellectual history of the period. Preoccupation with tracing the origins of feminism, however broadly defined, has led to an approach which treats the idea like a baton, passing from one thinker to the next. Scholars point to Rifa'a al-Tahtawi as one of the earliest modern Egyptian writers to consider the situation of women. The relevant works by him usually mentioned are *Takhlis al-Ibriz fi Talkhis Bariz* (Manners and customs of the modern Parisians, 1834) and *Manahij al-Amin li'l-Banat wa'l-Banin* (The faithful guide for girls and boys, 1873). That the two books were separated by almost forty years suggests that the importance of the woman question in his corpus of work may have been exaggerated.[8] Others have looked for connections between luminary thinkers, with one scholar arguing that the journal *al-Lata'if,* edited by the Syrian immigrant Shahin Makariyus, was the conduit of feminist ideas in the 1880s and 1890s linking Tahtawi and Qasim Amin, an Egyptian judge.[9] Though Makariyus's wife, Maryam Nimr, wrote many of the articles on women in *al-Lata'if,* she is seen as an instrument of the Masonic program rather than a thinker in her own right. Emphasizing the connections between well-known figures tends to marginalize women writers and their intellectual production.

Nowhere is the pattern of stressing male thinkers at the expense of female ones more apparent than in the focus on Qasim Amin as the central figure in the turn-of-the-century debate on women and society. In response to a French writer's criticism of the status of women in Egypt, Amin had defended Islam in 1894. But he turned to a reformist posture in *Tahrir al-Mar'a* (The emancipation of woman, 1899) and arrived at the secularist stance for which he is best known in *al-Mar'a al-Jadida* (The new woman, 1900). Among other positions, he advocated education for women, reform in marriage and divorce, and unveiling. Although he suggested that a woman be prepared for some profession, preferably one of high status should she need to support herself or her children, he favored a domestic vocation for her.[10]

Preoccupation with Qasim Amin and his cohort has led to a misconception that women were not actively engaged in the debate on women's role in society, or that they only joined a few years later when the Egyptian Muslim Malak Hifni Nasif began to write. "An irony of the early feminist literary debate among Egyptian Muslims in the years 1899–1902 . . . is that it was conducted by men," writes Juan Cole.[11] Robert Tignor acknowledges the participation of a few women in the women's rights movement in the prewar period but contends that of the participants "the majority were men from the urban areas."[12] Drawing on these assertions and others, many scholars credit men with founding and leading the women's movement not only in Egypt but in the Arab world. Yvonne Haddad notes that the Arab feminist movement's "most prominent advocates have been men who took up the cause of women."[13] The repercussions of such perceptions, in particular the seeming absence of a sizable coterie of female precursors, must certainly have had a negative impact on later female intellectuals and activists.

Why Amin became the center of attention and has been the subject of such frequent study remains to be explained by historiographers. No doubt his stature as a judge and license to speak as a man made many Egyptian women look to Amin to legitimize their positions. Yet Leila Ahmed has recently reexamined Amin's writings and concluded that he was not "the father of Arab feminism," as so many claim, but rather "the son of Cromer [British consul general in Egypt] and colonialism." Attempting to dethrone Amin by showing that many of his ideas echoed colonial thinking about women's status in Muslim society, she contends that his book *Tahrir al-Mar'a* "merely called for the substitution of Islamic-style male dominance by Western-style male dominance."[14]

The great irony is not that men helped or hurt women's struggle to advance, but that many of those women who were active in this cause have been pushed to the background or have been left out of the story altogether. Only a couple of poets, a few authors who published in the general press, and the noted feminist leader Huda Sha'rawi have received attention.[15] In fact, the debate on the rights of woman was well under way in the women's press and elsewhere when Qasim Amin made his mark. By concentrating on Amin, many scholars have missed the wider intellectual milieu and the complexity of the discussions on the role of women in Egyptian society. The debate grew lively among a certain segment of the population, reflected diverse opinions, and included numbers of women as well as men. *The Women's Awakening in Egypt* pulls back the camera that has been focused on a few male intellectuals and fewer female ones to reveal a wide array of female intellectuals engaged in thinking about women's roles and gender relations in Egypt in the decades before and after the turn of the century.

These female thinkers established agendas for reform and programs of action for the twentieth century. They are thus critical to our understanding of the roots of feminism in Egypt and, by implication, in the Arab world, where Egypt has taken the leading role in the struggle for women's rights. Yet whether one should label all these women as feminists is questionable. Coined in late nineteenth-century France, the word *féminisme* spread from there into other lands and languages.[16] In Arabic, the term *nisa'iyya* (women's) took on the added meaning of feminist, often generating confusion over the correct translation, which must be determined by context. But in pre-1919 Egypt this new meaning was not widespread, especially as Egyptian women's advocates generally tried to distance themselves from Western suffragettes and activists in this period.

Problems with the term *feminism* transcend the question of Arabic translation as scholars have debated the definition of feminism and its historical applications. Some have argued that expanding the roles of women within the family constitutes feminism, whereas others have seen the family as an anathema to women's freedom and focus on endeavors that strove to dismantle boundaries and to press for complete political, economic, and social equality as feminism. Women's advocates in pre-1919 Egypt usually fit into the first category (those seeking to enhance women's position in the home), and few into the second (with its focus on individual rights). Other men and women who claimed to speak on behalf of women defied this categorization altogether. Where do you place those who argued for stricter seclusion and heavier veiling in the belief that this would raise women's status? Is "Islamist feminist" a contradiction in terms? Conflating diverse positions and labeling all women's advocates as feminists obscures important differences of opinion as well as strategies for change. Moreover, positions fell along ideological rather than gender lines, with differences among men and women and not just between them.[17]

A range of opinion on the rights of woman evolved in the women's press in Egypt, with women's advocates falling roughly into three camps: secularist, modernist, and Islamist. The secularists, who proved few in number outside the circles of minorities, concentrated on matters such as language and education, which were less likely to provoke controversy. The modernists spoke of improving women's position within the family through innovative religious interpretations. The Islamists, in opposition to secularists, modernists, and religious conservatives alike, stressed the rights Islam had given to women and called for a return to "true Islam." Although arguments were often blended, the lines of debate were set in the early years of the women's press and have persisted, with one or another winning ascendancy at different moments.

The extent to which nineteenth- and twentieth-century intellectuals of different tendencies have been influenced by Western ideas has been debated.[18] That many of the earliest women writers in Egypt were Syrian Christians—a category that included women from present-day Lebanon as well as Syria[19]—has led some to conclude that they were little interested in the situation of Egyptian women and more concerned with the affairs of Western women.[20] This generalization comes mostly from an analysis of views expressed in the general monthly *al-Muqtataf,* though these cannot be said to be representative of opinions expressed in the women's press.[21] Syrian editors aiming women's journals toward Egyptian consumers ignored the interests of their reading public at their own risk. Although they served as transmitters of culture, they remained critical of the West, seeking a modernizing path with indigenous roots for the East. The Syrian immigrants provided a forum for Egyptians of Turkish background, Copts, and others, who soon started their own publications. The founders of the women's press were an ethnically and religiously diverse group, reflecting wide currents of Egyptian and Arab society, and their journals presented a wide range of views. They were no doubt aware of the Western colonial discourse, or more properly discourses, on gender but were not completely swayed by them. These writers wrestled with ideas in a critical fashion and grappled like other intellectuals of their day with problems of culture, identity, and change.

The Women's Awakening in Egypt situates the debates on the role of women in society in their specific historical settings. This approach was chosen to counter a popular tendency to treat Middle Eastern women ahistorically. For example, the Qur'an and contemporary Egyptian family legislation are invoked in the same breath to describe women's situation in spite of profound changes in their social concerns, economic conditions, and political circumstances over time. Another feature of the literature on Middle Eastern women has been frequent reliance on texts and treatises authored by men, as we have seen above, even when writings by women have been available. These latter works, and the information they contain, can often be used as a corrective to the tendency to abstract the issues and to lose sight of the individuals at the heart of the debate. To lay the foundation for further research, it therefore seems essential to reconstruct the lives of women writers and recover their texts, a process just beginning. There is a newer trend in the analysis of discourse to depict Egyptian and other Arab thinkers as passive recipients of colonial formulations, an approach that runs the risk of marginalizing women. Here the process of cultural contact is seen as more dynamic and complex. Female intellectuals were active agents, sifting and weighing various ideas, absorbing some and reacting against others, and shaping their own programs.

The first half of *The Women's Awakening in Egypt* focuses on the female writers who pioneered the Arabic women's press and their lives and literary output. It traces the process of creating Arabic literary texts, in this case journals, from production to consumption. Who were the intellectuals behind the women's press? How did they overcome the social and psychological obstacles to writing and publishing their works? Why did they turn to the crafting of journals and how did they deal with the financial constraints? What do we know about the consumers of the press—its readers—and their interaction with printed texts? The presumption here is that in order to understand the historical meaning and impact of a text, it is not enough to read the work, analyze it, and assume it had an influence. Only by examining the process through which a text was created and disseminated can we begin to assess its historical importance.

The second half of *The Women's Awakening in Egypt* sets texts in their social contexts. It turns to specific debates carried on in the women's press, placing them against the backdrop of late nineteenth- and early twentieth-century changes. What positions did these intellectuals carve out on the issue of "the rights of woman"? What sort of education did they advocate and who was responsible for delivering it? To what extent did their vision of domesticity and agenda for family reform reflect the needs and working conditions of most Egyptian women? How did the associations that emerged during this period nurture political activism and contribute to social welfare? Female intellectuals clearly served as astute observers and sharp social critics, but it is less clear how they affected and directed social change. This section explores that link, the relationship between intellectuals and society.

Taken together, information from the women's press, archival reports, census data, travelers' accounts, and other evidence show that the lives of urban middle- and upper-class Egyptian women underwent a significant transition in the late nineteenth and early twentieth centuries. This is apparent in their new literary, educational, economic, and associational activities. The cumulative weight of these experiences, and the sense that real improvement in women's lives was at hand, fueled belief in the awakening of women.

Part One

FROM
PRODUCTION
TO CONSUMPTION

1

PIONEERS OF THE
WOMEN'S PRESS

Women's journals appeared at a well-documented moment in Egyptian history. Yet the women who edited or owned journals generally sought to avoid the public eye and rarely left memoirs or autobiographical accounts. As a result, information about their lives is sketchy and must be patched together from a variety of sources, including biographical dictionaries, archival materials, and close readings of their own works. Syrians tended to write more about one another and left a longer trail than Egyptians, but even their record is sparse. This chapter sets the individual biographies of the women who founded the women's press in the context of Egyptian political history. The women's journals that were started by men will also be introduced.

The rise of the women's press paralleled the emergence of the nationalist movement in Egypt. Was this mere coincidence? The connection between the nationalist press and politics is clear, for the press was the leading medium for debating political issues. Yet the relationship between the women's press and national politics seems less apparent, especially as the writers in the women's press rarely discussed contemporary politics explicitly and made only passing reference, if any, to some of the most important events of the day. The writers were not oblivious to these events, however, or unaffected by them. National and regional politics formed the backdrop for the press, defined its parameters, and helped to shape the perspectives of writers. The emergence of nationalism meant a reimagining of the community and ties of loyalty, and, by implication, a rethinking of the family and gender roles.¹ The women's press took up the latter issues.

THE BIRTH OF THE WOMEN'S JOURNAL

The family of Hind Nawfal, the founder of *al-Fatah* (The young woman, 1892), arrived in Egypt from coastal Syria in the 1870s during the reign of Khedive Isma'il (r. 1863–1879). Although the mothers of most writers are absent from the historical record, Hind's mother proved exceptional. Maryam al-Nahhas (1856–1888) grew up in Beirut during a period of civil unrest and economic depression. At about the age of sixteen she married Nasim Nawfal, who was ten years her senior and from a Greek Orthodox Tripolian family. They joined the growing stream of Syrians leaving for different parts of the world.² Settled in Alexandria, Maryam al-Nahhas completed a biographical dictionary of Eastern and Western women, *Ma'rid al-Hasna' fi Tarajim Mashahir al-Nisa'* (The beautiful woman's exhibition for the biographies of female celebrities). She dedicated it to Princess Cheshmat Hanim, the third wife of Isma'il, who sponsored publication of the first volume in 1879. The second volume was never published, however, for the manuscript was lost during the chaos that accompanied the 'Urabi revolt.³

Isma'il spent large sums of money on building projects to transform Egypt into a modern society and on tributes to the Ottoman sultan to insure that his direct descendants would remain hereditary governors of Egypt. His borrowing at high rates from European lenders sunk the country deep into debt and ultimately, in 1876, into bankruptcy. Isma'il then tried to block the foreign commission created to oversee Egyptian finances and encouraged a free press in an effort to stir anti-European opposition. The late 1870s thus marked the birth of the political press in Egypt with the appearance of such papers as *Abu Nazzara Zarqa'*, *Mir'at al-Sharq,* and *Misr al-Fatah*. In 1879 the Ottoman government, pressured by the European powers, replaced the noncompliant Isma'il with his more docile son Tawfiq (r. 1879–1892).

Tawfiq's inability to curb European financial and increasing political control sparked Egyptian discontent. Provincial notables demanded a constitution and aligned themselves with a group of indigenous Egyptian officers, who felt blocked in promotions by the Turco-Circassian elite. European representatives in Egypt as well as the khedive viewed the alliance, led by an army officer named Ahmad 'Urabi, with mistrust. Tensions grew, spurred by poor harvests and peasant indebtedness, and disturbances broke out throughout the country, escalating into the Alexandrian riots of June 1882.[4] The British kept a close watch on unfolding events because the Suez Canal, inaugurated by Isma'il with great fanfare in 1869, had become the main artery of their empire, linking England and India. In the wake of the riots, the British decided to remove 'Urabi and his cohorts from power and restore the status quo. When the British navy bombarded Alexandria in July, Tawfiq sought their protection. 'Urabi rallied forces to counter the subsequent invasion, but British troops quickly routed the Egyptian army and by September had occupied the country. Sir Evelyn Baring (Lord Cromer) was named British agent and consul general. Cromer virtually ran the Egyptian government from 1883 until his retirement in 1907, although Egypt was still legally a province of the Ottoman Empire.

After the relative lull that followed the 'Urabi revolt, the press took off in the late 1880s with the foundation of *al-Mu'ayyad* (1889), among other papers.[5] In the absence of alternative outlets for discussion, such as a parliament or parties, the press gave the nascent nationalist movement and other currents in Egypt a voice. The new khedive 'Abbas Hilmi II (r. 1892–1914) encouraged nationalist activities in an effort to undermine the British and augment his own power, and this further boosted the press. There was an explosion of periodicals and newspapers, some of which were financed by 'Abbas, the British, and the French, or by other personalities and powers.

As Ottoman censorship in Arab provinces stiffened in the 1880s and 1890s, some Syrian writers moved to Egypt, attracted by the larger market of readers. There they found greater opportunity for free expression and joined Syrians who had migrated earlier for various reasons. Syrians proved influential in the early years of the Arabic press and owned close to 20 percent of the newspapers and journals founded in Egypt before World War I.[6] The Taqla brothers (Salim and Bishara) had started the daily *al-Ahram* in the mid-1870s, and Adib Ishaq helped to found *Misr* and edited *Misr al-Fatah*. Syrians also pioneered literary and scientific journals, providing a forum to debate social and cultural questions. Faris Nimr, Ya'qub Sarruf, and Shahin Makariyus moved the monthly *al-Muqtataf* from Beirut to Cairo in the mid-1880s (they also founded the daily *al-Muqattam*), and Jurji Zaydan started *al-Hilal* in 1892.[7]

That year marked the appearance of Hind Nawfal's *al-Fatah*, which came on the scene at a propitious moment. In spite of the variety of literary and scientific journals in 1892, none dealt specifically with women's issues or sought to express their views exclusively. Hind's father, who was also a writer, directed the office of the first Arabic women's journal, and her sister Sarah assisted. While still editing the journal, Hind, who had grown up in Alexandria and studied at one of the convent schools there, became engaged to a Syrian who worked in the legal section of the Ministry of Finance. The engagement was announced in *al-Fatah*, and Hind was married to Habib Dabbana in August 1893. The following year the last issue of the journal appeared. Hind withdrew to a life of domesticity and philanthropy, having launched a literary idea.[8]

THE IDEA TAKES HOLD

After a hiatus of two years, a second women's journal appeared in June 1896, Louisa Habbalin's *al-Firdaus* (Paradise). The Habbalin family came from the Syrian village of Zuq Mikha'il and boasted several literati. *Al-Firdaus* was the first journal of this sort based in Cairo and covered such topics as household management and childraising. It seems to have lasted at least until 1898; in that year it accused another journal of pirating material.[9]

Mir'at al-Hasna' (Mirror of the beautiful), edited by Maryam Mazhar, was first published in Cairo in November 1896, shortly after *al-Firdaus*. This bimonthly, which featured marriage notices, wedding reports, and serialized stories, ran for at least sixteen issues. Notices in other journals welcomed *Mir'at al-Hasna'*, although there was some confusion about the identity of the editor.[10] Ten years later Salim Sarkis (1867–1926), a male Syrian writer living in Egypt, cleared up the mystery. In an article entitled "Who is Miss Maryam Mazhar?" Sarkis confessed that he had created Maryam and explained the reasons for the ruse.[11]

When editing *Lisan al-Hal* in Beirut in the 1880s, Sarkis had run into trouble with the Ottoman censor, who blocked some of the articles he presented. He decided to leave politics aside and publish articles by women, but he had problems finding volunteers. To encourage women to write, he invented Maryam Mazhar and printed several articles under her name. Sarkis claimed that the censor had told him not to publish articles by women "because that will open their minds more than is necessary" and it was not for women "to be concerned with these matters." [12] But readers were curious about Maryam Mazhar and wrote in to find out who she was: "If the inquiry came from Damascus, I said she was from Cairo. And if it was from Beirut, I said Aleppo," Sarkis recalled.[13]

Sarkis assailed Ottoman censorship under the autocracy of Sultan 'Abdul Hamid and left Beirut for Cairo, where he hoped to find greater press freedom.[14] Yet before long he ran into legal problems again, this time on the journal *al-Mushir,* and decided to publish a family magazine to avoid political tangles altogether. He resurrected Maryam Mazhar, transforming her from writer to editor of *Mir'at al-Hasna',* and devised intricate schemes to maintain the fiction. When the post office held her mail, he had "M. M." delegate "S. S." to receive it, and he had "M. M." name him her assistant. He even told readers that Maryam's brother had been murdered (after an Iskandar Mazhar was killed in Beirut) to test their credulity. The condolence letters and telegrams that poured in, plus a marriage proposal and a note from someone claiming to be a relative, confirmed that the subterfuge was a success. But when his case at *al-Mushir* came before the courts in the fall of 1897, he received a prison term, which meant the end of his women's journal.[15] Although Sarkis considered *Mir'at al-Hasna'* a success, it was more concerned with social gossip than social progress and was one of the less serious journals of this sort. Still, Sarkis had perceptively recognized that a market for an Arabic women's journal existed in late nineteenth-century Egypt.

Alexandra Avierino also sensed this demand and founded *Anis al-*

Jalis (The intimate companion) in Alexandria in 1898. Unlike most of her female colleagues, Alexandra sought public renown and a role in contemporary events, and government dossiers record some of her activities.[16] Alexandra was born into an affluent Greek Orthodox family in Beirut in November 1872. On her paternal side, her grandmother was Egyptian and her grandfather a protected Russian subject, a status her father Constantine Khuri inherited.[17] (Members of minorities in the Ottoman Empire often sought protection from one consulate or another in an effort to enjoy the privileges of foreigners.) Alexandra came to Egypt at about the age of fourteen and continued her education at one of the convent schools there. At sixteen or seventeen she married Miltiades di Avierino, one of eleven children of a Spanish mother and Italian father, whose family had come to Egypt in the time of Muhammad 'Ali and had gained British citizenship in service to the Crown.[18] Through marriage Alexandra became a British subject. Shortly thereafter she had two daughters—Irene and Gisèle—and a son—Alexander.

Alexandra pursued a variety of interests. She traveled to Paris in 1900 to represent Egyptian women at a conference of the Alliance Universelle des Femmes pour la Paix (Universal Alliance of Women for Peace), held during the Paris Exposition.[19] Its founder, Princess Gabriella Wiszniewska, was an active proponent of international disarmament; and the support of socially prominent women made this alliance one of the more enduring peace societies in Europe.[20] Alexandra captured the Princess's affection, and the latter decided to adopt Alexandra and bequeath to her her title. After the Princess's death, and a subsequent trip to Rome to arrange the matter, Alexandra presented herself as "Princess Alexandra di Avierino Wiszniewska."[21]

Alexandra had started her journal *Anis al-Jalis* two years before her trip to Paris. She dedicated the first issue of the Arabic monthly to the wife and the mother of Khedive 'Abbas, presenting them with copies of the journal in a private audience.[22] She ran the journal with editorial assistance and her husband's help in the office. *Anis al-Jalis* thrived, carrying articles by Muslim and Christian men and women on a variety of topics. Alexandra Avierino received honors from the Ottoman sultan, the shah of Iran, the pope in Rome, among others, for—in her words—

"disseminating new ideas aimed at improving the situation of woman and serving her noble cause."[23] Alexandra started a French literary revue similar to her Arabic journal in 1901. She aimed *Le Lotus* at Egyptian francophiles and European readers interested in "the Orient." The journal attempted to fill a "lacuna in the intellectual life of Egypt" and was well received. The French government honored her for the enterprise. But the artfully produced journal proved too expensive to publish and did not last beyond its first year.[24] Alexandra continued to produce *Anis al-Jalis* for over a decade, until losses incurred in the 1907 economic crisis forced her to close it down.

In addition to producing two journals, Alexandra wrote poetry and a play. She also regularly held a salon at her home for male and female intellectuals, writers, and poets.[25] Alexandra cultivated literary and political contacts throughout her life. She contributed to pro-British newspapers like *al-Muqattam* and pro-khedivial ones like *al-Mu'ayyad*. She corresponded with Khedive 'Abbas and interceded with government officials to get appointments and grades for clients.[26] She was even deemed by a British official to be "of considerable use to our intelligence organisations in this country [Egypt] at various times."[27]

Yet the elite that came to dominate Egyptian politics after World War I had no sympathy for Syrians who had been actively pro-British or too closely allied with the now ex-khedive. In this changed political climate, Alexandra was considered a nuisance and became entangled in a web of legal difficulties. First the British questioned her status and that of her children as British citizens, and in order to resolve these and other matters, Alexandra spent eighteen months in England in the early 1920s. Then she was arrested in Egypt in July 1924, accused of complicity in the assassination attempt on the life of Prime Minister Sa'd Zaghlul. Government officials opened her mail, searched her house, read her diaries and papers, and examined her possessions. But prosecutors found no incriminating evidence, and after questioning her for several days brought no charges.[28] This interrogation proved part of an ongoing effort by Egyptian authorities to deport Alexandra, for they resented her activities on behalf of 'Abbas and her involvement in politics in general. They considered charging her with using her house for purposes of prostitution, suggesting that she and a British guest of hers had entertained a number of prominent men, among them the vice-president of the Wafd party. Again officials found no evidence for their claim.[29] A few months after the July inquiry, Alexandra left for England. She was later denied re-entry into Egypt and died in London in 1926.

Alexandra had become a victim of the fighting that erupted between the various parties that emerged in Egypt in the 1920s. Although she claimed to have worked for Zaghlul's release when he was in exile, he called her a "danger to public security" and initiated the move to deport her. Other government officials depicted her as an intriguer. Even Alexandra's son had told an administrator that his mother "was extremely fond of politics and intrigue and was, in these matters, 'like a child.'"[30] Yet women who were interested in influencing political affairs had few channels open to them, barred as they were from elections, parties, and the new parliament.

A FLURRY OF JOURNALS

A year after Alexandra Avierino started *Anis al-Jalis,* Esther Azhari Moyal (1873–1948), who had contributed to that journal and had earlier been a contributor to Hind Nawfal's *al-Fatah,* founded the bimonthly *al-'A'ila* (The family, 1899) in Cairo. Unlike most of the other early editors of the women's press, who were Syrian Christians, Esther came from a Syrian Jewish family from Beirut. She studied languages and other subjects at English and American schools and after graduation taught at Scottish Church Mission and Alliance Israélite Universelle schools and then directed the girls' school of a Muslim benevolent society. She was also active in the first Arab women's associations—*Bakurat Suriyya* (Dawn of Syria) and *Nahdat al-Sayyidat* (The ladies' awakening).[31] Her activities suggest that in certain educated circles in Beirut at the time, social and sectarian boundaries were permeable.

Esther's great foray into international women's affairs was her participation in the World Columbian Exposition in Chicago in 1893. Although Syrian correspondents had informed the head of the Board of Lady Managers that they could not obtain official government support, a small group, including Esther and Hanna Kisbani Kurani, mounted a Syrian

exhibit in the Women's Building.[32] Zaynab Fawwaz, a Syri/
in Egypt, encouraged Egyptian women to prepare handwⅎ
Chicago Fair and sent a copy of her own book for the exposition; but
she explained that as a Muslim woman she could not attend the mixed
gathering.[33]

A year after the exhibition and at about the age of twenty, Esther
married a young medical student named Shimon Moyal. Three years
her senior, he had come to Beirut from Jaffa. When he completed his
studies, they moved to Cairo, where Shimon practiced medicine. Interested in promoting intercommunal dialogue, he joined a Masonic Lodge
and translated the Palestinian Talmud from Aramaic and Hebrew into
Arabic.[34] Esther and Shimon had a son whom they named 'Abdallah after
the Egyptian nationalist 'Abdallah al-Nadim.[35]

Esther started *al-'A'ila* in 1899 and directed it at least until 1904 and
possibly through 1907, running articles on domestic and literary subjects.[36] Although it was not typical for a women's periodical to cover
world news, Esther discussed the Dreyfus affair in France and had a
keen interest in the novelist Emile Zola, who was one of Alfred Dreyfus's
defenders.[37] She wrote a biography of Zola, and his novels were among
the dozen or so that she translated from French into Arabic.[38]

At about the time of the 1908 Young Turk revolution that restored the
Ottoman Constitution, or shortly thereafter, the Moyals moved to Jaffa.
There Esther founded a women's organization and continued her literary
activities. She edited the paper *al-Akhbar* and helped her husband with
the bilingual Arabic-Hebrew *Sawt al-'Uthmaniyya* (The Ottoman voice).[39]
Like many Arab intellectuals before World War I, the Moyals probably
saw the Young Turk revolution as an end to despotic rule and an opening for greater political participation through decentralization. After her
husband's death in 1915, Esther and her family left the Middle East for
Marseilles, where she worked as a merchant. Sometime in the 1940s,
and probably fleeing the Nazi round-up of foreign Jews in France, Esther
returned to Palestine, then a British mandate, contributing once again to
the local press.[40]

The debate about women's status and role in society intensified at
the turn of the century, inflamed by the writings of Qasim Amin, whose

works must be seen in the context of the women's press and its concern with the rights of women.[41] Some of the half dozen or so women's periodicals that appeared at this time took part in these debates, although they also dealt with women's domestic lives and daily concerns. Cairo, by then the preeminent capital of publishing in Egypt, was home to at least three new journals dealing exclusively or partially with women's affairs. *Al-Hawanim* (The ladies) surfaced in 1900 as a weekly edited by Ahmad Hilmi, an Egyptian Muslim.[42] *Al-Mar'a fi'l-Islam* (The woman in Islam) appeared in March of the following year as a bimonthly, edited by another male Egyptian Muslim writer, Ibrahim Ramzi.[43] The bimonthly *al-Mar'a* (The woman) materialized in 1901, edited by Anisa 'Atallah, probably a Syrian Muslim woman.[44] Alexandria, the second publishing center of Egypt, was the site of Maryam Sa'd's *al-Zahra* (The flower) in 1902, and Salim Khalil Farah's *al-Muda* (Fashion) the following year.[45] According to press notices, these publications were generally by, for, and about women and ranged from social criticism to entertainment. Most proved ephemeral, however, and hardly left a trace.[46] Yet taken together with the other women's periodicals that circulated during this period, they show abundant female literary activity at the turn of the century. This should help to correct the misperception that women left the debate on their rights to men.

AN ECHO FROM THE PAST

One of the most intriguing journals that appeared in Alexandria was a bilingual Turkish-Arabic monthly entitled *Shajarat al-Durr* (1901) after the famed medieval sultana Shajar al-Durr.[47] Edited by Sa'diyya Sa'd al-Din Zadeh and including articles on women's rights, features, and correspondence, this journal was probably the first founded by a Muslim Egyptian woman.[48] An anonymous writer calling herself "Shajarat al-Durr" had earlier contributed several articles on Muslim women, marriage, divorce, and other topics to *Anis al-Jalis,* which was also located in Alexandria.[49] The coincidence of time and place suggests the hand of the same woman, about whom little is known. Perhaps her alter ego, "Shajar al-Durr," can provide some clues to her identity.

Shajar al-Durr (d. 1257) was the slave-wife of the medieval Ayyubid ruler of Egypt al-Malik al-Salih Najm al-Din 'Ayyub. During a Crusader onslaught, she hid her husband's death from his troops to prevent demoralization, and she issued edicts in his name until Turanshah, his son by another wife, returned from Iraq to succeed him. Turanshah quickly alienated his father's mamluks (slave-soldiers), who subsequently killed him and gave their backing to Shajar al-Durr. She then ruled as sultana, issuing coins and signing proclamations in her own name. But certain factions were unhappy about having a woman rule and forced her to marry one of the leading mamluks, 'Izz al-Din Aybak. Shajar al-Durr thus linked two dynasties that ruled Egypt for centuries, the Ayyubids (1171–1249) and Mamluks (1250–1517).[50] As one of a few Muslim women to have wielded open political power, Shajar al-Durr later became a symbol of female possibility.

Shajarat al-Durr was the only women's journal of this period whose title referred to a specific individual, and it was also the only bilingual Turkish-Arabic journal. We may infer that Sa'diyya Sa'd al-Din was an Egyptian Muslim of Turkish origin who identified with Egypt's earlier rulers. For centuries Egypt was run by Mamluks—Turkish or Circassian speakers who regularly replenished their ranks through the importation of male and female slaves.[51] Even after Egypt came under Ottoman control in 1517, the Mamluks regained autonomy and continued to import military and domestic slaves. Muhammad 'Ali, Ottoman viceroy of Egypt in the first half of the nineteenth century, finally decimated the Mamluk aristocracy and inaugurated a family dynasty in its stead. But Turco-Circassians continued to dominate key positions in the army and government for decades. Furthermore, the importation of female Circassian slaves for elite Ottoman and Egyptian harems persisted into the last quarter of the nineteenth century.

Some have argued that the status of these slaves was no worse, and sometimes better, than that of freed women, for they often belonged to wealthy owners and enjoyed certain comforts and rights. Although a man had free sexual access to his slave under Islamic law, if she bore him a child and he accepted paternity, she could not be sold and the child was free.[52] Circassian slaves were generally not responsible for heavy household work, which would have probably been left to servants or slaves of African origin. White slaves served as concubines and entertainers instead, and many were eventually married into elite families.[53] Through private tutoring and enrollment in schools, women of Turco-Circassian background and their daughters were among the earliest to have access to education and thus among the first to write in modern Egypt. For example, the poet 'A'isha al-Taymuriyya (c. 1840–1902), who had a Circassian mother and Kurdish father, composed diwans in Turkish, Arabic, and Persian; and slaves of the royal family entered one of the first state-sponsored schools for girls in 1873.[54]

With the signing of the Anglo-Egyptian Convention for the Suppression of the Slave Trade in 1877 and the transition to wage labor, domestic slavery began to fade. Many slaves were manumitted, while others lived out their lives with their owners. The elite became more Arabicized over time, and French and English gradually replaced Turkish in importance. Thus when Sa'diyya Sa'd al-Din published her journal in Turkish and Arabic, one otherwise enthusiastic reviewer wondered about "the benefit of founding it [the journal] in Turkish in this land after the Turkish language has almost completely disappeared."[55] Sa'diyya straddled two worlds, an old one that was passing and a new one that she was not quite ready to accept. Given the special privileges of those of Turkish descent in Egypt, it is not surprising that the first attempt by an Egyptian-born Muslim woman to start a journal was by a woman of Turkish background. Like many periodicals of the time, however, Sa'diyya's venture proved short-lived, possibly because there was little demand for a bilingual publication of this sort. Subsequent journals by women of similar background were published in Arabic.

OTHER SYRIAN VENTURES

Syrians remained prominent in the second decade of the women's press. Three women's journals started by Syrians in this period stressed Eastern or Arab unity and generally avoided Egyptian politics. Yet the first took a strange turn when hijacked by a family member for polemical purposes. Regina 'Awwad's monthly *al-Sa'ada* (Happiness, 1902), founded in Cairo, preached moderation and modesty. It contained instructional material as well as social commentary, both by now standard fare in a women's journal. Three volumes appeared from 1902 through 1904, printed on the press of Amin 'Awwad, a brother or a husband.

The journal reappeared in 1908 when Amin used it to publicize a new society calling for the equality of Ottomans—by which he meant Syrians—with Egyptians.[56] A number of political parties had been formed around newspapers in Egypt in 1907, advancing different Egyptian nationalist visions. Mustafa Kamil's al-Hizb al-Watani (Nationalist party) was linked to the paper al-Liwa' (1900). Calling for an immediate end to the British occupation, it emphasized Egyptian-Ottoman loyalties and proved the most popular nationalist party of the prewar period. Hizb al-Umma (Party of the Nation) championed a more secular territorial nationalism based on a break with the Ottomans. The organ al-Jarida (1907), edited by Ahmad Lutfi al-Sayyid, disseminated its views. A third party—Hizb al-Islah al-Dusturi (Constitutional Reform party)—formed around Shaykh 'Ali Yusuf's al-Mu'ayyad and was connected to the khedive.[57]

With the increasing vocalism of Egyptian nationalists, Syrians in Egypt who promoted Arabism and similar ideologies found themselves on uncertain ground, for Egyptian-Ottomanist and territorial nationalist tendencies were far stronger than an Egyptian Arab allegiance.[58] Many Egyptians resented the Syrians in Egypt, due to their success in various economic and cultural endeavors, their competition for government jobs, and their occasional support for the British occupation. Amin 'Awwad started his society to push for improved conditions for Syrians. He probably used al-Sa'ada as an outlet because Regina had a license to publish a journal at a time when such licenses were not easily obtained from the Ministry of Interior. Amin may not have fooled the Ministry's Press Bureau in altering the mandate of the journal, however, when after the 1909 reactivation of the 1881 Press Law the bureau became more vigilant. In any case, al- Sa'ada's second life proved short.

A year after Regina 'Awwad's al-Sa'ada appeared in Cairo, Rosa Antun's al-Sayyidat wa'l-Banat (Ladies and girls, 1903) came out in Alexandria. Rosa Antun (1882–1955) was born in the coastal city of Tripoli, one of five children of a Greek Orthodox family. Her mother Karima came from the Yaziji clan, which produced a number of well-known writers and poets, and her father was a lumber merchant. After her father's business began to fail, the family followed her brother Farah to Alexandria. There Rosa taught for a few years at the American missionary school in Ibrahimiyya, helping to support the family. (Rosa had attended American schools as a student.) She also assisted her brother in the production of his periodical *al-Jami'a* (1899).[59]

Rosa's journal fared better than her brother's, for Farah had alienated many readers by debating Muslim reformers. With his career stalled, he left for New York, where Rosa joined him in 1906 to help edit the now daily *al-Jami'a*. Three years later she married Niqula Haddad (d. 1954).[60] Haddad, a prolific writer who was ten years her senior, had studied pharmacy in Beirut but had taken up the pen. He contributed articles to the press (including the journal of his future wife and that of Esther Moyal), and authored more than thirty books over the years. Like his brother-in-law, he advocated socialism and similar progressive ideas.[61] But the bachelor Farah had apparently found his advanced ideas on marriage, presented in the book *al-Hubb wa'l-Zawaj* (Love and marriage, 1901), indecent.[62] Shortly after their marriage, Rosa and Niqula returned to Egypt, where Rosa had a son named Fu'ad and possibly more children.

Denied a permit to start a new journal in the 1920s, the husband-wife team resuscitated *al-Sayyidat* after a fifteen year interlude, and they later appended *al-Rijal* (men) to the title to signify its new scope.[63] When her brother died in 1922, Rosa published his biography in the journal he had helped her to found and later reprinted it as a book.[64] She died in Cairo in 1955, one year after her husband. Although she was quite prolific, Rosa has never received the attention that either her brother or husband has received.

At about the time Rosa left Egypt for New York, Labiba Hashim (1882–1952) started *Fatat al-Sharq* (Young woman of the East, 1906). Labiba was the most successful of the Syrian editor-writers, producing a journal that ran without interruption for over three decades. Born in Beirut into a Maronite family by the name of Madi, Labiba studied with Lazarite nuns and at English and American missionary schools. At about

the age of sixteen she married 'Abduh Hashim, twelve years her senior,
a trader, and a Freemason. They migrated to Egypt at the turn of the
century and shortly thereafter had at least one son and one daughter.[65]
Labiba contributed to *Anis al-Jalis, al-Hilal, al-Muqtataf,* and other journals before she started her own monthly in Cairo in 1906. *Fatat al-Sharq*
offered biographies of famous women, literary works, social commentary, and domestic instruction, along with other features. Labiba was
also active in women's organizations and toured Egypt and Syria giving
speeches. She delivered a series of lectures to women at the Egyptian
University a few years after it opened, and many of her lectures and
speeches were later published as pamphlets and books or printed in
her journal. She also wrote novels, short stories, and poetry, as well as
accounts of travels to Istanbul and elsewhere.[66]

Labiba had long had an interest in education. After the Ottoman Constitution was reinstated in 1908, she sent an open letter to the Ottoman
Parliament calling for a broadening of girls' education.[67] Her husband's
death during World War I left her free to serve as inspector of girls'
schools in Faysal's short-lived Arab nationalist government in Damascus after the war. Upon Faysal's ouster by the French, she left for South
America, where in Santiago, Chile, she founded *al-Sharq wa'l-Gharb* (East
and West, 1923). She returned to Egypt after a year and to *Fatat al-Sharq,*
which had been left in the hands of her daughter, Elise As'ad Daghir.[68]
Labiba's journal ran for an impressive thirty-four years, right up until
the eve of World War II, outlasting many other journals of its era. Labiba
died in 1952, the year the Free Officers toppled the monarchy. *Fatat al-
Sharq* was one of the last such journals launched by a Syrian in Egypt,
but one of the most enduring. The Syrian wave had crested.

EGYPTIAN ENTERPRISES

Although Egyptian women had contributed to the women's press from
its inception and had founded a few journals in its early years, 1907
marks a turning point in their participation in the press. The timing
reflected growing nationalist activity among Egyptians. Two events had
stirred national consciousness in 1906. In the first, the 'Aqaba incident,

the British and Ottomans argued over the demarcation line between Egyptian and Ottoman territory in the Sinai. Many nationalists backed the Ottoman position in spite of the implication of loss of land for Egypt, for they sought to reaffirm the legal sovereignty of the Ottoman Empire over Egypt and to oust the British. In the second episode, the accidental shooting of a woman in the village of Dinshaway by British officers out pigeon-hunting provoked an attack on the officers, which left one injured and one dead. A hastily held trial resulted in the hanging of seven villagers and the flogging and imprisonment of others.[69] Together these incidents angered Egyptians and fueled anti-British protest, sparking the formation of political parties the following year. The incidents also helped to generate the foundation of a cluster of periodicals by Egyptian women.

Jamila Hafiz, an Egyptian Muslim about whom little is known, started the monthly *al-Rayhana* in 1907 in Helwan, a town close to Cairo. Jamila edited the journal and appointed a male director, 'Abd al-Hamid Hamdi, to assist in production.[70] The journal was well received by readers, who sent in letters of praise and articles for publication. The following year Jamila appointed a new editor, Ibn Yahya, and changed the journal's format to a weekly. Those behind *al-Rayhana* supported the Ottoman-Islamic orientation of the Watani party rather than the more secularly minded territorial nationalism of the Umma party, and *al-Rayhana* called for women's rights within the context of Islam.[71] This was the first in a series of periodicals whose Islamist path to raising women's status showed that neither secularists or modernists had a monopoly on the sympathy of women's advocates.

A group of Egyptian Muslim women met in early 1908 in the home of Fatima Rashid (d. 1953) in Cairo to form Jam'iyyat Tarqiyat al-Mar'a (the Society for Woman's Progress). This was the first such organization in Egypt. Members founded a journal to promote their program and named Fatima editor.[72] The monthly *Tarqiyat al-Mar'a* published articles only by women who were willing to sign their names; contributions came from members in Cairo and affiliated women throughout the country. The journal called for the application of the rights of woman granted by Islam, supported veiling and the separation of the sexes, and demanded a religious education for girls. The women behind the journal backed the Watanists and their pro-Ottoman policy. Upon restoration of the Ottoman Constitution, for example, Fatima Rashid noted that the entire Egyptian nation welcomed the event, and another member praised those Turkish women who had demonstrated in Istanbul in its support.[73]

It is unclear how long this organization or its journal lasted, and what little can be gathered on Fatima Rashid's life must be derived from information about her husband, Muhammad Farid Wajdi (1875–1954). A writer who urged a return to the Islamic values of the first generations of Muslims, his literary career spanned over half a century. Wajdi had joined the attack against Qasim Amin early on with the book *al-Mar'a al-Muslima* (The Muslim woman). His *al-Madaniyya wa'l-Islam* (Civilization and Islam) showed an Islam "dissolved" into modern thought and an attempt to argue that "*true* Islam is in conformity with civilization."[74] In 1907 Wajdi started the newspaper *al-Dustur,* a mouthpiece of the Watani party, to which Fatima contributed the column "Minbar al-Awanis" (Pulpit of the young ladies). She also published her organization's journal *Tarqiyat al-Mar'a* on the press of *al-Dustur.* Although the couple had no children, they had a long life together, with Fatima predeceasing her husband by one year, a year after the 1952 revolution.[75]

Malaka Sa'd, a Copt from Cairo, launched *al-Jins al-Latif* (The gentle sex) in late 1908, adding a new dimension to the women's press. The Coptic community, estimated at 6 percent of the population by the 1907 census and 15 to 20 percent by some Coptic accounts, formed the largest minority in Egypt.[76] Although most Copts (like Egyptian Muslims) were peasants, some large landowners had emerged in the course of the nineteenth century. This group felt that their political role was not commensurate with their economic strength. In their view, furthermore, some of their privileges, as well as their general position, seemed to be eroding under the British. Yet appeals to British officials brought only increased suspicion in the eyes of Muslims and few results.

After the untimely death of Watani party leader Mustafa Kamil in 1908, the pan-Islamic rhetoric of the nationalists intensified and religious hostility escalated. Coptic organs like *al-Watan* (The nation, 1877) and *Misr* (Egypt, 1895) exchanged insults with papers like *al-Liwa',* now edited by Shaykh 'Abd al-'Aziz Jawish, a radical of Tunisian background. Tensions climaxed in February 1910 when Prime Minister Butrus Ghali, a Copt, was assassinated by a partisan of the Watani party. Ghali's role in the Dinshaway trial and his identification with other unpopular government policies had led to his vilification in the nationalist press. Copts viewed him as a martyr and blamed the pan-Islamists for creating an atmosphere of hatred and violence. In an attempt to air their communal grievances, Coptic delegates convened a congress in Asyut in March 1911. Muslim leaders countered with an Egyptian congress in Heliopolis one month later. Religious tensions began to subside only after the two congresses.

Copts continued to explore different strategies for increasing their political participation in Egypt. Whereas some wanted to maintain group autonomy by forming separate Coptic parties, others argued that the time had come to dismantle communal divides. The latter group pushed for inclusion in the nationalist movement and greater integration in the envisioned independent nation-state, and identified the Umma party, with its more secularist ideology, as a possible partner. The structure of separate autonomous communities was eventually sacrificed as Copts joined the Wafd, the postwar heir to the Umma party, in the fight for national independence, and then opted for individual rather than communal rights, becoming minority citizens in a Muslim state.[77]

In the prewar period and at the height of the tensions, some Copts had difficulty obtaining licenses to publish periodicals or newspapers.[78] This may explain in part why Malaka Sa'd covered news of special interest to Copts in *al-Jins al-Latif,* including a report on Butrus Ghali's death. Malaka published co-religionists such as Olivia 'Abd al-Shahid of Luxor in her journal, but she also carried articles by Muslim women, and Muslim writers such as Malak Hifni Nasif contributed essays. *Al-Jins al-Latif* lasted into the mid-1920s, almost two decades, providing a regular forum for men and women of diverse backgrounds. Malaka also authored a manual on household management, *Rabbat al-Dar* (Mistress of the house, 1915), which she dedicated to her daughter.[79] That she had a daughter is only a small piece in the puzzle of a life of which little is known.

In March 1909, Sir Eldon Gorst (Cromer's successor as British consul general) responded to the growing nationalist activity and spreading religious hostility by reactivating the dormant Press Law of 1881. Earlier he had noted the increase in the "virulence of the vernacular press" and "the false news and intemperate criticism of the actions and motives of the Government."[80] There was a certain irony in his course of action. Although Cromer had run Egypt as an autocrat, he had favored freedom of the press, considering it a harmless outlet and trusting the British garrison to restore public order in case of trouble.[81] Gorst preferred a less restrained policy and enacted a number of reforms, but he could not keep the balance that Cromer had so studiously maintained and blamed it in large part on the press.[82]

Originally enacted around the time of the 'Urabi revolt, the Press Law of 1881 empowered the Egyptian Ministry of Interior to issue warnings to papers in the interests of public order, religion, or morality, and to suspend or suppress papers after two warnings without trial and without previous warning by a decision of the Council of Ministers.[83] Upon proclamation of the revived law, thousands of workers and students demonstrated against it in Cairo.[84] Labiba Hashim joined the chorus of protestors in print, assailing the government's attempt "to stifle the atmosphere of Egypt after the light of freedom has shone for so long."[85] After reactivation of the law, a few papers (*al-Liwa'* and *al-Watan,* among others) received warnings or were suppressed. Some editors tried to evade government action through the fiction of foreign ownership and the protection of capitulations. But the British government successfully pressured the European powers to cooperate so that the Egyptian government could tighten control of the press.[86] The government could now bypass the courts to suppress a publication if it so desired.

Yet the law and a subsequent decision not to issue new licenses to Arabic newspapers except under exceptional circumstances had no discernible affect on the women's press.[87] Women's journals were not considered seditious or threatening to the government's program or to public order, and a handful of new journals came out in 1909. Among them were two Coptic ventures: Angelina Abu Shi'r's *Murshid al-Atfal* (The children's guide), a Cairo weekly instructing mothers on infant care, and *al-'A'ila*

al-Qibtiyya (The Coptic family), an Alexandrian monthly in Arabic colloquial for younger readers.[88] A bilingual Arabic-French journal *al-A'mal
al-Yadawiyya li'l-Sayyidat* (Handiwork for ladies, 1909) appeared in Cairo
under the names of Mademoiselle Vasila and her sister, who were most
likely Greek. It specialized in drawings, patterns, music, literature, and
art.[89] Fitna Hanim, an Egyptian who was probably of Turkish Muslim
background, produced the monthly *al-Brinsisa* (The princess, 1909) in
Mansura "to discuss affairs of the gentle sex and cultural events." Three
years later Fatima Tawfiq, an Egyptian Muslim, started *al-Jamila* (The
pretty one, 1912) in Cairo.[90]

Most of these journals ran for one issue to a few years, though it is
usually easier to say when they started than when they stopped. Little
is known, moreover, about the women behind them. Nonetheless, they
point to new directions in the women's press. Instead of one journal
dominating the field, a number competed and a few found specialized niches. Editors experimented with colloquial language and French-
Arabic bilingualism to attract wider audiences. With journals appearing
in Helwan and Mansura, production had moved outside of Cairo and
Alexandria. Yet at the end of the first decade of the twentieth century,
the predominance of female Egyptian editors proved the most significant
development in the women's press.

NEW MUSLIM VOICES

With *Fatat al-Sharq* and *al-Jins al-Latif,* among other journals, corner-
ing a certain share of the market, Sulayman al-Salimi started a different
sort of women's periodical in 1910, the biweekly then weekly paper *al-
'Afaf* (Virtue). Unlike some of the other periodicals of the time—one- or
two-man or -woman operations relying on contributions and help from
outsiders—*al-'Afaf* was set up with an active female staff from the start.
Not surprisingly, it recreated the gender divisions of Egyptian society
in its internal structure. The official female representative of *al-'Afaf* was
available to meet female readers in secluded quarters of the paper's office
or in private homes. Men and women did not mix when the newspaper held receptions, and they organized separate clubs. The sexes only

mingled in print, though even there they emphasized morality. *Al-'Afaf* presented itself as "the voice of the Egyptian woman" and ran at various intervals for over a decade.

A number of Egyptian Muslim women writers gained literary experience in the pages of *al-'Afaf,* and at least two of these later founded their own journals. The circle of eight staff reporters included Zakiya Kamil al-Kafrawiyya, a representative of the paper, and her sister Fatima; Sarah al-Mihiyya and her sister Khadija; Ihsan Ahmad; Fatima Ahmad Thabit; and Malak Hifni Nasif. They generally followed the line established two years earlier by Fatima Rashid and her colleagues in *Tarqiyat al-Mar'a,* promoting women's rights within the context of Islam, stressing modesty and morality, and assailing the trend toward greater integration apparent in contemporary Egyptian society. Among other articles, *al-'Afaf* carried reports on lower-class neighborhoods, which were used to critique social and sexual behavior and illustrate arguments for reform.

Writers in *al-'Afaf* supported Egyptian-Ottomanism and rallied to the empire's side during the Ottoman-Italian War in Tripoli in 1911–1912.[91] Yet the new wave of European imperialism revealed just how impotent the Ottoman Empire was in defending its lands. The Balkan Wars of 1912–1913 further chipped away at Ottoman territorial integrity, undermining Egyptians' confidence in the empire's ability to assist them in their quest for autonomy. Rather than wait for Ottoman aid, members of the Umma party pushed internal reform as the path to Egyptian independence, receiving a boost with the creation of the Legislative Assembly in 1913. Made from a merger of the General Assembly and Legislative Council, the project had been supported by Lord Kitchener, who replaced Gorst after his death in 1911. Although the new assembly of lawyers and landowners had little more than consultative powers, it became an important center of governmental opposition and gave leaders like Sa'd Zaghlul (who was elected vice-president) greater legitimacy to represent Egypt later on. The body debated issues of specific interest to women, such as a bill raising the age at marriage, which women had called for in the press.[92] But women were not invited to participate, nor is there any evidence that they pressed to do so at a time when many still adhered to the rules of segregation.[93]

The year the new assembly was convened, Sarah al-Mihiyya, an Egyptian Muslim who had been a regular columnist for *al-'Afaf,* started her own monthly *Fatat al-Nil* (Young woman of the Nile, 1913) in Cairo.[94] It was among the first women's journals to incorporate a central symbol of the Egyptian landscape—the Nile—in its title, reflecting the growth in national identification among a certain strata. A portrait of Sarah emerges from the pages of the journal. A woman deeply steeped in Islamic subjects, learning, and prayer, she condemned as un-Islamic popular practices such as the *zar* (a dance ceremony designed to rid the body of spirits) and elite habits such as Westernized wedding celebrations. She also viewed with alarm the unveiling of women in Egypt and the increased mixing of men and women. Sarah had a younger sister, with whom she seemed quite close, and studied with a private tutor, whose death she described in moving detail.[95]

The eve of World War I was not an auspicious time to start a journal. After the Ottomans joined the forces allied against the British in late 1914, the British declared Egypt a protectorate and placed the country under martial law. Khedive 'Abbas Hilmi II, who was abroad at the time, was ousted in favor of his uncle, Husayn Kamil, who was named sultan (r. 1914–1917). British troops repulsed two German-Ottoman attacks on the Suez Canal and later went on the offensive in Palestine and Syria. Since Egypt was a staging area for operations, food and animals were requisitioned and men forced to join labor corps. This created severe shortages and hardships and sent prices soaring. While a few profited from the circumstances, the general population suffered.

Restrictions on and censorship of the press increased under martial law.[96] Faced by multiple pressures, many periodicals folded, and sometime in 1915 *Fatat al-Nil* also disappeared. Still, a few new ventures were started. In May 1915, a group similar to that gathered around *al-Jarida* (which was discontinued shortly thereafter) launched *al-Sufur* (Unveiling), a Cairo weekly.[97] Although the title suggested a central focus on women, its goals were "the creation of a literary awakening aimed at freeing the mind, delivering Egyptian nationalism from weak elements, and freeing woman from the chains of ignorance and unsound traditions," in an order that reflected its priorities.[98] To the writers of *al-Sufur,* women were a symbol of the backwardness of the nation and thus a subject of concern. Contributors included such men of letters as Muhammad Husayn Haykal, Mansur Fahmi, and Taha Husayn, as well as women who signed their names only as al-Misriyya (the Egyptian), 'Aliya, and Zahra. The editor, 'Abd al-Hamid Hamdi, was on the list of those deported to Malta in 1916, but *al-Sufur* continued publication through the war and into the 1920s.[99] Those journals that survived the war showed amazing diversity and tenacity.

The British persisted in the suppression of nationalist activity even after the war had ended, having resolved not to relinquish control of Egypt. British officials refused to negotiate the country's status with the delegation (*Wafd*) formed of members of the Legislative Assembly (which had been adjourned during the war) and then exiled Sa'd Zaghlul and other nationalist leaders. Egyptian frustrations with British promises and treatment exploded in nationwide marches, strikes, and protests in 1919. Many women joined these demonstrations, with some leading their own, a story that has been frequently recounted. Whereas the extent of women's participation in the 1919 revolution is debated, the event is considered a pivotal one for women. For the first time in Egyptian history, according to many accounts, women were thrust from the private realm onto the public stage. The revolution is thus often taken as the first expression of nationalist sentiment on the part of women, as well as the crucible of the women's movement. Yet women's participation in the events of 1919 were a continuation and extension of the activities of the previous decades.[100]

When the negotiations that were eventually held stalled in 1922, the British unilaterally declared Egypt independent, encouraging the creation of a parliamentary monarchy and the naming of Ahmad Fu'ad king (r. 1917–1936). Britain maintained a military presence along with political influence and left the status of the Sudan, the protection of foreigners, and other thorny issues unsettled.[101] The defeat and dismemberment of the Ottoman Empire destroyed Egyptian-Ottomanism as a nationalist ideology and option for independence and led to the Wafd's adoption of a more secular territorial nationalism. This move had broad implications for women, opening the door to greater integration in society. With calm and the economy restored in the early 1920s, the press revived. Those few women's journals that had survived the war continued, an older journal was revived, and new enterprises were started.[102] After three decades and close to thirty publications, the women's press had become firmly entrenched in Egypt and had nurtured a generation of writers.

As long as ulama at al-Azhar (the preeminent center for Sunni Islamic studies for men of all classes) and similar schools had held a monopoly on formal learning, intellectuals in Egypt had come from their ranks espousing a religious worldview. The appearance of secular schools alongside religious ones in the nineteenth century created a new cadre of thinkers, often of middle-class background. This new generation of male intellectuals studied subjects like law in government schools; they visited Istanbul, the Ottoman capital, and went to Europe for higher degrees, spending time in Paris, London, and Geneva. When they returned they took jobs as lawyers, judges, teachers, and journalists. They often gathered around influential figures to discuss their ideas, meeting in clubs, cafes, and newspaper offices. Many subsequently started their own newspapers and periodicals.[103]

The lives of female intellectuals in Egypt diverged from this pattern. Although much of what we know about them is sketchy, a composite portrait of the Syrian and Egyptian women who participated in the first quarter-century or so of the Arabic women's press can be constructed. Their fathers and husbands were merchants, pharmacists, doctors, teachers, journalists, or government employees. If a title appeared in their father's or husband's name, it was *effendi* more often than *bey* or any other. Titles and professions placed most of these women squarely in the new middle class, and, as we shall see, their journals reflected the concerns of this class. Their fathers or brothers often encouraged them, sisters sometimes wrote, but mothers were typically silent or illiterate. These women attended sectarian, missionary, and new state schools or were tutored at home. In their studies they focused on history, geography, language, and other subjects; but they could not earn advanced degrees in Egypt or pursue them in Europe, though some traveled abroad. A few of these women were among the first teachers and administrators in girls' schools, almost the only career options available. They organized their own circles and associations, meeting in private homes and secluded settings to exchange ideas, and they started women's journals to promote social change.

A clear pattern emerges in the first quarter century or so of the women's press. Syrian women, many of whom were Greek Orthodox, dominated the production of women's journals in the first fifteen years. They were roughly of the same generation, born in the mid-1870s to the early 1880s in coastal Syria. In 1907 the balance tipped toward Egyptians, who from that time on produced most of the women's periodicals in Egypt. These women were probably born in the late 1880s and early 1890s. In both phases, national origins presented few obstacles to contributors and readers linked by language. A second trend that emerges from a survey of the press shows the interconnectedness of periodicals. Editors had often contributed to other journals earlier in their careers, as a thread of continuity wound through the women's press. Finally, although the periodicals were not ostensibly concerned with national politics, they were interested in hierarchies of power posited on gender and the redefinition of male-female roles and family relations that accompanied the rise of nationalism in Egypt.

CREATING
LITERARY TEXTS

Although women had composed Arabic verse from pre-Islamic times and written throughout Islamic history in Spain and elsewhere,[1] women began writing in greater numbers in Egypt at the end of the nineteenth century. This first generation of women writers overcame social, psychological, and ideological obstacles to break out of isolation and generate printed texts. By 1920 observers no longer wondered why so few women wrote but marveled instead at the numbers of women who had joined the *nahda*.

Many aspects of the general Arabic cultural revival known as the nahda remain matters of dispute. Was it a "renaissance" of classical Arabic literature, or a "rising up" more influenced by modern Western writing and modernization of Arabic language, style, and technique? Should its start be traced to the arrival of General Bonaparte's troops in Egypt in 1798, or located in Syria sometime in the 1800s?[2] With the origins, points of reference, influences, and end of the nahda all open to debate, focus on the literary aspects of *al-nahda al-nisa'iyya* (the women's awakening) provides important insights into the cultural history of this period.

Various factors fueled the literary awakening, but appropriate technology was a necessary precondition to the explosion of print culture in late nineteenth- and early twentieth-century Egypt. Texts had been produced and copied by hand in premodern times, resulting in manuscripts that circulated only among small circles of the elite. This culture was transformed by the introduction of the Arabic printing press, which widened the potential audience of readers. The press was first brought to Egypt by Bonaparte's troops in 1798, and although the French took the press with them when they left a few years later, the new technology was firmly established under Muhammad 'Ali. After having sent a mission to Italy to learn printing, the Ottoman viceroy had an Arabic printing press installed at Bulaq by 1820. This press printed the government journal along with other official publications. To facilitate the production of printed texts, a paper mill was established in the 1830s.[3]

Private presses began to multiply in Egypt after 1860 as the state surrendered its monopoly on printing. Individuals could now run their own printing operations or use other privately run presses. By the first decade of the twentieth century, there were over 130 presses in Egypt, a figure that did not include small shops of no more than two people. Although the presses were concentrated in the two major cities—half were in Cairo and one-third in Alexandria—there were presses in other locations as well.[4]

The replacement of manuscripts by printed materials gave readers greater access to literature. At the same time, it offered writers, including women with literary aspirations, more opportunity to publish. They entered the world of print culture at a dynamic moment in Arabic literary history. Through the creation of literary texts, they hoped to encourage social reform and fuel the women's awakening.

LEGITIMIZING THE ENDEAVOR

Many Muslim and Coptic women, particularly those of the middle and upper classes, were still veiled at turn of the century and could not move about without escorts or justifiable purpose. Women of the lower classes were not veiled or secluded to the same extent, of course, but practiced segregation and accepted the ideal of separation of the sexes. These measures effectively silenced women, for people without a public presence were certainly not expected to have a public voice. Given these and other social restrictions, they faced attacks by opponents when they picked up the pen. "Such extremism is not expected from a girl like you," a female friend told a girl named 'Aziza when an article of hers first appeared on the "Girls' Page" of *al-Jins al-Latif.* The young critic expressed a view common in 1909, that it was wrong for women to write in a journal "and correspond with strangers!" 'Aziza's reply suggested that she had not crossed sexual boundaries or broken social taboos. "What is extreme in that?" asked 'Aziza. "Isn't this journal made for those of our sex in order to improve their situation?"[5] Newly arrived on the literary scene, some women felt compelled to explain to their audience why they broke injunctions to be silent. Their rationales illuminate attitudes toward writing, as well as society's stipulations about acceptable behavior.

Women could not legitimize writing simply as an act of individual artistic expression, although no doubt some were so inspired. Nor could they admit to writing in order to earn a living or to supplement the family income, in spite of the fact that some ran journals, produced translations, or wrote books for just that purpose. (Labiba Hashim, for instance, helped her husband after he had suffered financial losses.)[6] Writing had to be presented instead as a service to others and linked to larger causes, such as the progress of women. Some, therefore, claimed that writing was a bridge from house to house, a way to combat domestic isolation and loneliness, and was meant only for the eyes of other women (although clearly men read texts by women). Prefaces abounded with dedications "to the girls of my sex," to "my sex, the gentle one," and similar phrases. The authors usually inserted the possessive *my* in these dedications to show their identification with other women.[7] Whether they meant Egyptian, Eastern, Muslim, or women in general depended on the author and the context. Writers of different perspectives used similar legitimizations, for in spite of their disagreement on the extent and direction of change, they agreed on the necessity for social reform in order to improve women's lives.

A second rationale frequently invoked by women was the desire to help the nation. "Do not reproach me, for I am not a person of rhetoric and not from among those who excel in the art of composition and writing," wrote Munira Suriyal, a young girl from Asyut. She confessed that she had neither the skills nor the license to write because of her youth but was inspired by a higher goal, her love for the nation.[8] The wave of nationalism was a convenient one for women to ride, arguing that all Egyptians had to be mobilized in the struggle for independence. Patriotism served those who might otherwise have been prohibited from a literary vocation. Fatima al-Kafrawiyya, for example, explained that she wrote "to add her voice to those of others in order to help the Egyptian nation," after Egypt had been named a British protectorate.[9] Writers discussed women's patriotic duties, which included imbuing their sons with love for the nation and cultivating patriotism in the home through song. Using nationalism as an excuse did not confine them to this subject, however. Rather it gave them greater freedom to pursue literary and other endeavors.[10]

The conditions under which women wrote often added legitimacy to the enterprise. Malaka Sa'd may have been depicting her own work environment when she printed a picture of a woman sitting at a desk in a private study, pen in hand, in her manual on housekeeping. The ideal study, she wrote, should be far from noise and furnished with a desk, a swivel chair, an electric light or gas lamp, bookshelves, a clock, a calendar, maps, a wastepaper basket, paper, and writing instruments.[11] Alexandra Avierino revealed that she had an Arabic typewriter at home, which she apparently used.[12] The poet Khadija al-Maghribiyya composed verse, we are told, while seated in bed under a mosquito net.[13] In whatever posture chosen and with whatever instrument selected, women undertook writing in private quarters away from the male public and without challenging gender segregation, thus making a literary avocation more acceptable.

Writers still had to account for how they spent their time. That is, women could not dedicate themselves exclusively to writing—or admit to that—but had to present writing as an activity that was only undertaken when domestic chores were done. Malaka Sa'd assured her readers that she made the visits in which she gathered material for her journal after having finished household chores, and she presented herself as a mother, housekeeper, and journal owner in that order, emphasizing her priorities.[14] Women were judged for their domestic accomplishments, as well as their literary achievements, by male critics who followed female writers into the home. One wrote of Labiba Hashim that "her family chores do not prevent her from writing at opportune moments."[15] But women also internalized this standard. Labiba Hashim noted that Maryam al-Nahhas's "intellectual and literary work had not interfered with managing her home and raising her children well."[16] Writing was allowed because it did not disrupt women's real vocation—domesticity—and often complemented or enhanced it.

Women claimed that they wrote to help advance the nation and women, and that they did so without neglecting their domestic duties. They turned to the past to further legitimize this endeavor, pointing to women such as the pre-Islamic poet-elegist al-Khansa' and others.[17] They depicted themselves as heirs to an Arabic female literary tradition, or were depicted in this way, implying that they had not set a precedent. Yet this was not entirely true, for most of the female predecessors they pointed to were poets—not prose writers—whose recited works had survived in manuscript form with limited circulation. These late nineteenth- and early twentieth-century writers represented the first generation of women to exploit a medium with a much larger circulation. And they became particularly adept at new forms like the essay, which they helped to develop.

Setting themselves in a female literary tradition, some writers argued that inherent differences in male and female writing existed. This difference gave women an authority to write on certain topics, particularly those that pertained to them.[18] It also linked them to such writers as Jane Austen, Charlotte Brontë, and Juliette Adam, whom they admired and depicted in biographical sketches.[19] Writing mostly in literary Arabic, they placed themselves in a chain of writers of the "high" tradition and did not connect themselves to female producers of oral culture, the reservoir of storytellers, singers of ballads, and other indigenous women whose medium was colloquial speech.[20]

Writers presented visual images of women creating literary texts to suggest that it was a natural and noble act that could have a broad impact on society. The cover of *al-Jins al-Latif,* for example, showed a young girl sitting at a desk penning the words: "What can I do to improve?" The repetition of similar phrases connecting writing to change indicated the high regard these women had for the power of the pen. Behind this phrase was an implicit belief that producing texts could generate personal and social transformation, for these middle-class women sought social mobility as well as social reform through writing. They claimed that many of the problems women faced were rooted in traditions and beliefs, and their situation would improve through education, argument, and persuasion.

Belief in the power of the word was also linked to its novelty. This was not only the first generation of literary women, but also the first generation of literate ones. Literacy opened a new world to many, multiplied possibilities, and enhanced the sense of awakening. The faith of these writers in the ability of ideas and the written word to reshape reality fed their enthusiasm and drove them to recruit new writers. These were women with a mission for whom writing was a weapon. Armed with political, social, and historical defenses to counter injunctions to be silent that transcended class and religious divides, women entered the literary arena.

TO SIGN OR NOT TO SIGN

Writing was one thing. Signing works was another altogether. As women began to write, many chose to hide their identities, leading to debates about the benefit of using pseudonyms. Two issues converged in these debates: the status of the writer in Egyptian society and the position of women. The discussions and the patterns of use of pseudonyms shed light on the sociology of writers and the psychology of writing, as well as on differences in the experiences of male and female writers.

Writing did not exist as a separate profession at the turn of the century. There were no training schools, writing associations, or other signs of professionalization. Indeed, it was nearly impossible for writers to support themselves through writing alone, and writers without independent means usually practiced professions such as journalism, law, and teaching. Journalism seemed the most practical choice, for editing a periodical or newspaper left time for writing and provided a place for publication. Yet journalism was still not a prestigious career. This was illustrated by the scandal that surrounded Shaykh 'Ali Yusuf, editor of the popular *al-Mu'ayyad,* when he married the daughter of a notable in 1904. Her father went to court to block the marriage, arguing that Shaykh 'Ali Yusuf was her social inferior, and the khedive eventually became involved in the attempt to reconcile the two sides.[21]

Since writing was not a stable, lucrative, or highly regarded profession, it was not carefully controlled or regulated either. Had it been like law, which organized the earliest professional syndicate in Egypt (the National Bar Association) in 1912, women might have been barred from the practice. But individuals needed no special schooling or certification to write, and the closest thing to a writers' association (the Journalists' Syndicate) was not founded until the 1940s.[22] Women could therefore write and publish without being blocked by male writers trying to guard their professional advantages.

The prestige of writing, which was relatively low compared to other professions, varied somewhat according to genre. Poets still won the highest acclaim and dramatists the lowest. Prose writers fell somewhere in between, depending on whether or not they produced fiction, a form which though increasingly craved was generally not respected. Fiction writers tried to distance themselves from popular storytellers, who were associated with folk culture and whom the "genteel public loathed." One strategy authors used to mute objections to fiction was to argue in their introductions that their story had an educational value or moral purpose.[23]

Muhammad Husayn Haykal's literary path shows some of the problems faced by writers in the early 1900s. When his novel *Zaynab* first appeared on the eve of World War I, Haykal signed it "Misri Fallah" (an Egyptian of peasant origin). Then practicing law in a provincial town, Haykal did not want to harm his legal career, or so he explained in 1929 when the book came out under his own name. In the interim he had left the provinces and the legal profession and taken up writing and politics full time. Signing the book showed his greater identification as a writer, as well as the increased acceptance of the novel.[24] Writers of a variety of genres faced the risk of negative reaction from government officials, religious authorities, and the general public. Pen names or deletions of names altogether were used to avoid real or potential problems. Salim Sarkis had used the pseudonym "Maryam Mazhar" to avoid government censors in the 1880s and 1890s. Two decades later an *'alim* (cleric) writing for *al-'Afaf* did not divulge his identity, possibly fearing the opprobrium of conservatives from al-Azhar, who occasionally attacked the paper.[25]

Women writers developed a particular affinity for pseudonyms, often hiding their names for reasons related to reputation and family honor. According to convention, a woman's name was not to be mentioned in public, for it would shame her and impugn her family. Often a man would not acknowledge the individual identity of female relatives, or even their existence.[26] Wedding announcements gave the names of the father and the groom but listed the bride only as "holder of chastity and modesty" or some such appellate.[27] Silence was meant to signal respect, but respect for the ideal of woman showed total disregard for individual women. Furthermore, silence negated their existence outside the home. Women of a certain strata were thus physically secluded and psychologically cut off; they had no public persona. Hiding a name in public by not pronouncing it was also akin to hiding a face in public by veiling and part of the same symbolic system. Both acts pretended to shelter women, yet both functioned to control women's movements, actions, and thoughts.

Many of the women writing in Egypt in this generation used pseudonyms to hide their family ties, with false names serving as veils. Cloaked in anonymity—faceless and nameless—the writers continued to deny their public existence. While masking their real names, the names they chose revealed other aspects of their identities. Most invariably indicated their sex by the gendered (feminine) Arabic ending or by word choice. Some of the names reflected a sense of belonging to a female circle and showed a growing identification with women. "A woman from among you" drew a reply from "another woman from among you" in one journal.[28] The names also reflected a developing sense of national consciousness. "An Egyptian woman," "a Muslim Egyptian Ottoman woman," "a young woman of the Nile," and "one faithful to her nation" were among those pseudonyms expressing patriotic pride.[29]

Other patterns in the use of pseudonyms appeared among women that were similar to those of men. The decision to use a pen name might be based on genre. When Zaynab Fawwaz (c. 1860–1914) published the story *Husn al-'Awaqib* (The happy ending, 1893), she signed it "an Egyptian woman," although she was a Shi'i from Jabal 'Amil in south Lebanon who had migrated to Alexandria at about the age of ten. Her decision to sign her own name to her biographical dictionary when it appeared in 1894 may have reflected the greater respectability of a genre with roots in Islamic literary tradition. Many writers also used pen names when starting their careers, revealing their names only later when they felt more secure. Upon the reissue of *Husn al-'Awaqib,* Zaynab in fact signed her real name.[30] Labiba Hashim used a pen name when she first contributed to the press but later had little hesitation in signing her own name.[31]

Those writers who started journals also revealed their names. Sa'diyya Sa'd al-Din, editor of *Shajarat al-Durr,* had probably been "Shajarat al-Durr," the turn-of-the-century essayist. A decade later, Sarah al-Mihiyya, editor of *Fatat al-Nil,* was probably "Fatat al-Nil," a contributor to the press.[32] Since newspaper and periodical owners had to register their names with the Ministry of Interior in order to obtain a government license, they had already revealed their names publicly. Most editors then published their names on the cover of their journal. Registering and publishing names were therefore steps toward greater professional awareness.

Most authors never became editors, however, and never faced this particular imperative to reveal their identity. Malak Hifni Nasif (1886–1918) had earned a primary school diploma and taught for a few years before marrying 'Abd al-Sattar al-Basil, a bedouin tribal leader. When she moved to the oasis of Fayyum, Malak took the pen name "Bahithat al-Badiya" (searcher of the desert). Her choice of pseudonym, which she used for most of her literary career, gave readers a clear clue to her identity.[33] That many readers probably knew who she was suggests that a pseudonym was sometimes a translucent rather than a thick veil. The metaphor is apt, for at about the same time women's face veils were getting lighter, to the point that some critics contended they were almost transparent.[34]

No set pattern emerged for the use of pseudonyms along religious lines. Although Muslims practiced seclusion more strictly than Copts, they shared similar cultural views on sexual morality. Coptic women were still veiled in the early years of the twentieth century, and some Copts used pseudonyms throughout this period. Olivia 'Abd al-Shahid, a prolific writer whose works appeared in a number of periodicals, often used the name "al-Zahra" (the flower).[35] Princess Nazli Fazil, a Muslim woman from the khedivial family known for hosting salons in her home for the leading political and intellectual figures of the day, contributed articles to the press without signing her name.[36]

Syrian Christians unveiled sooner than Copts and Muslims (those in Beirut had stopped covering their faces in 1890)[37] and probably started using their own names sooner as well. When Hind 'Ammun's book on Egyptian history was accepted for use in state schools in 1913, the Ministry of Education asked permission to change the name on the title page to that of a man. State authorities may have been trying to hide her Christian identity as well as her gender, but Hind refused and her name appeared on the text.[38] Considerations about signing or not signing a name were informed by a number of variables, including sex, religion, class, content of the work, politics, and personal disposition, in no fixed order.

Yet use of pen names or initials created ambiguity about authorship and sometimes raised suspicions about authenticity. While hiding identity, pseudonyms may thus have inadvertently harmed credibility. Amina Z., who did not give her own family name, asked the editor of *al-Sufur,* "Is the name of the director of *al-Sufur* a name of a real man, or is it a young woman, like me, who has borrowed a name? And Doctor Haykal? And M.? And Q.? And Mansur?" The editor assured her that they were all men (writers at *al-Sufur* included Muhammad Husayn Haykal, Mustafa 'Abd al-Raziq, Muhammad Taymur, and Mansur Fahmi), and suggested that if she doubted them, they might in turn doubt her claim to be a woman.[39] The use of initials, abbreviations, or pen names could mask gender as well as identity, and many found "literary transvestitism"—male and female writers posing as the opposite sex—disturbing. When *al-'Afaf*'s editor Sulayman al-Salimi discovered that he had received a letter from a man who had forged the signature of a woman, he assailed the forgerer for "wearing the names of women and hiding behind their clothes."[40] Even in print, or especially so since trust was implicit, "cross-dressing" threatened gender boundaries. Readers and editors wanted to know if a man or woman had authored a text, whether or not they knew the exact identity of the individual. This led al-Salimi and others to set newspaper policies that allowed pseudonyms in print only if the authors had signed their real name to a cover letter.[41]

The question of authenticity, like identity, stirred debate. Whether women signed their names or not, some male critics doubted that they had authored the works they claimed as their own. A writer in *al-Mu'ayyad* in 1898 dismissed all the women's journals prior to Alexandra Avierino's *Anis al-Jalis* as women's "in name only, in reality they were written by others," implying that fathers, husbands, brothers, editors, or publishers had produced them.[42] But no evidence exists that men authored any women's journal other than *Mir'at al-Hasna'* in that period. The close partnership of Rosa and Farah Antun caused detractors to question her literary ability. Farah admitted that he helped his sister with her journal *al-Sayyidat wa'l-Banat,* marking his contributions with three stars. Whereas observers mentioned his help to her, they did not acknowledge the reciprocity of the relationship. He confessed that he was "indebted to her for her unparalleled and invaluable assistance" and "did not publish a line in *al-Jami'a* or other books until she has looked at it," yet no one questioned Farah's originality.[43] Officials later challenged Alexandra Avierino's writing ability as well. When she appeared before the Parquet in 1924, investigators insinuated that she had not really written some of the articles, letters, and poems found in her possession, and they questioned her on the conditions under which she composed texts.[44]

Many assumed that women did not have the ability or language skills to write. Although some of the literature produced by this generation, male and female, was admittedly not very good, writing well was no solution, for critics then claimed that men had authored the texts. Female

writers were thus trapped, condemned if they wrote poorly and disbe-
lieved if they wrote well. However, few challenges held up under close
scrutiny, and the motives of assailants were often suspect. "Look at the
one who writes under the signature 'Bahithat al-Badiya,' for example, or
'Nabawiyya Musa' or 'Sarah al-Mihiyya' and others," wrote one critic in
al-'Afaf. "The first won fame in several days that would have taken a man
long years to find," and the others had views which were "idle prattle
in relation to the ideas of men." Jealous of the ready attention given to
some women writers, this critic sought to undermine their achievements.
But others quickly came to their defense, forcing the critic to later re-
tract his statements.[45] In spite of the danger of feeding the suspicions of
opponents, women writers often thanked those who had helped them.

Attacks harmed the egos of individual writers, the prestige of women
writers, and respect for women in general. More women had to start
signing their works to prove that real women stood behind them and
to show by their numbers that women could write. This transformed
the question of whether or not women should sign their names from a
personal issue for a few individuals seeking or disavowing credit to a
collective one with social implications. The members of Jam'iyyat Tarqiyat al-Mar'a (the Society for Woman's Progress) adopted the cause of
signing and announcing their names in 1908 in order to fight a tradition
of referring to women only by "scornful allusions or whispers" and to af-
firm their existence in public. Their charter stipulated that every member
must reveal her name. Turning to Islamic law to defend their position,
they argued that signing a woman's name was not only permissible but
obligatory, and that the appearance of women's names in the Prophet's
time had set a precedent. After a year, Fatima Rashid, the president of the
society, declared that the campaign had succeeded. Women had begun
to sign their names publicly in newspapers and journals "that are read
by thousands of men."[46]

Some of the women's organizations that followed Jam'iyyat Tarqiyat
al-Mar'a had similar stipulations in their charters about revealing the
names of members, confirming the importance of this issue for women.[47]
The debate over signing names paralleled that over whether or not
women should remove the face veil.[48] Although positions did not neces-

sarily coincide—some of those for revealing names were against unveiling—both debates touched on the question of women's public presence and integration in society. Signing their names and removing their face veils should be viewed as steps along a continuum toward greater integration and greater choice rather than complete negations of segregation and an absolute immersion in society.

These debates reflected questions about the greater mobility of urban women in late nineteenth- and early twentieth-century Egypt. Young girls of certain strata were going to schools in growing numbers and attending theater and the opera. New department-style stores in the modern sections of the larger cities attracted female clientele. Trams and cars facilitated transport to distant quarters of the city, and steamship and trains made travel to other parts of the country and beyond possible. More women, particularly those from the classes that had most carefully practiced seclusion, moved increasingly through the expanding public space.[49] At the same time, and in part in order to comment on these changes, women sought to break into literary space, first veiled by pseudonyms and then later lifting their "veils" and revealing their identities.

Did signing their names raise the prestige of writers? Did it convince critics that women were capable of authoring texts? Did it enhance the stature of women by acknowledging their existence as discrete individuals? Women began to write in numbers when the literary profession was in flux and not strong enough to bar them, but they still faced critics who questioned their ability to write. As individual writers developed confidence and writing gained greater respectability, more women began to sign their names. They proved by their sheer numbers that women could write, which increased the stature of women as well as their prestige as writers. Signing their names helped secluded women who had previously had no public presence break a psychological barrier. Through this act they acknowledged their individual existences and gained public recognition. Affirming their own separate identities, moreover, was a necessary first step to forging a positive collective identity. For the most part, however, women's writing remained on the sidelines of the literary mainstream.

FEMALE LITERARY CULTURE

Although al-nahda al-nisa'iyya paralleled and occasionally intersected with the general nahda, few women of the first generation of writers broke into the male world of letters. Instead, they created a female literary culture, exploiting the new print medium and responding to the growing number of readers hungry for texts on social and domestic topics. Women writers worked in traditional forms and helped to pioneer new ones. Poetry remained a popular genre for many, inspired by the memory of female poets from the pre-Islamic and early Islamic periods. 'A'isha al-Taymuriyya (c. 1840–1902) composed diwans in Arabic, Persian, and Turkish; and Warda al-Yaziji (1838–1924), a contemporary Syrian poet who also resided in Egypt, composed in Arabic.[50] Both women were born before the middle of the nineteenth century and set an example for the generations that followed. But most younger writers, some of whom composed poetry on the side, chose to express themselves in other forms.

Two women of the generation born after mid-century, Maryam al-Nahhas (1856–1888) and Zaynab Fawwaz (c. 1860–1914), turned to another genre with long historical roots—the biographical dictionary—using a traditional medieval form to present new contents. For although some biographical dictionaries had included women and a few dedicated separate volumes to them, most excluded women. In an effort to document women's lives, Maryam al-Nahhas produced *Ma'rid al-Hasna' fi Tarajim Mashahir al-Nisa'* (The beautiful woman's exhibition for the biographies of female celebrities) in 1879, and Zaynab Fawwaz followed fifteen years later with *al-Durr al-Manthur fi Tabaqat Rabbat al-Khudur* (Scattered pearls of the classes of secluded women). Both encyclopedic works portrayed the lives of great women—including literary figures—from around the world.[51] The biographical dictionary seemed an appropriate form for these women, for like poetry, it was a respected genre. Zaynab Fawwaz was at work on a biographical dictionary of famous men when she died.[52] Women continued to write biographies in the following decades, although they were more influenced by Western examples than by medieval Arabic ones.[53]

New literary genres were introduced into Egypt in translation in the course of the nineteenth century. Women writers, who were often well suited for translating due to their language training, became active in this movement. Most notably, Esther Moyal translated over a dozen novels from French into Arabic. She also translated many shorter works and was on at least one occasion commissioned to translate a specific book.[54] Many other writers translated selections for publication in their own journals and elsewhere. In this way they introduced new scientific and humanistic ideas to the Arabic reading public.

Writers experimented with the new fictional forms to which they had been exposed through original works and in translations. Labiba Hashim may have been one of the first writers in Egypt to publish short stories with "literary pretensions," according to J. Brugman. Her works appeared in the journal *al-Diya'* (1898), as well as in her own *Fatat al-Sharq*.[55] Short stories became standard fare in the women's press, as the genre moved from old-style Arabic anecdotes toward the European-style short story. Many editors serialized fiction, including their own works, although it is sometimes hard to determine whether the work was original or adapted. Sarah al-Mihiyya published a story called "Thurayya" over a few issues. In a pattern that had become common, the installments were later gathered, bound, and sold as a book.[56]

The boundaries between genres are not always clear in any language, and Arabic is no exception. While Haykal's *Zaynab* (1913) has often been regarded as the first authentic Arabic novel, this view is considered a simplification by Brugman. Works that appeared prior to that date, many of which were written by Syrians in Egypt, could be considered novels.[57] Although Brugman does not specifically mention Labiba Hashim's *Qalb al-Rajul* (The heart of man) in this context, the work falls into that category. When it appeared in 1904, one reviewer urged men to read it in order to learn a woman's view of the heart. Labiba may have had slight misgivings about writing a romantic novel, for she promised to donate all the profits from the book to charity.[58] The fictional works of the early women writers have received little attention, and their incursions into drama have not been studied either. Zaynab Fawwaz wrote a play in four acts on love and honor, and Alexandra Avierino also wrote a play. Although Egyptian and Syrian women writers tried their hands at drama, little is known about adaptations of their works for the stage or whether any were ever produced.[59]

Writers mostly churned out works of nonfiction. With the spread of girls' education and growing female literacy, there was a demand for Arabic literature on health and related topics. Recognizing the acute shortage of instructional materials, writers moved to fill the void with translations and original works, transmitting the new sciences of health, childcare, and household management to young readers. Not surprisingly, *hakimas* (female health practitioners) were among the first women in Egypt to write and publish in their field. Jalila Tamarhan, a graduate of the School of Hakimas, contributed to a medical journal in the 1860s. An anonymous hakima from Qasr al-'Ayni Hospital contributed pieces to the first woman's journal, *al-Fatah,* in the 1890s; and Sayyida Sabri, "among the most famous experienced Egyptian women doctors," wrote for *al-'Afaf* in the 1910s. Women were instructed during pregnancy and after childbirth, as well as in hygiene and first aid.[60]

The new domestic literature gave increasing attention not only to producing a healthy child, but also to mothering and housekeeping. Labiba Hashim delivered a series of lectures on childraising at the Egyptian University, which she later published as *Kitab fi'l-Tarbiya* (1911).[61] In addition to translating British and American advice manuals, Olivia 'Abd al-Shahid wrote a study on the Egyptian family, *al-'A'ila al-Misriyya* (1912).[62] There was also a greater focus on running the household efficiently. Malaka Sa'd's text on housekeeping, *Rabbat al-Dar,* went into a number of printings and was used by the Ministry of Education in state schools.[63] Many of these writers responded to the needs of school girls and young graduates. Teachers also provided an array of educational materials for the classroom, including primers, grammars, and histories. Nabawiyya Musa, who became known for her advocacy of women's education and work, was prolific in this field, with one of her grammars going into at least nine printings. Another Muslim school teacher, Zaynab Mursi, also wrote primers. In the process of teaching students to read, these texts socialized young children and had an enormous potential to redefine gender roles and relations.[64]

The first half of the twentieth century was the heyday of the essay, a form that was eclipsed by the newspaper article only in the second half of the century.[65] Essays often dominated the pages of periodicals and newspapers and were occasionally gathered together into collections. Two of the best-known female writers, neither of whom started journals, had their essays collected and published. Zaynab Fawwaz had contributed works from 1891 to *al-Nil, al-Mu'ayyad, al-Fatah,* and *Anis al-Jalis,* among other publications, and her essays were reprinted as *al-Rasa'il al-Zaynabiyya* (Zaynab's essays, 1906).[66] Malak Hifni Nasif followed four years later with *al-Nisa'iyyat* (Women's affairs, 1910). Although her articles occasionally appeared in women's periodicals such as *Anis al-Jalis, al-Jins al-Latif,* and *al-'Afaf,* essays from *al-Jarida*—the organ of the Umma party—formed the bulk of her collection. It was introduced by the newspaper's editor, Ahmad Lutfi al-Sayyid, and printed on its press.[67] Both of these essayists published in the women's press and in the general press, but they earned greater renown through publication in the latter. Furthermore, their decision to have their essays collected and published as books has made their writings easily accessible to later generations. As a result of their literary strategies, they have received more recognition than most of their female contemporaries.

The essays that filled the pages of the women's press provided commentary on society, morality, and domestic life. The women's press also integrated poetry, biographies (often excerpted from biographical dictionaries), short stories, serialized novels, jokes, and letters. After 1890, women's journals quickly became the main outlet for the writings of women. In the pages of the women's press, writers explored a variety of forms, developed new styles, and helped modernize the written language.

A few forms were noticeably lacking in the early years of al-nahda al-nisa'iyya. Although biographical dictionaries and biographies appeared, autobiographies were almost nonexistent. Some editors encouraged women to write about their private lives, arguing that women's stories had been suppressed and that discussing their personal affairs would improve the situation of women.[68] Women occasionally told their stories and narrated personal episodes in the press, usually anonymously.

Letters between friends and relatives published in the journals also give glimpses into female bonds and sentiments. But the published memoir had not yet emerged as a form in which women, or men for that matter, chose to express themselves. The first published Arabic autobiography— Taha Husayn's *Ayyam*—appeared only in 1926 (with two subsequent parts released in the following decades).[69] The line between public and private had shifted after the turn of the century as women wrote and signed their names, but they still did not reveal certain aspects of their private lives through autobiography or in other forms.

Foreign influences and indigenous concerns reshaped Arabic language and literature in this period, and the press played an important role. Language, which had traditionally been the preserve of religious scholars, underwent an evolution. Just as it was sometimes necessary to rediscover or invent words to convey new political concepts, a new vocabulary was created for the domestic realm. Phrases emerged for "housewife," "women's progress," and "domestic economy," or existing terms took on a new resonance. At the same time, writers developed a new aesthetic in prose that avoided the use of the more arcane vocabularies of the past, encouraged new forms stripped of rhyming schemes and other rigid structures, and emphasized directness and fluidity. Obscure words were cut back, and formalized writing gave way to a clearer style. The essay, more than any other genre, aided in this transformation.[70] A revitalized language and new forms helped literature reach a wider audience, as writing became an activity that more people could practice. The evolution in language and literature coincided with the entry of a new group of writers onto the literary stage.

Wondering why there were so few articles by women in the first issues of *Anis al-Jalis* in 1898, Labiba Hashim asked whether there were "only three educated Eastern women or can only three of them write?" and chastised literate women for their apathy.[71] But the ranks of women writers began to swell in the late nineteenth century. That women started to write then—in the midst of the nahda—was no coincidence. They entered the literary world at an opportune moment, when the profession was porous and literature itself in flux. Suddenly writers, male and female, seemed to be everywhere. "No sooner do you raise a rock on Egyptian soil then out from it pops a writer or a poet," joked Alexandra Avierino in 1906.[72]

The reaction to the phenomenon of women writing, as well as to the literature they produced, was generally positive. Literary and scientific journals such as *al-Muqtataf, al-Hilal,* and *al-Manar,* whose editors were generally predisposed to the cause of women's progress, reviewed women's writings favorably. Rashid Rida's response to Malak Hifni Nasif's *al-Nisa'iyyat* can be taken as characteristic of the receptiveness of many male colleagues to women's writing. Noting that what this author had written at the outset of her career was better in terms of style and content than the work of many men, Rida acknowledged the significance of the questions she posed. Moreover, he was convinced that these questions were the most important social issues of the day in Egypt and the Islamic world.[73]

How did male and female literary experiences compare? Many women of this pioneering generation felt compelled to link their writing to the nationalist struggle or to reform movements; others pointed to the domestic duties they had performed before taking up the pen. Men, on the other hand, seemed to feel less of a need to legitimize their writing. Women's justifications, as well as their use of pseudonyms, eased them onto the literary stage. Both men and women occasionally used pen names to hide their identities, though men seemed motivated by practical, pecuniary, and political reasons whereas women seemed to struggle with psychological and social obstacles. As the ranks of women writers began to swell, more began to sign their names to articles and books, showing their growing self-confidence and consciousness as writers and as women.[74] The greater sense of collectivity that grew out of these steps was also manifested.

If male and female experiences of writing in Egypt differed somewhat, the only real difference in the literature produced was in its emphasis. Women participated in the nahda, cognizant of the changes in forms, style, and language, and sometimes at the forefront of these changes. The general nahda and al-nahda al-nisa'iyya diverged only at the choice of contents, with women often but not always preferring domestic and social topics. The limited variations that existed in male and female writing arose out of cultural considerations, not as a reflection of any inherent sexual differences. In spite of their own occasional claims, women writers were not part of a completely autonomous literary chain, nor were they oblivious to general literary trends and traditions. To the contrary, they influenced and were influenced by a large circle of male writers. Yet women writers remained mostly on the edges of the literary stage, where they developed the women's press. For as more women picked up the pen, they encountered the classic dilemma of the modern writer: where to publish?

3

THE MAKING
OF A JOURNAL

The story of the emergence of the Arabic women's journal as a recognizable form is one of transmission and appropriation of culture. The idea came from abroad but was reshaped according to regional tastes. In the hands of female editors and owners, it became a vehicle for giving women greater access to print culture. Women's journals provided a group on the margins of the literary world with an opportunity to produce texts and disseminate ideas and thereby to promote their programs for social reform.

Producing a journal was an economic as well as a cultural undertaking, a business made possible by a confluence of factors in nineteenth-century Egypt. The transition to capitalism created new opportunities, and though many businesses were in the hands of foreigners (due to their access to capital and protection through capitulations), openings for smaller enterpreneurs existed. This was particularly so in fields in which Europeans could not compete so readily, such as those requiring a knowledge of Arabic. Arabic newspapers and periodicals presented an option to Egyptians and other Arabic writers. This was a business that could be run by one or two people, required little initial investment, and might return a profit.

By the late nineteenth century the infrastructure necessary for the development of the press existed in Egypt. Telegraphic connections had come, and sometime between 1860 and 1870 Reuters initiated their wire news service in the country.[1] A postal system capable of delivering a rising volume of mail, including periodicals and newspapers, was in place.[2] And a modern banking and credit system was in operation by the end of the century, facilitating the export of periodicals.[3] Telephone communications were even on the way. The legal mechanism was also set: the state allowed private presses to multiply and set few restrictions on the press, at least until the 1909 renewal of the 1881 Press Law. The boom in the economy at the turn of the century further stimulated consumers to buy new products. The rise in literacy gave newspapers and periodicals an expanding market.

Women found new opportunities in the business of periodical production. To some extent this was continuous with past entrepreneurial endeavors undertaken by women in Egypt. Elite women in the Mamluk period had developed astute investment strategies to safeguard and multiply family assets.[4] Rural and urban women of the middle and lower classes in the nineteenth century had been involved in petty trade and other business enterprises. They were occasionally assisted in their ventures by male family members or representatives who handled their legal affairs and found protection in Islamic laws that guaranteed women's share of inheritance and their property rights. Court records show many women coming to court in person or by proxy to defend these rights in the nineteenth century.[5]

Building on past patterns, the founders of women's journals took advantage of contemporary economic opportunities to try their hands at a new venture, one which tested their business acumen. Women writers gained literary experience through these journals and learned to produce print culture. In the process, they inaugurated a new profession—journalism—for women. This chapter will consider the making of women's journals as a literary exercise and business enterprise.

FROM IDEA TO PRODUCT

The Arabic women's journal need not have emerged as a form. From the 1880s, journals such as *al-Lata'if* and *al-Muqtataf* had published articles by and about women. These were usually written by female relatives of the editors, including Maryam Nimr, Farida Hubayka, and Ya'qut Barakat.[6] In addition, women occasionally managed general publications. Most notably, the widow of the publisher of *al-Ahram* assumed control of that newspaper in 1901 and ran it for seven years until her son was old enough to manage it.[7] Arabic periodicals might have started women's pages and stopped there, or women might have directed general publications but not have initiated specialized periodicals. Yet women's journals were launched, and the source of inspiration for this idea as well as the course of its development are of interest.

Hind Nawfal opened the first issue of *al-Fatah* in November 1892 by discussing the need for a women's journal. She pointed out that in contrast to the plethora of magazines for women in Europe and the United States, none existed in the East.[8] Although the founder of the Arabic women's press sought to fill a lacuna, *al-Fatah* folded in 1894. The next two women's journals had fitful starts. When Alexandra Avierino began *Anis al-Jalis* in 1898, she also noted that "the learned ladies of this land are lacking a journal especially for them."[9] From that time on, a continuous stream of Arabic women's journals circulated in Egypt. The early women's journals fused indigenous needs and foreign influences into a new form, *al-majalla al-nisa'iyya* (the women's journal). These influences were acknowledged, particularly in the first years of the press. Hind Nawfal, Rosa Antun, and other editors listed European and American women's magazines among their sources, citing some by name.[10]

The idea for separate women's journals, like the original inspiration for Arabic periodicals and newspapers, came from abroad, where the periodical had specialized by gender almost a century and a half earlier. The *Female Spectator,* an English periodical started in 1744, is usually considered the first periodical written by a woman for women. According to one scholar, the early English periodicals of this sort "made themselves necessary to their audience by elevating an ideal [of domesticity] and promising to train their readers to live up to it."[11] By the late 1800s, women's periodicals had flourished in Europe and America for more than a century. Over two hundred and fifty magazines for women existed in England and France alone in the last quarter of the nineteenth century. Although there were significant variations between the periodicals of different countries and among them, general patterns emerged. These included an interest in family and marriage and a promotion of domesticity.[12] Derived from foreign example, the idea of a separate women's journal suited the segregation of Middle Eastern society.

A second or alternative source of inspiration for some Egyptian editors may have been the Turkish women's journals circulating in Istanbul and elsewhere in the Ottoman Empire. Fatima Rashid wrote that she preferred Islamic Turkish literature to the corrupting influence of European works, and she translated selections from Turkish texts for *Tarqiyat al-Mar'a*.[13] Turkish women's journals included *Hanımlara Mahsus Gazete* (Women's gazette, 1895), *Mahasın* (Good moral qualities, 1908), *Kadın* (Woman, 1909), *Kadınlık Hayatı* (Life of womanhood, 1913), and *Kadınlar Dünyasi* (Woman's world, 1913).[14] According to a contemporary report, Belkıs Şevket Hanım, one of the editors of *Kadınlar Dünyası*, rode in a military airplane throwing "feministic literature" on the crowds below; she was received as a hero and her picture placed in the military museum.[15]

Turkish women's journals were probably not as numerous as Arabic women's journals in the years before the Young Turk revolution of 1908 due to Sultan 'Abdul Hamid's heavy hand on the press. *Shajarat al-Durr*, the bilingual Turkish-Arabic journal founded in Alexandria in 1901 by Sa'diyya Sa'd al-Din, may have found a market in Istanbul as a result. Both Turkish and Arabic women's journals covered subjects such as health, education, and the home and stressed women's maternal, conjugal, and religious roles. Both attempted to define a new Ottoman or Egyptian-Arab womanhood.[16] Yet these parallels probably arose from the simultaneous development of the form in similar societies and inspiration from the same source, rather than from conscious copying of one another.

From the 1880s an increasing number of literary and scientific journals were in circulation in Egypt. This in turn helped the production of women's journals as more people learned about publishing and could turn to local monthlies like *al-Muqtataf* as blueprints. In general, female editors kept a close watch on developments in the Arabic press, studying innovations and reporting regularly on new publications. Women's journals were thus a hybrid: the idea from abroad was merged with the examples at hand. Over time the European roots of the Arabic women's press faded as women's journals were adapted to suit Egyptian needs.

The Arabic women's journal took on a recognizable shape and form and established its own conventions as it became part of the local literary landscape. Editors first signaled their purposes through their covers, attempting to attract readers through bright pinks, reds, greens, purples, and other hues. Drawings next caught the eye, with the sphinx, pyramids, palms, and the Nile showing the Egyptian context or flowers suggesting the feminine content. Although a few covers featured drawings of girls or women, representations of women were problematic for Muslim-owned or oriented journals until the 1920s. This was not because of religious injunctions against depicting humans but rather due to conventions on veiling. A lightly veiled woman on the cover of an early issue of *al-'Afaf*, for example, had her veil thickened, and the picture was subsequently removed as a result of conservative attacks on that periodical.[17] Covers mostly announced that these were women's journals with local loyalties.

The titles described the subject matter as well as the audience that editors hoped to attract. *Al-Fatah* (The young woman), *al-Sayyidat wa'l-Banat* (Ladies and girls), *Fatat al-Sharq* (Young woman of the East), and *Fatat al-Nil* (Young woman of the Nile) all emphasized youth. Another series of titles, possibly but not necessarily geared to a slightly older audience, centered on women. These included *al-Mar'a* (The woman), *al-Mar'a fi'l-Islam* (The woman in Islam), and *Tarqiyat al-Mar'a* (Woman's progress), the organ of the organization by that name. (An earlier *al-Mar'a* had been founded by Nadima al-Sabuni in 1893 in the Syrian city of Hama.) *Al-'A'ila* (The family) shifted attention from women to the family, although family was a subject covered by most of these journals.

Whereas these titles were literal, announcing their subject and audience in a word or phrase, other titles were more metaphoric and tended to stress gender polarity. *Al-Jins al-Latif* (The gentle sex) stood in opposition to *al-jins al-nashit* (the stronger sex) and reinforced the complementary but polar roles of men and women. *Anis al-Jalis* (The intimate companion) suggested female bonds and intimacy. Other titles linked women to certain virtues: *al-Firdaus* (Paradise), *al-Sa'ada* (Happiness), and *al-Jamila* (The pretty one). Whether literal or metaphoric, the titles of women's journals generally emphasized youth, womanhood, and gender difference.

The banners below the titles reflected the range of material that editors intended to print in the periodical. Most were identified as "women's" journals, a marker occasionally combined with or replaced by "family," for the line between women's and family journals was blurred. To this was added "scientific" or "literary," which described many contemporary monthlies. A few were "educational," "humorous," or "historical," and the odd one was "social," "moral," or "critical." Absent from the lists were the labels "political" or "religious." Periodicals that intended to discuss issues of this nature were more tightly regulated, especially after the revival of the 1881 Press Law.[18] All of these adjectives gave readers some sense of the contents of the journals, although editors did not always stay within the bounds of their concessions or deliver what they had promised.

Most women's journals, like other literary and scientific periodicals, were published at monthly intervals with a consequent size and shape. Editors faced no pressure to publish with greater frequency, for they rarely dealt with timely news items. Monthly periodicity also suited editors who balanced literary and domestic tasks. The monthly format came to typify a women's journal. Most appeared in the form of six-by-nine inches with one column per page and ran from sixteen to forty-eight pages. They were journals, not magazines, not only because of their smaller size but because of their contents and emphases. The magazines that developed later included more advertisements and pictures, stressed consumption and entertainment over instruction and debate, and featured shorter articles. Although most early women's journals were similarly shaped, the covers and the information that they conveyed revealed to the discerning eye that not all journals were alike. Editors took the liberty of fashioning their periodicals according to their own tastes and temperaments, generating an array of publications that broadly fell into the category of al-majalla al-nisa'iyya.

SUPPLYING THE CONTENTS

Although Sarah al-Mihiyya had initially declined when her teacher asked her to contribute to *al-'Afaf* (she wrote regularly for another paper and had little extra time), she eventually joined the staff. Realizing that many of her submissions to this and other periodicals never appeared, however, Sarah decided to start her own journal, *Fatat al-Nil,* in 1913. She planned it as a "school for girls and ladies" and "a field for their pens."[19] Hind Nawfal had similarly promised to adorn the pages of her journal with "pearls from the pens of women," and Labiba Hashim hoped to print the "cream of women's thoughts."[20]

Editors opened their pages to women's voices. When she learned that Sarah al-Mihiyya wrote in newspapers, a friend came to tell her "what grieves me in order that you publish it in the pages of the press."[21] Such women believed that they would receive redress if they told their stories and expressed their views in print. Moreover, many considered articulation and publication the first steps in the process of women's awakening and the promotion of progress. Editors sought to provide these women with a literary outlet and readily printed their essays, letters, speeches, stories, and poems. Some journals went one step further and only published material by women. Rosa Antun announced that *al-Sayyidat wa'l-Banat* will "publish all that is useful for ladies and girls . . . and will not publish essays that are not theirs." This was her policy in spite of the desire expressed by some men to print their views in her journal.[22]

Editors solicited material from their own circle of acquaintances. Sarah al-Mihiyya published a column of letters in *Fatat al-Nil* that included correspondence from her sister, her teacher, and school friends. When articles were not forthcoming, editors devised strategies to encourage contributions. They set contests and offered prizes. The editor of *al-'Afaf* started a competition that was "restricted to ladies only to encourage and stimulate them."[23] Huda Sha'rawi, founder of al-Ittihad al-Nisa'i al-Misri (the Egyptian Feminist Union, 1923), promised a prize to the reader of *Fatat al-Sharq* who wrote the best essay on ways that women could participate in the struggle for Egyptian progress on the eve of World War I.[24] Some editors apparently faced an overabundance of contributions, as solicited and unsolicited manuscripts poured into their offices. They then apologized to readers for not printing all the articles that were sent due to lack of space.[25] Most of the material in the women's press came from women, fulfilling the dreams of pioneers of the press. The "field for women's pens" had proven fertile.

It remained for editors to shape these contributions, find supplementary material, and draft the rest. Although they did not necessarily sign all their own pieces—a literary convention understood by readers— editors often wrote the balance of each issue. They drew on their own experiences and their observations of the lives of family and friends. In addition, they gathered materials from various sources, "borrowing" from the press and translating foreign literature. Though a few protested the piracy from local periodicals—"a disgracefully widespread practice among some of our newspapers"[26]—copying foreign texts was more acceptable, especially given the absence of copyright restrictions.

As the women's journal developed a standard shape and size, readers came to have certain expectations about content. That editors understood this was clear from their notes to readers. Fatima Rashid apologized in the first issue of *Tarqiyat al-Mar'a* for not printing any essays on child-raising, women's manners, or household duties because of limited space. By the middle of the second decade of the women's press, readers anticipated articles on these topics, and Fatima promised coverage in future issues.[27] Journals usually included essays on work, education, marriage, and similar subjects, as well as biographical and historical sketches and sections on household instruction in cooking, cleaning, managing servants, raising children, and sewing. Literary selections, either prose or poetry, often followed, frequently serialized at the end of an issue. News sections generally proved brief, reporting on communal, regional, or world affairs, and letters from readers often appeared. Notices, sayings, jokes, and pictures were interspersed with the rest of the material. Editors also sought to distinguish their journals from others by adding special columns on health, customs, travel, or some other feature.

While no journal was typical, and certainly no single issue was representative, a look at the contents of *Fatat al-Nil* in the third issue of its second year (Rabi' I, 1333/January 1915) shows the range in one of the more Islamicly oriented journals:

> Historical Section: al-Imam Ali and al-Sayyida Nafisa
> Social Study: Letter from a Father to a Daughter
> The Smoking Habit (part 3): Coffee and Smoking
> Justice as the Basis of Sovereignty
> The Japanese Woman (part 2)
> To the Wife
> Literary Section
> Household Management
> To the Father
> Sad Illustrations: A Child's Elegy
> Scattered Bits from Greek Philosophers
> Questions Calling for an Answer

Fillers included useful household lessons, advice, and *hadith* (traditions attributed to the Prophet). The disparate parts of this issue added up to a whole, attempting to educate and to argue for reform.

The journals evolved over time. The earliest borrowed more heavily from European sources for stories and subject matter than later ones. Biographical sketches—a standard piece in the press—shifted from a focus on Western women to Arab, Muslim, and Egyptian women, a change corresponding to the "indigenization" of the journal. Arabic women's journals also broadened their targeted audience beyond a small community, dropping news of limited interest, like birth and wedding announcements, as circulation spread beyond the city of origin and the initial core of readers. Although editors continued to author a good deal of the periodical, outside contributions multiplied over time, and some journals were almost exclusively made up of contributions. Periodicals tended to increase in size as editors added columns, sometimes by specialists, and advances in technology generally improved production. Drawings eventually gave way to photographs, although photos of Muslim women rarely appeared at a time when many still covered their faces.

The journals set out to educate middle- and upper-class women and to advocate on their behalf. Most of the education effort was geared to domestic instruction, reflecting a consensus about women's priorities and duties. An ideology of womanhood emerged from the early women's press that reinforced women's roles as mother, wife, and homemaker. Discussions of women's responsibilities were balanced with ones on the rights of woman, by which they mostly meant access to schooling and greater autonomy within the family. The domestic component of the press remained central, distinguishing women's journals from literary and scientific ones. Nonetheless, not all women's journals were alike. Editors often took contending positions in contemporary debates and offered varied agendas for reform. Yet they shared the experience of making a women's journal and also shared the risks and challenges inherent in such an undertaking.

FUNDING A JOURNAL

Although built on a tradition of women owning property and managing small enterprises in Egypt, running a journal was still a new profession for women in the late nineteenth century, one that combined literary skills and business talent. Whereas one or two editors may have been independently wealthy and used their own resources, most were from the middle class and had limited means; they needed financial assistance to capitalize their project and meet the costs of production. These costs included paper, postage, and renting an office, in addition to the fees of writers, editors, and printers. Some of the costs might have been waived, particularly if the owner was also the editor, if she had free access to a press, and if she received contributions or generated enough copy on her own to avoid paying writers by the word. Costs also varied under different circumstances. Editors' pay generally ranged from eight to ten Egyptian pounds a month, and only in a few rare cases did their monthly salaries reach forty or fifty pounds. (When Shaykh 'Abd al-'Aziz Jawish became editor of *al-Liwa'* after Mustafa Kamil's death, he received forty pounds a month, a handsome income.) Yet editors who were owners of a publication, particularly a new one, probably could not afford to set aside a regular salary for themselves.[28]

What about the cost of a press or the fees of printers? One printer offered to sell his press for twenty-five pounds in 1919, but leased it instead at two pounds a month, a price that included the salaries of the printers.[29] Other costs are equally hard to determine but added up. When the British started up a weekly Arabic paper for propaganda purposes during World War I, they estimated an initial expenditure of sixty pounds and recurrent expenditures of two hundred pounds per month, which turned out to be good approximations. The government press printed the weekly for free, but paper for one thousand issues had to be bought specially and writers had to be paid at a rate of one pound per five hundred Arabic words.[30] Moreover, wartime prices had boosted costs. Twenty years earlier, a subvention of twenty-five pounds a month plus one hundred pounds for starting up was considered enough for launching an Arabic paper.[31]

Faced with many if not all of these costs, editors of the women's press employed different strategies to fund their periodicals. Some of their colleagues in the general press, particularly editors of a few well-known dailies, relied on subsidies from patrons (the British, the French, the khedive, the sultan) in return for support in print. These subventions usually ranged from about twenty-five to one hundred pounds a month, with donations sometimes thrown in, and were offered to some monthlies as well.[32] One scholar has suggested that Malaka Sa'd received funds from Coptic societies in exchange for covering Coptic communal affairs but presented no evidence other than the coverage itself.[33] Because editors of women's journals usually avoided discussions of the sort that patrons sought and because they lacked connections to those in a position to give subsidies, they were generally unlikely clients.

Those who obtained outside support probably got it in the form of a purchase of a block of subscriptions. Prince Muhammad 'Ali Pasha, for example, gave copies of *Fatat al-Nil* to several girls' schools, and other backers bought blocks of subscriptions.[34] Yet these were not on the scale of some government grants. The Ministry of Interior gave the Muslim Benevolent Society seven hundred pounds a year for 4,100 subscriptions of its journal.[35] But editors of the women's press did not receive large contracts of this sort. Nor could they rely on the smaller gifts sometimes given to sustain their publications. The virtue in the lack of large subventions was that editors were more or less free to express their own views rather than argue a patron's position and could write more independently than those at newspapers and periodicals indebted to outside interests. This enhances the value of these journals as a historical source.

An alternative strategy used to finance publications was to form a company to raise capital. Some sixty or so notables founded such a company in 1906 to produce the newspaper *al-Jarida,* which was started the following year (when these men also formed the Umma party). The group raised £E 20,000, of which 80 percent was paid up at the outset, and was therefore not dependent on outside sponsors. The origins of this paper were not typical, however, for the shareholders of the company were a particularly wealthy group.[36] The members of Jam'iyyat Tarqiyat al-Mar'a (the Society for Woman's Progress) may have followed a similar model but on a much smaller scale when they started the organ of their group in 1908. Yet most newspapers or periodicals were the output of one or two individuals, not the products of companies or organizations. They were started with limited capital and had to find a way to pay quickly.[37]

Another technique to raise funds was through advertising. Some editors placed ads on the back pages of their journals or at the bottom of a page of text. One of the earliest advocates of advertising, Alexandra Avierino, tried to convince other periodical owners of its benefits. She argued that advertising linked buyers and sellers in the free market that had emerged in Egypt as the fixed prices and monopoly on labor of the guild system disappeared.[38] Alexandra devoted almost 20 percent of the space in *Anis al-Jalis* to ads, far more than similar women's, literary, and scientific journals. These advertisements promoted clothing shops, pharmacies, and a variety of other stores, as well as the services of music teachers, governesses, seamstresses, and others. Yet women's journals were neither consumer-oriented nor consumed by fashion. Though advertisements added some revenue, they probably could not sustain a journal before World War I.

Most editors of women's journals seemed to rely on subscriptions as a main source of income for their periodical. Agents—who were sometimes book dealers, printers, or friends—were appointed to sell subscriptions. Unfortunately, they were not always trustworthy: *al-Jins al-Latif* reported that one former agent was forging subscription forms and withholding funds, and *al-'Afaf* redistricted the regions of its representatives after a problem with "immoral" agents.[39] The zeal with which editors called upon readers to pay their bills showed their reliance on these funds. An agent of *al-'Afaf* assailed those who did not pay "under the pretense of some that the newspaper goes to them free of charge because of their personal connection to the director of *al-'Afaf*," and called on subscribers to pay late bills so that they could cover operating costs.[40] Editors wanted subscription fees in advance and when they felt particularly pressed by lack of funds, they might reduce the rate if subscriptions were paid immediately.[41] Other editors begged and pleaded with readers, offering incentives to those who submitted the names of new subscribers. In short, a women's journal had little chance of surviving without at least some revenue from readers.

In whatever fashion they financed their journals, editors had to keep an eye on changing economic circumstances, nationally and internationally. Egypt had few industries and her economy was essentially tied to the price of cotton—her main cash crop—on the world market. The economy boomed from 1895, with many thinking that the possibility for reclaiming land was endless. But the 1907 recession, linked to a recession in Europe, ended this period of prosperity. Agricultural yields peaked, and two years of poor cotton harvests followed. Various problems began to manifest themselves, including soil depletion, underproduction of necessary foods, and infestation of canals by parasites.[42] Although there was some recovery, World War I plunged the nation once again into economic turmoil, sending the prices of various commodities and foods soaring.[43] These fluctuations affected the press and tested the financial skills and staying power of periodical owners. During the 1907 economic crisis, Labiba Hashim delayed a planned expansion in the size of *Fatat al-Sharq*. Later during the war she apologized to readers when she cut a section, "for a reason that the readers know," the scarcity of supplies and the price of paper.[44] Faced with similar wartime shortages, Malaka Sa'd cut back columns, started combining issues, and printed *al-Jins al-Latif* on a poorer quality paper. She urged subscribers to send in their money right away and even requested donations.[45] Editors adapted to the exigencies of the moment and scrambled to balance the books so that they could continue producing their journals.

RUNNING THE OPERATION

Editors also balanced their time, a feat that intrigued readers. Some had apparently asked Labiba Hashim how she managed to produce her journal while taking care of her children and tending to the housework. In an article entitled "How I Edit My Journal!!!" she explained that she spent two hours every morning beginning at ten o'clock (after she had completed her domestic chores but when some women were just awaking) writing, editing, and arranging the affairs of the journal. The routine was broken only during the summer when, like many editors, she suspended publication for two months.[46]

Running a journal was a business that could be conducted from the home. Yet editors also listed offices, which were sometimes directed by family members. Hind Nawfal's father ran the office of *al-Fatah,* and Alexandra Avierino's husband administered the office of *Anis al-Jalis.* Other editors shared offices with siblings and spouses. Rosa Antun and her brother gave one address for their twinned periodicals *al-Sayyidat wa'l-Banat* and *al-Jami'a,* and Fatima Rashid's *Tarqiyat al-Mar'a* and her husband's *al-Dustur* shared a space. Offices were occasionally located in Fajjala, a popular section in Cairo for printing, binding, and bookselling. Although newspaper offices were gathering spots in certain intellectual circles and the sites of lively discussions and debates, it is difficult to know if the offices of the women's press served the same function. That editors dutifully informed readers when offices were moved suggests that their locations were important to readers, whether or not they occasionally visited.

Editors stored current and back issues of the journals in their offices and offered them for sale. If a journal became popular, readers might request earlier issues, which then increased in value. The remaining issues of the first volume of *al-Manar,* for example, were sold at four times the original price in the journal's twelfth year.[47] Malaka Sa'd repeatedly called for back issues of *al-Jins al-Latif*, presumably to make complete sets for patrons. In the journal's eighth year, she called for an issue from the fourth year and offered to replace single issues with books, indicating that the value of past issues had increased.[48] Editors also occasionally sold books publicized in their periodicals or stories serialized over a number of issues and later bound as books from their offices. In addition, they provided a clearinghouse for information, linking consumers and advertisers through messages left at the office. Correspondence directed to the journal ended up there as well.

Some women's journals were printed on a family press. Fatima Rashid's journal came out on the press of her husband's newspaper, and Regina 'Awwad's monthly was published on Amin 'Awwad's press. A few papers, such as *al-'Afaf*, owned their own press. Yet most women's journals were printed on the press of an unrelated paper or at an independent printer, which was not an unusual practice. *Al-Manar*, for example, had been printed early on at the office of *al-Mu'ayyad*.[49] Two journals—*al-'A'ila* and *al-Jins al-Latif*—were published on the Tawfiq Press, whose owner, Francis Mikha'il, was the author of the popular book *Tadbir al-Manzil* (Household management).[50] Since the print trade was predominantly male, segregated women sought help in dealing with printers. This sort of arrangement was consistent with the practice of appointing agents as proxies in business. The author Zaynab Fawwaz turned to her brother, a lawyer, to oversee publication of her biographical dictionary at the government printing office.[51] Muslim editors like Sarah al-Mihiyya probably had a similar arrangement with a family member or male agent.

Editors also saw to the distribution of their periodicals, which moved mostly through the post. In the nineteenth century the postal system in Egypt had developed under an Italian concession from an array of foot messengers traveling between Alexandria and Cairo into an organized system based on the railroad. The Egyptian government purchased the Italian concession in 1865 and then proceeded to absorb the independent European postal services, a process that was nearly completed by 1900. The government office printed its own stamps (featuring the sphinx and pyramids), kept accounts, and issued money orders. The postal system expanded rapidly to accommodate the increased demands placed upon its services, which resulted in part from the multiplication of periodicals and newspapers in Egypt. The rural, branch, and main post offices numbered about eight hundred in 1898; fifteen years later this number had more than doubled. Rural and urban areas now had access to mail service, homes and offices had delivery, and people could obtain post office boxes. Even with the increased volume and weight of the mail, difficult terrain, and diversity of languages, the Egyptian postal system made a profit at the turn of the century.[52]

Journal owners followed the affairs of the post closely, recognizing that the distribution of their periodicals depended upon its efficient functioning and that journals gone astray could be problematic. Readers of *al-Manar* complained about late and missing issues, and the editor, Rashid Rida, noted in 1899 that delivery from Egypt to Tunis had increased from nine to seventeen days.[53] Readers of *al-Afaf* also reported missing and delayed papers, which were investigated as the editor pressed the postal authorities to improve services.[54] Others applauded this branch of the government. Jurji Zaydan, editor of *al-Hilal,* reviewed postal reforms and praised the director. Labiba Hashim later thanked the director for having taken an interest in the mailing of her journal.[55]

Were the journals lucrative? Did editors make money or expect to? Editors recognized the investment in time and money involved in producing a periodical. Labiba Hashim highlighted the importance of material published by newspapers at the cost to editor-owners of physical exhaustion and enormous expenditure.[56] None of these women stated profit as their main motive for starting a journal, however, and clearly some lost money. (This was the case for Rashid Rida through his years of producing *al-Manar.*)[57] Yet not all editors shared the same motives or had the same financial concerns. Those who had no independent source of income to fund their journal—and few had unlimited funds—certainly expected some return. Perhaps they only hoped to break even. While calling for subscription fees to cover costs, *al-'Afaf* disavowed profits and contributed extra funds to the building of schools and shelters for girls, or so it claimed.[58] Others argued that the prices they set for publications were fair. In marketing a book available at her journal's office, Alexandra Avierino insisted that it was priced at cost, denying that she was motivated in any way by profit.[59] Most editors probably expected to make at least enough money to keep on publishing and possibly to draw a salary or small return from their enterprise. Although some editors had independent means, we cannot assume that all journalists, male or female, worked for free or continuously subsidized their own publications.

Without records of income and expenditures, it remains hard to ascertain the profitability of women's journals—or any other periodicals or newspapers for that matter. Lord Kitchener estimated in 1914, when there were over sixty daily and weekly Arabic newspapers in Cairo alone and more elsewhere in Egypt, that "two may be said to bring in a fair return, one pays its way, a few of the others are subsidized by high personages or political parties, and the rest eke out a miserable existence with unpaid staffs and rent in arrears. They appear, disappear and appear again spasmodically."[60] Alexandra Avierino, who was closer to the business, had a more optimistic assessment. She found that many who published periodicals became rich from the profits or at least received remuneration.[61] Based on the length of their publication and other evidence, some journals seemed to be successful business enterprises, making journalism a viable option for those women with the requisite skills.

Yet a new direction in journalism loomed on the horizon: the building of large companies and conglomerations of papers. By 1919 at least eight Arabic and foreign-language newspapers in Egypt (including the popular daily *al-Ahram*) were owned by the Société de Publicité Orientale, whose major shareholder was Maltese.[62] This trend would turn the production of journals from a small business, in which an owner was often the editor and had a good deal of autonomy, into a large industry, in which one company produced a number of publications. In the early twentieth century, however, opportunities for the small businessman and businesswoman still existed. A new profession for women was established, and a new medium for their expression born.

COMPETITION AND CAMARADERIE

The founders of the women's press saw themselves as professionals. Both Esther Moyal and Malaka Sa'd presented themselves as owners of journals, and Alexandra Avierino posed for a photograph with a copy of her periodical in hand, in a posture suggesting pride of ownership.[63] Editors featured foreign female industrialists and entrepreneurs in biographical sketches. They admired their business acumen, something they needed in dealing with the practical problems of producing a journal.[64]

These writers entered journalism at a time when educated women had few professional options. Blocked from becoming doctors, women could get some health care training or could become teachers.[65] The first professions opened to women were ones that served other women while helping to preserve the system of segregation. Women's journals were also presented as a service to women. "From the time that I could move the pen," remembered Labiba Hashim, "I thought of founding a women's journal to serve the ladies and girls of the nation." Labiba had started her journal "in service of the fair sex and advance of Eastern woman."[66] Malaka Sa'd had dedicated *al-Jins al-Latif* "to that which improves the situation of Egyptian woman in particular and Eastern woman in general."[67]

As the number of women's journals multiplied, editors might have seen newcomers as competitors. But this does not seem to have been the case. Editors welcomed new women's journals in literary notices, promoting the development of the literary form they had pioneered. Alexandra Avierino introduced *Shajarat al-Durr* as "the new companion to our journal" and listed new women's journals throughout the tenure of her *Anis al-Jalis*.[68] Upon the appearance of Malaka Sa'd's *al-Jins al-Latif*, Labiba Hashim welcomed her "new colleague" and wished the journal "endurance and success," and the two editors greeted subsequent newcomers.[69] These notices suggest that an atmosphere of congeniality and camaraderie characterized the women's press, in contrast to the spirit of hostility that sometimes typified the daily press. New journals were not necessarily competing, for they often catered to a special audience or found a specific niche. The appearance of a new women's journal, moreover, confirmed the legitimacy of the endeavor, and numbers assured the survival of the women's press even if a particular journal failed.

The fact that some men started women's periodicals provides further proof of the growing acceptance of the literary form. An analysis of those periodicals founded by men reveals, not surprisingly, the different ways in which male and female journalists crafted women's periodicals. Some of the periodicals edited by men appeared in tabloid form with more columns on fewer pages than those journals edited by women. Bimonthly, weekly, or biweekly publication was preferred to monthly periodicity, showing that men were not as constrained by domestic obligations as their female colleagues. Male editors also often chose names for their periodicals that differed from those selected by their female counterparts. Whereas the latter generally preferred literal names, male editors most often turned to abstractions, such as *Mir'at al-Hasna'* (Mirror of the beautiful), *al-'Afaf* (Virtue), and *al-Sufur* (Unveiling). Even *al-Mar'a fi'l-Islam* (The woman in Islam) implies a timelessness and a viewing of woman through an unchanging prism. These names suggest that male editors were generally more attracted by the ideal of woman than by the concrete realities of women's lives, a pattern usually borne out by the contents of their pages.

Front-page banner descriptions like "nationalist" suggested greater attention to politics, and male editors often placed the question of women's status in the context of political debate. *Al-Rayhana,* for example, coupled "Egypt for the Egyptians" with demands for the rights of woman guaranteed by Islamic law.[70] Mixed with the nationalist debate, or subsumed by it, women became a metaphor in the struggle for independence. "Women are not the only ones who are veiled in Egypt," wrote 'Abd al-Hamid Hamdi, editor of *al-Sufur.* "We are a veiled nation."[71] Although *al-'Afaf* and *al-Sufur* contested the boundaries of modesty and separation, both periodicals shared a concern for the symbolic meaning of woman in society. Both politicized the issue of the rights of woman and both used women's progress as a means to measure morality or modernity. Female editors by contrast were less preoccupied with issues like the veil and more attentive to ones like marriage, divorce, work, and education. Editors of both sexes nonetheless hoped to improve women's lives, and their positions on the "woman question" were not set by sex. Finally, whether produced by female or male editors, women's periodicals formed a cohesive body.

From the appearance of the first Arabic women's journals, observers were aware of the originality of the endeavor. The editors of *al-Muqtataf* applauded *al-Fatah* as an "incomparable pearl" when it came out for "it restricts itself to that which concerns woman and opens its columns only to the pens of women."[72] Jurji Zaydan welcomed the arrival of *al-Fatah*, which appeared the same year he started *al-Hilal*, as "the first Arabic paper founded by an Eastern lady," and he continued to announce the arrival of new Arabic revues of this sort.[73] These editors were probably pleased that a fellow Syrian had conceived and initiated the first Arabic women's journal. Rashid Rida argued that the nation might benefit more from the new periodicals than from the political papers that were so rife.[74] The endorsement of these male journalists—editors of important literary and scientific monthlies—no doubt eased the entry of female journalists into a field that might have been hostile or, equally unfortunate, might have ignored their existence altogether.

The notices that appeared regularly in such journals as *al-Muqtataf,* *al-Hilal,* and *al-Manar* charted the growth of the women's press. One of the closest watchers of the women's press was Jurji Niqula Baz (1882–1959), a Beiruti nicknamed "Nasir al-Mar'a" (the supporter of woman) and son-in-law of the poet Warda al-Yaziji.[75] A biographer compared Baz to Qasim Amin in Egypt, Jamil Sidqi al-Zahawi in Iraq, and al-Shaykh 'Abd al-Qadir al-Maghribi in Syria "in relation to feminism and the call for the liberation of Arab woman from the chains that bind her."[76] Baz edited the women's journal *al-Hasna'* (The beautiful) in Beirut from 1909 to 1912 and published a series of articles on the women's press in various periodicals. One of his most exhaustive studies appeared in *Fatat Lubnan* and listed the names, editors, and places of publication of twenty-five Arabic women's periodicals produced up to 1914: twenty had been published in Egypt, three in Syria, one in Algiers, and one in New York.[77] Although he missed a few short-lived publications, Baz captured the growth and vitality of the early Arabic women's press. His articles documented the birth of a new sort of journal and testified to its acceptance in the literary world. The women's journal had taken root.

The close to thirty periodicals and newspapers produced in the first quarter century of the Arabic women's press demonstrated its strength and, at the same time, revealed its frailty. Although many tried their hand at this business, few succeeded for a long stretch. About half the journals did not survive the first year, and another fifth did not mature beyond three years. This attrition rate reflected the situation of the general press during a period in which many periodicals and newspapers competed for a limited number of readers, and most proved of short duration. This rate is also probably little different from the start-up rate of other sorts of new businesses, especially in uncertain economic times.

Many journals succumbed in the face of financial difficulties. Because of her losses in the 1907 recession, Alexandra Avierino closed *Anis al-Jalis* after a decade of publication.[78] Fatima Rashid's appeals for more subscribers a year later, at the end of *Tarqiyat al-Mar'a*'s first year, may not have been answered, and it is unclear how much longer, if at all, this journal lasted.[79] World War I, with its severe shortages and skyrocketing costs, brought down other journals, including Sarah al-Mihiyya's *Fatat al-Nil,* which folded after less than two years of operation. Other women's journals were silenced for family reasons. Hind Nawfal's *al-Fatah* stopped some months after her marriage, and Rosa Antun's *al-Sayyidat wa'l-Banat* was suspended when she followed her brother to the United States.[80]

Still, some journals thrived. *Anis al-Jalis* (1898–1908) had appeared for over a decade before closing; Malaka Sa'd's *al-Jins al-Latif* (1908–1925) lasted for eighteen years; and Labiba Hashim's *Fatat al-Sharq* (1906–1939) surpassed them all, running for thirty-four years. The longevity of their publications should be ascribed to the editors' talent for business, as well as to their literary abilities. Their successes show, moreover, that producing a women's journal was more than a hobby for a few wealthy women. Regularly turning out a periodical was a serious undertaking requiring a commitment of energy and resources. By making women's journals, these writers helped to establish a new profession and to provide women with greater access to print culture.

Understanding the conditions under which editors labored and turned out these periodicals establishes a context for the ideas put forward in their pages; these will be explored at greater length in the second part of this book. Acknowledging the constraints surrounding the production of a journal generally confirms the independence of action of editors and increases the value of the women's press as a historical source. It also highlights the accomplishments of those who were instrumental in the making of journals. In their struggle to succeed, editors bridged literary and business worlds, following both intellectual trends and market conditions. Most of all, they kept a close watch on the consumers of their product—their readers.

4

THE COMMUNITY
OF READERS

Reading was not a new phenomenon for women in Egypt. Daughters of the ulama and others had occasionally been taught by tutors in medieval times,[1] and this pattern persisted into the early nineteenth century. Edward Lane found in the 1830s that although female children were seldom taught to read or write, a *shaykha* (learned woman) sometimes instructed the girls of the wealthiest families, and that a few middle-class girls attended school with boys. The central text for these lessons was the Qur'an.[2] In the 1860s an *'alim* (cleric) in Luxor told a traveler that he was teaching his little girl of six or seven to write, claiming that no one else thought of doing such a thing outside of Cairo.[3] White slaves, destined for the homes of the elite, received religious instruction and were taught to read but not to write.[4]

Still, oral transmission of culture predominated in the nineteenth century, and women were probably more accustomed to texts being read aloud, or more accurately recited (for the text itself may have been absent if memorized), than to the thought of reading themselves. Female professional readers of the Qur'an were sometimes hired to recite from the holy book at gatherings, and some wealthy women set aside money for the reading aloud of prayers at their tombs.[5] If taught to read at all— and few were—women were taught in order to read religious works. Yet it was difficult to ensure that women, once literate, would restrict themselves to religious books, especially as Egypt became a market for new genres. Most women were discouraged from learning to read, or if they became literate, not encouraged to read widely, for it was thought that reading improper texts would lead to immoral behavior. Suhayr al-Qalamawi, a writer born in 1911, recorded her grandmother's words: "This habit of reading is an ailment which women of my generation did not suffer from. Bless our good old times! I never allowed my daughters enough time a day to read. Free time only brings devious ideas and thoughts in the minds of girls. Reading to me is like doing nothing. I never let my daughters read a book that their father or elder brothers had not read before them."[6]

This attitude began to change in the late nineteenth century as the middle and upper classes increasingly viewed reading as a necessary skill for women. Rather than a road to immorality, reading became a way to build moral character and domestic expertise. Permissible reading expanded beyond religious texts into a broadening world of secular works, which included domestic literature and women's journals. This chapter focuses on the rise of women readers, the new consumers of literary culture. It shows how, in spite of low literacy, the early women's press disseminated ideas in Egypt. Yet it challenges the assumption that the new literary medium created public opinion by simply stamping ideas on a passive audience. Readers of the women's press, to the contrary, showed themselves to be active and loyal.[7]

TOWARD GREATER LITERACY

The data provided by censuses reveal very low literacy rates for men and women in late nineteenth- and early twentieth-century Egypt, a situation probably exacerbated by the difference between colloquial and literary Arabic. According to the 1897 census, 8 percent of Egyptian men and 0.2 of Egyptian women were literate, by which census takers meant sedentary Egyptians above age seven who could read and write.[8] Alexandra Avierino figured that there were 31,200 potential female readers of her *Anis al-Jalis,* which included Syrian and other non-Egyptian Arabic readers.[9] In the next ten years Egyptian female literacy jumped 50 percent compared with a 6.25 percent increase in male literacy.[10] By 1917, the figures for women had climbed again, with the number of literate Muslim women more than tripling and literate Coptic women increasing at an even higher rate.[11]

The censuses of 1897, 1907, and 1917 should be compared with caution, however, for they were supervised by different directors and did not have uniform definitions and variables. For example, the cut-off age for literacy was seven in 1897, ten in 1907, and five in 1917. Moreover, individuals who could read but not write—such as the slaves mentioned earlier—would have been counted by census takers as illiterate. (Whether a widespread pattern of readers of this sort existed might be checked by examining instruction in schools.) Observers were nonetheless impressed with the percentage increase in female literacy, although the absolute number of readers remained very small.

Whereas the censuses should not be taken as completely reliable sources on male or female literacy (census takers were men who queried male heads of household), the statistics still showed some interesting patterns. The most striking was the concentration of literacy in major cities, which was not surprising given the greater number of schools and greater support for education in urban areas than in the countryside.[12] Two cultures had emerged in Egypt by the turn of the century: an urban one, constituted by 17 percent of the population, which was partially literate, and a rural one, representing most of the population, which was overwhelmingly illiterate.[13] Yet pockets of female readers could be found away from the larger centers: there were close to three hundred in Bani Suwayf in 1907, for example, and two hundred in al-Mahalla al-Kubra. Readers were also scattered in more remote towns, villages, and oases: there were thirty-three in Kafr Saqr and one in Kharja.[14]

Literacy rates rose most rapidly among the young—also not surprising given the spread of girls' education in this period. The percentage of female literacy was higher between ten and fourteen than twenty and over, and highest at fifteen to nineteen.[15] In addition, literacy among Coptic women was proportionately higher than that among Muslim women, primarily because the drive to send girls to schools began earlier in the Coptic community. (In 1907 the literacy of Coptic men per 1000 was 2.5

times greater than that of Muslim men, and the literacy of Coptic women per 1000 was 8 times greater than that of Muslim women. Seen from another angle, there were thirty-eight times more male Muslim readers than female Muslim readers and twelve times more male Coptic readers than female Coptic readers.) [16] Taken together, the statistics suggest that an evolution in literacy had begun among the young in urban Egyptian centers.

Articles arguing for female education filled the press as certain strata began frowning upon illiteracy. One Muslim housewife told Zakiya al-Kafrawiyya, who was reporting for *al-'Afaf*, of her regret at being unable to read. She thought that she had learned "all that a mistress of the house needed" to know and had not thought that she needed to master reading and writing, but she confessed that "now not a single month passes without my feeling bored." [17] Her sense of inadequacy contrasted with what teachers called "the intense conceit" of girl students who were sometimes the only ones at home who could read. [18] Literacy raised the status of readers in the family and in society, and as reading became more respectable for women, writers pointed to pioneers in this endeavor. *Al-Fatah* celebrated Rahil al-Bustani as the first woman to learn to read in a Syrian school. [19] Although daughters of notables had studied privately in the past, new schools made literacy attainable to larger segments of the population and in particular to the new middle class.

Still, literacy did not necessarily imply Arabic literacy. One British traveler returning to Europe by steamship in the early 1900s seemed surprised at the conduct and reading matter of Muslim women, who had stayed "shrouded up to the eyes" until they reached the ship and then appeared the next morning at the public meal "unveiled, bareheaded, clad in the latest Parisian travelling fashion" and supplied with French novels. [20] The American traveler Elizabeth Cooper, in Egypt before World War I, found Coptic women often fluent in English and French and observed them reading Browning and Tennyson. [21] Some of these Egyptian women could not read Arabic, however, a phenomenon that disturbed many intellectuals. Labiba Hashim illustrated the grave danger of Arabic illiteracy through the story of a young woman who applied carbolic acid to her hand thinking it was cologne. When asked why she had not read the label, she replied that she had studied French not Arabic.[22] Nationalists of various tendencies called for the expansion of Arabic education in state and private schools.

Debates over the benefits of Arabic versus foreign-language education suggested, nonetheless, that opposition to female literacy among the middle and upper classes had eroded. Parents no longer questioned whether their daughters should learn to read and write but wondered what languages they ought to be taught. Once perceived as dangerous, female literacy became not only accepted but expected. Literacy inspired a new group with pride, and sometimes conceit, opening the door to a new literary culture. As Suhayr al-Qalamawi's grandmother confided to her, "You already know more than I ever knew or would even like to know."[23] The meaning of reading had changed in the space of two generations and with it the attitude toward printed texts.

LITERARY TASTES

Books became a symbol of the times, signifying the new attitude toward literacy and literature. Labiba Hashim noted in 1912 that it was rare to see a woman without a book or a journal in hand.[24] Although no guarantee that she read it, carrying a printed text showed that a woman identified with the new literary culture. In her often reprinted manual on household management, *Rabbat al-Dar* (Mistress of the house), Malaka Sa'd advised women to place books, journals, and newspapers on a table in the reception hall.[25] Again, visitors may not have read the works while awaiting their hosts, but the presentation of the literature signified that this was a house of readers, or at least a home where family members respected the new literary culture. Even Elizabeth Cooper noticed the proliferation of Arabic periodicals, newspapers, novels, and books, finding these "popular educators" in every home now that education for women had become such "a fetish" in Egypt.[26]

What exactly were women perusing? What were the literary tastes of young female readers in early twentieth-century Egypt? Conduct books tried to guide them in their selections. Zaynab Mursi, a Muslim schoolteacher, told girls to study the life of 'A'isha, Mother of the Believers, as well as other worthy women in history books. At the same time she warned them "to stop reading nighttime stories, for they are a source of corruption."[27] Although steered toward historical texts with religious themes, women may have preferred the novels that bothered Zaynab. These included translations, adaptations, and originals of foreign works readily available in Egypt in the early 1900s.

Readers could find a rich assortment of works at the Khedivial Library, which was founded in 1870. In the last decades of the nineteenth century, books were purchased in literature, medicine, history, geography, and politics, among other fields. Hundreds of readers came to browse through the collection, consisting of thousands of titles in Arabic, Turkish, Persian, and European languages.[28] The library, which eventually became the Egyptian national library Dar al-Kutub, was run by a succession of German Orientalists until World War I, when Ahmad Lutfi al-Sayyid became the first Egyptian director.[29] But this library, as well as those of the Geographical Society, the Municipality of Alexandria, and the new Egyptian University, probably remained out of bounds to women at least until the 1920s. By the 1930s, the situation had changed, causing Suhayr al-Qalamawi's grandmother to observe, "What a difference between your generation and ours. All these public libraries open to you where you can read anything that pleases you."[30]

Late nineteenth- and early twentieth-century women readers who had no access to public libraries turned to whatever was available at home. Huda Sha'rawi remembered purchasing books clandestinely from peddlers who came to the door "even though I was strictly forbidden to do so." Her system for evaluating and sorting them was simple. She kept a book if it was easy to read, "otherwise I tossed it in the cupboard." Frustrated by the limitations of the literature she found in this way, she broke into the bookcase of her late father, a patron of poets and scholars. Taking two books at random, one of which was a collection of poems, she kept them throughout her life. She loved poetry and continued to buy all the books of poems that she could find.[31]

'Anbara Salam al-Khalidi, a Muslim writer from Beirut who grew up in a social milieu similar to that of educated urban Egyptian women, also recorded her early memories of reading. Hers was a case of an obsession: she admitted that she was "passionately in love with reading, taking refuge in it," and in the absence of children's books used to read anything that her hands fell upon, "even the pages of the almanac." Like Huda Sha'rawi, she was forced to content herself with what was available at home. When she found a voluminous book of prayers and invocations in the house, she "read it avidly and did not put it down until I finished it." She persisted because, as she wrote, "the important thing to me was to read." Among her favorite works was *Alf Layla wa-Layla* (A thousand and one nights).[32] Yet 'Anbara was not the first woman in her family to read. Her grandmother had been literate, and her mother had a collection of books that she carried from the home of her father to that of her husband upon marriage. These included Ibn al-Athir's *al-Kamil fi'l-Ta'rikh* (A complete history) and Muhammad Ibn Musa al-Damiri's *Hayat al-Hayawan* (Animal life).[33] 'Anbara also collected books. When she traveled with her family to Cairo in 1912, she visited bookshops to purchase the historical novels of Jurji Zaydan as well as the works of other authors. 'Anbara also read Arabic journals, including *al-Muqtataf, al-Hilal,* and *al-Zuhur,* and the women's monthly *al-Hasna',* edited by Jurji Niqula Baz in Beirut.[34] As a reader, 'Anbara Salam al-Khalidi started young, read with great zeal, developed an interest in history and culture, and added books and journals in these and other fields to her collection.

Scattered comments give glimpses into the contours of women's private libraries. Khadija al-Mihiyya reported that she used the library of her elder sister Sarah, which contained works by women in addition to religious texts. But Khadija did not cite any specific titles.[35] Lists of titles from women's libraries that were recorded in a will or trust would yield quantitative data about literary tastes and cultural outlooks in the early twentieth century.[36] Until such lists are located, however, it might be helpful to consider the books and journals that Malaka Sa'd thought were essential for any home library. In giving advice on furnishing and decorating rooms in her household manual *Rabbat al-Dar,* this Coptic writer described the contents of the shelves in the study. And although Copts comprised only 6 percent of Egypt's population according to the 1907 census (and double that or more by some Coptic accounts), Coptic women made up a much higher percentage of literate Egyptian women, suggesting that Malaka Sa'd was not an untypical reader.[37]

All of the works that Malaka Sa'd mentioned were in Arabic, although a few were translations from other languages. Most of the authors and editors were men, with the exception of Olivia 'Abd al-Shahid, Labiba Hashim, and Malaka herself. The texts ranged from older classics to contemporary works, arranged in categories of health, morality, society, and history (but notably there was no category of politics). The first book was not listed by title, for apparently everyone knew what Dr. 'Abd al-'Aziz Bey Nadhmi had written on health. Other books in that category gave information to pregnant women and new mothers, as well as first aid instruction. Under morality Malaka mentioned among other works *Kalila wa-Dimna* (a popular mirror for princes that instructed by means of animal fables) and the Shafi'i jurist 'Ali Ibn Muhammad al-Mawardi's *Adab al-Din wa'l-Dunya* (Religious and worldly refinement).[38] In the largest category, that of society, books ranged from Olivia 'Abd al-Shahid's *al-'A'ila al-Misriyya* (The Egyptian family) to a text on personal status laws. But Qasim Amin's books on women came first, confirming observations that Egyptian women had read *Tahrir al-Mar'a* (The emancipation of woman) and *al-Mar'a al-Jadida* (The new woman).[39] Several selections by Jurji Zaydan dominated the section on history.

When it came to journals, Malaka's list, like that of 'Anbara Salam al-Khalidi, included *al-Muqtataf* and *al-Hilal*. To these Malaka added her own *al-Jins al-Latif* and Labiba Hashim's *Fatat al-Sharq*, as well as *al-Hayah*, the journal of Fatima Rashid's husband, and two other periodicals. Missing from this list were Arabic novels, a genre just emerging, and Arabic poetry, a well-established form, although both genres would have appeared, serialized or complete, in journals. Since only two dozen or so titles of books and a handful of journals were recorded, the list was no doubt meant to be suggestive rather than comprehensive.

Malaka revealed something of her attitude toward print culture in her discussion of the arrangement of the shelves and the care of the books. The latter were objects to be respected and preserved and ought to be well ordered. She placed the historical texts on one end, followed by those of the other categories. To prevent moth worms from devouring the pages—evidently not an uncommon problem—she suggested that the books be well ventilated and sprinkled with naphthalene. But Malaka did not speak of first printings, page quality, or letter types. She was more concerned with the utility of a book than its value as an aesthetic object. Books were to be used and passed along to friends and relatives. To facilitate borrowing and at the same time try to ensure that the books were returned, Malaka recommended that the volumes be numbered and that these numbers be recorded when they were loaned. This suggests that books circulated from hand-to-hand among an informal network of readers in certain circles in Egyptian society, a practice that may have been especially important to those who lacked access to public libraries.

Journals were also saved, bound in annual volumes, and numbered to become part of a permanent collection. As an editor, Malaka frequently called for back issues of *al-Jins al-Latif* to complete sets.[40] Since back issues rose in value if the journal became a success, journals were not quickly discarded. Rashid Rida reported coming across several copies of *al-'Urwa al-Wuthqa* in his father's papers nearly a decade after the periodical had ceased publication.[41] Journals were thus read well after their original issue, giving them more than a transitory value.

Our knowledge of literary tastes in late nineteenth- and early twentieth-century Egypt remains sketchy. As a result it is easier to say what a few women read or recommended than to establish what most literate women read with great certainty. The women presented here selected religious, historical, scientific, and social texts; prose; and poetry. As their mobility increased in the early 1900s, they were no longer reliant on peddlers or forced to read the books in the house. They could borrow from friends, find books in school, go to stores to make their selections, and eventually they gained entry to public libraries. At the same time, the publishing industry expanded to cater to the growing number of literate Egyptians, offering readers a wider choice of Arabic original and translated materials. Writers also recognized the growing market of women readers and began producing works of special interest to them, including domestic literature and women's journals.

READING HABITS

Since individuals in different times and places have read in different ways, a look at reading habits may provide some clues to a reader's relationship to, and interpretation of, a text. An analysis of reading habits and postures also illuminates attitudes toward print culture and its place in society. Reading for women in the late nineteenth and early twentieth centuries was often a sociable experience carried out among family members. Journals and books were read aloud at home. "If the mother cannot read them—and few of the women of the older day can read— the daughter and the grand-daughters can read to them," noted Elizabeth Cooper.[42] Husbands were encouraged to discuss the contents of relevant texts with their wives if the latter could not read.[43] Texts were often absorbed through the ears and not the eyes. This meant that the literary work might be discussed by the family or a reading circle.

Reading was not always sociable, however. As literacy grew, it became a private, occasionally even an antisocial, affair. Labiba Hashim's young son resented the newspaper, or so she tells us, for he could not bear to see his mother sit staring at it for hours.[44] Reading was an activity that could be undertaken in the absence of company or could substitute for it, and writers depicted books and journals as "friends." Alexandra Avierino named her journal "the intimate companion" (*Anis al-Jalis*), and Zaynab Mursi considered a book to be "a companion in the evening."[45] Gas and electric light provided new possibilities for reading into the night in the wealthier quarters where they could be found. Malaka Sa'd even advised readers of her household manual exactly where to place different sorts of lighting for nighttime reading.[46]

Women generally read at school or at home. In school they sat on benches, which were no doubt uncomfortable but kept students awake, and at home they sometimes read at desks. Yet mostly they read more at ease, probably reclining in the European-style chairs and couches furnishing many middle- and upper-class Egyptian homes. When Labiba Hashim complained that people relaxed at home reading the paper and did not need anything except half a piaster to do so—in contrast to newspaper owners who invested time and money—she revealed something of the reading habits of her audience.[47] Egyptian readers maintained their leisure habits when they traveled abroad. As an observer on board a ship bound for Europe noted, Egyptian women not only brought reading matter but came "supplied with the latest thing in steamer-chairs."[48]

Reading aloud or silently, sharing a work or consuming it in private, affected the rate of reading. Sociable reading was inevitably slower, and silent reading meant one could consume more. Still, in the absence of large libraries and long lists of titles and in light of accounts of the ways in which women spent their leisure time, it is doubtful that women read extensively, digesting massive quantities of literature. Literate women probably read a limited number of works, including periodicals. Reading less may have meant that they retained more of what they read, and some readers do speak of "devouring" books and becoming totally absorbed in literary texts. One woman reported that every time her mother read sections of Qasim Amin's *Tahrir al-Mar'a* "unrestrained tears poured from her eyes," for it upset her.[49] Other descriptions suggest a similar personal involvement in reading. The effort that some women had to invest in order to find reading matter may have also meant that they did not take the works, once found, lightly. In any case, monthly journals seemed to suit Egyptian women's habits of reading, aloud or silently, at home and at leisure.

CIRCULATION OF THE PRESS

A young woman who described herself as a "very devoted" reader of *al-'Afaf* from its inception wrote that she waited impatiently for the day it appeared each week, claiming that "all the young women of Egypt" read it.[50] What did she mean by *all*? Although most figures are speculative, the most popular daily newspapers in Egypt in the early twentieth century had circulations (copies sold through subscriptions and individual sales) in the thousands. For example, in 1903 *al-Liwa'* sold 1,500 to 2,000 copies a day, *al-Muqattam* 3,500 to 4,000 copies, and *al-Mu'ayyad* 6,000 to 7,000 copies.[51] In 1907 *al-Liwa'* was just short of 10,000, and *al-Jarida,* in its first year, was at 3,000.[52] By 1911 *al-Jarida* had climbed to 4,200 copies a day.[53] Circulation figures for the two leading dailies in 1919 were in the tens of thousands, with *al-Afkar* at 12,000 to 14,000 copies and the best-selling *al-Ahram* at 20,000 copies a day.[54] Most of these newspapers were affiliated with political factions or parties, which gave them a subvention and provided a ready audience.

The scientific and literary periodicals that appeared monthly or so had smaller circulations than the daily newspapers. Lists have survived of nearly a hundred regular recipients of *al-'Urwa al-Wuthqa,* the journal Jamal al-Din al-Afghani and Muhammad 'Abduh published briefly in Paris in the mid-1880s. This was not a very large number given the influence the journal was said to have had, and it may be only a partial list.[55] *Al-Muqtataf,* one of the most popular journals of its day, had a circulation of about 3,000 in 1892, after over ten years of publication.[56] In 1901 and after three years in print, Rashid Rida's journal *al-Manar* had a circulation of 300 to 400, a figure that rose in subsequent years.[57]

In spite of significantly lower literacy rates among women than men —male readers reached close to one-half million in the 1907 census while female readers hovered slightly above 60,000 (including non-Egyptians)[58]—many women's journals held their own. Of the 1,500 copies of *al-Sayyidat wa'l-Banat* printed per month in its first year (1903), 1,100 were distributed, which the editor Rosa Antun considered a very large number for a new women's journal.[59] *Tarqiyat al-Mar'a* was distributed in its first year (1908) to the over 165 members of the organization by that name.[60] *Al-'Afaf* estimated its female readership at a hundred.[61] Longer-running journals such as *Fatat al-Sharq* and *al-Jins al-Latif* probably had higher circulations than those periodicals mentioned here. Rather than concrete figures, however, we are left only with Labiba Hashim's assertion that schoolgirls and women did not read daily newspapers but "all read her *Fatat al-Sharq.*"[62]

Although it is nearly impossible to determine precise circulation figures for most Egyptian periodicals, circulation should not be confused with the size of a journal's audience. Listeners must first be added to any estimate. Rashid Rida related that he initially came into contact with *al-'Urwa al-Wuthqa* when he heard some articles from it read aloud by Egyptian political exiles who were staying with his family in Tripoli.[63] Reading aloud multiplied the size of a periodical's audience many times and provided an important source of information in the days before news was broadcast over the radio. As reported in *al-Hilal* in 1897: "We often see servants, donkey-rearers and others who cannot read, gather around one who reads while they listen. The streets of Cairo and of other towns in the region are full of this."[64] This practice was evident in Egyptian villages ten years later as well, much to the chagrin of the British Consul General Eldon Gorst, who found the masses "far too ignorant to appreciate the absurdities and the falseness of the diatribes which are read out to them daily in the villages."[65]

Female listeners were not necessarily found in the streets but rather in schools and at home. Since teachers often subscribed to journals and schools were given them as gifts and prizes, articles may have been read aloud in class. Schoolgirls were also often the ones who read "the news of the world" aloud at home.[66] Reading aloud was frequently carried out in the context of the family, as we have seen, and all it took was a single literate family member. One woman offered to read a journal to her sister, who "unfortunately did not know how to read," in an effort to convince her to share a subscription.[67] The audience of a newspaper or journal was also extended by passing the printed text around. Although subscribers in Egypt numbered 20,000, according to the writer in *al-Hilal*, the number of readers reached almost 200,000, "since a single copy of a newspaper is touched by many hands, and is read by tens or scores of people."[68] Copies circulated among friends and relatives, which may explain why Malaka Sa'd recommended cataloguing one's library and recording the number of a book loaned.

The audience of women's journals was probably larger than the few figures available on circulation suggest given the likely large number of listeners, the shared subscriptions, and the practice of passing periodicals around. Still, the journals did not reach vast numbers of people, or even strive to, and instead seemed to target a specific strata. Estimates of the number of readers should thus be blended with a profile of real readers. Reaching a small but influential portion of the population could go a long way toward affecting change, providing the periodical received sufficient funds to stay afloat.

PROFILE OF READERS

Editors targeted a potential audience based on their own perceptions of Egyptian society and its readiness to consume print culture. Their distribution, pricing, and advertising policies all give clues to their ambitions—and the aspirations of advertisers—to reach a certain group. Although they reflect perceptions about ideal readers, they also suggest contours for a rough profile of readers.

To start, how were women's journals distributed? Newspapers were often sold in Egypt by hawkers, who worked the streets, cafés, squares, and railroad stations.[69] Although this was an effective way to sell daily papers to men, it was not necessarily a good way to reach women buyers, particularly middle- and upper-class ones, who expected goods to be brought to their homes by servants, peddlers, male members of their family, or the post. Women's journals probably came to them at home through the post.

Since women's journals did not usually receive subsidies, they depended mainly on subscriptions, with prices varying according to periodicity and size. An average annual subscription to a women's monthly ranged from fifty to sixty piasters. With most editors producing ten issues a year (suspending publication during the summer months), this broke down to one issue for five or six piasters. This was not much less than the cost of a book, which ranged from five to ten piasters. Yet it meant that a female factory worker, who made three to four piasters a day, would have had to pay more than two weeks' wages for an annual subscription.[70] In short, this was not a penny or popular press; subscribing to a periodical was beyond the means of the lower classes.[71] But pricing the journals for mass circulation did not make much sense when lower-class literacy was so limited. Editors geared their journals toward the middle and upper strata instead, pricing them accordingly. They then offered discounts to students, who benefited from 25 to 50 percent reductions. *Fatat al-Nil* even gave half-price rates to religious scholars, showing Sarah al-Mihiyya's interest in reaching this group.[72] Almost all the journals also listed a separate price for subscribers outside Egypt, anticipating or hoping for foreign circulation.

Subscriptions were sold in Egypt and abroad through a network of agents—sometimes other publications or bookstores—whose locations indicated intended distribution. Syrian editors had male and female agents scattered throughout Egypt, Syria, and wherever there were pockets of Syrian emigrants. Rosa Antun, for example, shared agents with her brother Farah Antun and his *al-Jami'a* throughout the Middle East and North Africa and as far away as Brazil.[73] Egyptian editors tended to have a different network of agents. Malaka Sa'd, a Copt, had an agent in the Sudan, and Sarah al-Mihiyya, a Muslim, had one in Mecca. The greatest concentration of agents was naturally in Egypt. Agents did not necessarily generate sales, however, and sometimes diverted them. When unscrupulous or unauthorized agents sold false subscriptions, editors quickly reported the scams and advised readers of authorized agents' locations.[74]

Advertisements, although rather limited in this period, reveal information about readers, or at least about advertisers' perceptions of the location and interests of readers. Unlike agents, most advertisers were local, based in the main urban centers of Egypt and usually in the city of publication. Most of the advertisers in *Anis al-Jalis,* which pioneered advertising and published more ads than any other journal, were situated in Alexandria (more specifically on the fashionable avenue of Sharif Pasha), with a few in Cairo and the odd one in Mansura, Tanta, and Port Said. Advertisers assumed that most readers of this journal had access to these markets and offered goods that appealed to those of modern tastes, including European-styled clothing, jewelry, perfume, pianos, light fixtures, photographs, insurance, medicine, sewing machines, and telephone service.[75] Yet advertisers in journals such as *Fatat al-Nil* recognized the special needs of female buyers who remained secluded. They extended such services as home delivery, private showings, and female photographers.[76] The goods and services advertised suggest, nevertheless, that readers of these journals defied easy categorization.

The imagined audience of editors, agents, and advertisers can be compared to actual readers, especially those who responded actively to the women's press. Readers sent in queries, wrote essays, solved puzzles, and won prizes. Whether or not they gave their names—and some sought anonymity—they invariably disclosed some details about themselves, such as their sex, profession, age, class, religion, and region. These data prove useful in constructing a profile of readers who through their correspondence with the press left evidence of their reading.

Although predominantly female, readers of women's journals were not exclusively so, for the rights of woman and other issues covered in the journals concerned men as well. Moreover, given the limited pool of potential female subscribers, male readers had to be tapped in order to sustain a publication. Male contributors identified themselves as doctors, lawyers, bankers, school officials, government employees, or *shaykhs,* placing themselves primarily in the ranks of the middle class. Women were less likely to identify themselves by profession because they were less likely to have practiced one. Nevertheless, from time to time they presented themselves as school administrators, teachers, and students, with the latter sometimes giving their ages. One thirteen-year-old wrote to *al-Sayyidat wa'l-Banat,* and a ten-year-old sent a letter to *al-'Afaf.* [77] Most women readers were from middle-class homes, but women from less advantaged backgrounds or those whose families had fallen on hard times sometimes wrote. Wealthy and even royal women numbered among the occasional readers. One chronicler claimed that *Anis al-Jalis* was "read in the palaces of sultans, kings, princes, and notables in all the Eastern countries." Its owner, Alexandra Avierino, had presented the journal to members of the khedivial family and received a variety of prizes.[78]

A quick survey of the names, interests, and outlooks of those corresponding with the journals shows a mixture of Muslims and Christians. Many of those writing from abroad were Syrian emigrants; but most of the readers of Arabic women's journals were urban Egyptians. This readership also extended to such towns as Zaqaziq, Asyut, Suhaj, and Jirja; and while the names of small villages rarely appeared, some contributions came signed "from the countryside." The composite picture of readers of the women's press that can be drawn from the signatures of contributors and their stories is that of a young, unmarried, middle-class Muslim or Christian woman from Cairo or Alexandria.

AN ACTIVE AUDIENCE

Pseudonyms revealed other information about consumers of the press—that they not infrequently identified themselves as readers. Some of those who chose not to give their own names signed themselves as "a reader from Tanta" or some other town, or simply as "a reader," with the gendered ending indicating that they were female. Others identified themselves in relation to the journal, as "one of the readers of *al-'Afaf*," for example. They also established connections with other readers: a woman in *al-Jins al-Latif* signed herself "one from among you" to which "another one" replied.[79] Readers thus forged a community, an active audience with shared outlooks and interests and with links to one another.

Editors cultivated such sentiments and tried to build a loyal circle of readers through a number of devices. They strove, first of all, to publish on schedule, for readers were subscribers who supported the journal with an annual fee, and erratic publication was sure to undermine their trust. Editors urged readers to report instances of issues that had gone astray in the post.[80] When issues were published late, editors apologized and offered explanations, sometimes giving some sort of compensation in an effort to prevent defections to competitors. In turn, they demanded payment of subscriptions on time, particularly in hard times, and were not averse to threatening to reveal the names of delinquent subscribers to shame them into paying their fees.[81] Still, shaming was only effective as a tactic when individuals feared the condemnation of those who knew them, suggesting that editors and readers perceived themselves as part of a close circle.

Yet the relationship between the producers and consumers of the press was not defined in economic terms. The bond between editors and readers was developed over time as readers came to expect certain columns from an editor, and editors called for the active participation of readers. Women's journals strove for dialogues, not editor's monologues. The contact between a journal's editor or delegate and readers was sometimes personal. For example, the male editor of al-'Afaf appointed a female agent to meet regularly with members of the public in secluded quarters of the newspaper's office, and Zakiya al-Kafrawiyya later became the paper's official representative at functions. Al-'Afaf also held a reception for its readers.[82] Alexandra Avierino met some of her student readers on a visit to a girls' school, where one told her that they always read Anis al-Jalis.[83] Other editors and writers mingled with their readers in lectures, at philanthropic gatherings, during association meetings, and on similar occasions. Just how intimate some writers might be with their readers is revealed by a notice for a book by Zaynab Fawwaz informing those interested in purchasing it that they could do so at the home of the author.[84]

Nevertheless, many readers probably had little or no personal contact with a journal's editor. They reacted instead to an editor's literary persona and generally saw editors as authorities on a range of domestic and social issues. Editors displayed their expertise in a variety of forms, including the advice column. Most questions addressed to these columns by readers dealt with proper conduct in Egyptian society. Rosa Antun responded to the following queries with rather conservative advice: how to handle harassment in the streets; whether women should work l,ke men; and proper behavior riding trams, dancing, and during engagements.[85] Most of the questions stemmed from stresses caused by socioeconomic and technological change. Readers also asked editors, or specialists they had recruited, about financial, medical, and legal problems. In response to a reader's letter, for example, Sarah al-Mihiyya provided guidelines for balancing a household budget.[86] Al-'Afaf asked a female doctor to answer inquiries about health and a religious scholar to respond to questions about family law. Women wrote in looking for solutions to a variety of pressing problems. Their willingness to confide in editors indicates that they viewed the journals as authoritative sources and trusted them to give good advice. The journal thus sometimes served as an outlet when all else had failed, a refuge of last resort.

Readers also sent in letters and essays expressing their views on a range of topics, including marriage, divorce, veiling, education, and work. Although these contributions may not have all been authentic, it is doubtful that more than a few were fictive. The evidence of reader participation is too extensive and in too many journals for collusion between editors to have been possible or even likely. Moreover, editors often required contributors to disclose their real names even if they did not wish these printed.[87] The letters and essays of readers were frequently published with a short explanation or introduction by the editor. When limited space or editorial policy meant that not all contributions could appear, editors usually apologized. These introductions and apologies, as well as instructions to readers on submitting works, suggest that some journals received too many rather than too few contributions from readers.

Some readers became regular contributors, which blurred the line between readers and writers and sometimes resulted in heated discussions among contributor-writers. For example, two Muslim readers debated marriage practices for over a year in *Anis al-Jalis,* each calling for the last word.[88] A critic's attack in *al-'Afaf* on several women writers drew a flurry of responses from angry readers, who defended the writers.[89] Similar exchanges frequently appeared, as secluded women who had few opportunities to discuss their views with men or women outside their household used the women's press as a forum for debate. And some journals were turned over almost completely to reader-contributors.

Readers responded to the journal itself. Comments sometimes took the form of a poem congratulating an editor or a letter of encouragement. One female reader who signed herself "the sincere one" applauded Regina 'Awwad, editor of *al-Sa'ada,* for her efforts.[90] Another young woman calling herself "daughter of the Nile" commended *al-'Afaf* for its role as a women's advocate.[91] Praise also came from such well-known literary figures as Zaynab Fawwaz and Warda al-Yaziji, as well as lesser-known readers. Other tributes came from a woman in Europe who but for her inability to read Arabic would have subscribed, and from a woman in New York who bought subscriptions to the journal and had them distributed in Egyptian schools.[92] From the notices of editors, it seems that they received a stream of letters commenting on the endeavor of publishing a women's journal. But not all readers expressed support or approval.

We learn that one reader was "astonished" by *al-Sayyidat wa'l-Banat*'s having taken a position "against women," while another reader criticized its editor for having provided husbands with a rationale for enhancing their power in the home.[93] Editors issued rebuttals to some of their detractors, apologized to others, and adjusted the contents of their pages accordingly. Yet critical comments also showed that the journals were taken seriously.

Journal owners encouraged the sense that real proprietorship lay in the hands of contributors. *Al-Fatah* aimed to be "women's one journal in the East," and *al-'Afaf* called itself the "mouthpiece of woman." Editors presented the journals as forums for readers that were awaiting the products of their pens. Readers and editors of the women's press thus made a tacit compact with respect to their roles. Readers were expected to participate in the journal, which was ultimately a joint enterprise, while editors would offer their authority and expertise on a wide range of topics and would endeavor to respond to readers' demands. This pact downplayed the economic dimension of their relationship—that readers were subscribers who paid a fee for the periodical, which it needed for continued publication. For readers were not ordinary consumers of a product but active architects in its production who shared in shaping the press.

Reading had triumphed in Egypt, becoming a mark of prestige and opening a new world of meanings and interpretations to the newly literate. With the rise of female literacy, a small but increasingly significant group of mainly young, urban women and men began to read women's journals, in addition to other literature. The journals focused on such important issues as the rights of woman, education, domestic versus waged work, and the activities of associations—issues that we will take up in turn in the coming chapters. Although the journals disseminated ideas, they did not create public opinion by imposing it on their audience, for this audience was not a blank slate. As their literary tastes reflected, women readers chose their reading matter carefully. Their habits of reading showed, moreover, that they read the selected material with zeal.

Those who drafted written responses to women's journals found editors eager to publish their contributions and fellow readers ready to listen. Producers and consumers of the press both played active roles in defining this new literary medium. The women's press in turn enlivened the intellectual debates of the period through its social criticism.

Part Two

TEXTS AND
SOCIAL CONTEXTS

5

THE RIGHTS OF
WOMAN

Articles on *huquq al-mar'a* (the rights of woman) appeared in the women's press from its first years.[1] Yet debates about women's roles and rights in Egyptian-Islamic society were hardly new. A tradition of literature prescribing roles for women and criticizing behavior as Islamic or un-Islamic stretched back centuries and included juristic works, behavioral guides, and biographical dictionaries, among other texts. The medieval 'alim Ibn al-Hajj, for example, wrote a polemic attacking women's customs and manners in fourteenth-century Cairo, evidence that Muslim scholars disputed women's interpretations of social and sexual boundaries.[2] The historical record preserved only the male accounts of the exchange, however, and not the direct voices of those women with whom they argued. There were two important changes in the content and context of the debate on women's role in society in the nineteenth century. First, the contours broadened beyond the Islamic framework with the introduction of Western ideas and references. Second, for the first time women participated extensively in the literary debate through writings that were often published in the women's press.

Female intellectuals wrote in the tradition of nineteenth- and twentieth-century intellectuals responding to the challenge of the West. With the first European conquest of Middle Eastern territory in modern times—the French invasion of Egypt in 1798—Egypt encountered the military superiority of the West. The Egyptian state that subsequently emerged borrowed military techniques, science and technology, industrial organization, and, later, political ideas in an effort to modernize and compete with the West. Intellectuals—some of whom were sent abroad on educational missions—reacted to the West with varying postures. But the response to Western values became more charged after the British occupied Egypt in 1882 and Egyptians experienced Western imperialism as the flip side to Western civilization. The woman question could never be examined outside of this context and thus became entangled in religious and political issues and explanations for the current state of weakness in Egypt and the Muslim world. The debate was also fueled by socioeconomic change in Egypt; it did not arise simply as a reaction to Western stimuli. The discussions in the press showed attempts to slow or accelerate these developments.

The responses of intellectuals to transformations in Egyptian society and to Western contact ranged across a continuum. Ideologies were often more precise than an individual's posture, which sometimes shifted over time depending on the situation, the audience, and the moment. As a result of witnessing the introduction of secular educational and legal systems that broke their monopolies and eroded their economic and social power, most of the religious establishment, on the one hand, tended to cling to the past in an attempt to block change and preserve the status quo. Westernizers, on the other hand, attempted to jettison traditional culture and emulate foreigners. Most views fell somewhere in between, including Islamist, modernist, and secular tendencies, and female intellectuals in particular avoided the extremes.[3]

Yet conflating women's views and labeling this pole *feminist* presumes that these women presented a unified voice and obscures real differences of opinion. Due to their special education and socialization, female intellectuals saw the world through a unique prism, but they did not all see the colors refracted in the same way. An examination of the positions and aspirations of women writers in the early years of the women's press shows that the phrase "the rights of woman" had many meanings and that the views of female intellectuals also covered a wide range. The spectrum of opinions that existed from women's earliest participation in the press, foreshadowing future splits, cannot be reduced to a mere clash of personalities. This chapter explores areas of consensus and difference among female intellectuals and examines the influence of nationality, religion, class, gender, and culture on their positions.

SYRIANS AS MEDIATORS BETWEEN EAST AND WEST

Many of the Syrian women who migrated to Egypt played an important role in transmitting ideas and suggesting new possibilities to Egyptians. Syrian women were the first to appear on the stage (replacing men who had played female parts), the first to train in medicine, and the first to take jobs as teachers and administrators.[4] Syrians contributed to periodicals from the 1880s, started Arabic women's journals in the 1890s, and pioneered in political journalism.[5] Syrian women—especially Christians—were at the forefront of transforming traditional activities into modern professions, often investing them with a new status. Their earlier access to education through a network of missionary and sectarian primary schools in Syria had prepared them for these roles.[6]

Syrian writers in Egypt proved adept at bridging European and Arabic cultures, translating foreign scientific and humanistic ideas for local readers. Their journals carried biographies of foreign women and news of women's struggles from Russia to America, as well as articles on the history of women in the West. Many had contact with Western women at a time when foreigners made up 10 percent of the population in the larger urban centers.[7] Travel also gave Syrian writers firsthand experience of Western culture. Esther Moyal, Rosa Antun, and Labiba Hashim all spent time in North or South America, and other writers visited Europe. Still, they tended to depict Western women in monolithic terms and dissociated themselves from Western women's political demands.

These Syrian intellectuals closely identified with the East and continuously criticized irrational imitation of the West. Rosa Antun urged her friends "to copy what is useful and appropriate for ourselves and reject . . . whatever reason judges as corrupt."[8] Syrian writers tried to dampen blind love for the West and to protect the core of their own culture, curtailing the impulse to dismiss many local customs and practices.

Most important, they sought to safeguard Arabic. That they battled over language was not surprising, for language tied Syrian Christians to other Arabs and Egyptians. They argued for more Arabic education in schools in lieu of French and other foreign languages. They also discussed contemporary choices in names and titles, both symbols of cultural identity. Rosa Antun wondered what excuse they had for copying foreign names, while Labiba Hashim challenged the use of the French *madame* instead of *sayyida* for a married woman.[9]

Although undoubtedly influenced by foreign discussions of women's role in society, Syrian intellectuals looked for indigenous models for women's progress. By locating golden ages for women in the past, they hoped to show that the idea of the rights of woman was part of their own history and therefore make it more acceptable. Syrian editors often carried abstracts on the lives of ancient Eastern and pre-Islamic Arab women in their journals. Hind Nawfal pointed to Samiramis, an Assyrian queen, and Bilqis, queen of Sheba, and praised women of Pharaonic times, who "for a period of two thousand years showed extreme gentleness and refinement and demonstrated achievements and perfection which women of the West have not yet reached." She argued that Eastern women should look to their own past for inspiration and that they need not plant a foreign idea in Eastern soil.[10] The male Syrian writer Jurji Zaydan helped in this endeavor by popularizing Arab history in a series of romantic historical novels that featured famous and fictitious Arab women.[11]

Syrians faced the imperative of not only showing that the rights of woman was an indigenous idea, but of defining it in such a way that it included Syrians as well as Egyptians. Although Syrian immigrants had lived more or less amicably with Egyptians for generations, antipathy toward Syrians in Egypt increased in the latter part of the nineteenth century. This was due in part to resentment of the economic success of Syrian merchants and moneylenders who had profited from the cotton boom. The perceived close links of Syrians with the British occupation also generated hostility. Muslim and Coptic Egyptians complained, according to Lord Cromer, that young educated Syrians came to Cairo and won the best state appointments, and, in fact, the number of Syrians in the administration exceeded that of Egyptians at one point.[12] Tensions were exacerbated by Syrian opposition in the press and elsewhere to Egyptian nationalism, which they feared would exclude them. Egyptian nationalists in turn attempted to block Syrians through nationality restrictions and to discredit them in articles and speeches. The nationalist leader Mustafa Kamil attacked the Syrians as *dukhala'* (aliens) in Egypt; and although he later specified that he meant only pro-occupation Syrians, he had effectively branded most as unwanted outsiders.[13]

The Syrian-women writers strove to overcome regional divisions by emphasizing a shared Eastern identity, a common language, and a collective past. In an article entitled "The Two Women" (al-Mar'atan), Labiba Hashim wrote that after long consideration, she found "the woman one in Egypt and Syria," a small wonder "for both live beneath the Eastern sky and both have the same customs and language."[14] Authors stressed the sisterhood of Syrian and Egyptian women as well as the relatedness of their endeavors. When two journals appeared almost simultaneously—*Fatat Lubnan* in Beirut and *Fatat al-Nil* in Cairo—they were considered sister enterprises.[15] The wider role Syrians prescribed for women in society was set in the context of regional history and showed seeds of Arab nationalism. Easternism, the precursor to Arabism, was meant to link Syrians and Egyptians, although the concept proved more popular among the former than the latter.

"A Syrian by birthplace and native land, an Egyptian by upbringing and abode," is how Zaynab Fawwaz described herself in her biographical dictionary published in 1894.[16] As a Muslim she had greater chances for integration in Egypt than Syrian Christians, especially after her marriage (her third) to a colonel in the Egyptian army. Her writings showed support for women's education, endorsed segregation, and argued for women's right to work.[17] Yet most Syrian writers in Egypt were Christians in a country with a majority Muslim population. A few, like Hind Nawfal (who insisted that her journal had "no aim in religious controversies"),[18] chose to ignore religious issues altogether in their writings. This seemed to be the path that Alexandra Avierino initially followed. The German scholar Martin Hartmann considered Alexandra "the head of the feminist movement in the Orient" but admitted that as a Christian, "she naturally could not touch on the religious ideas of the Muslims." This strategy would have backfired, he explained, and damaged the cause for which she fought. "But today [1901] that the alleged command relative to the veil is stigmatized as an invention of the theologians by the most outstanding Muslims, she may speak freely." [19] Hartmann no doubt referred here to, among others, Qasim Amin, whose works Alexandra reviewed favorably. [20] Critiquing Islamic practices became more difficult for Syrian Christians in tense times, however, and at those moments some chose to defend Islam. Pointing to the number of knowledgeable Muslim women who wore the veil, Labiba Hashim argued that this religious custom was not an impediment to learning. [21]

Syrian writers focused on lack of education, a problem that transcended nationality and religion, as the main obstacle to women's progress. They argued that education would better prepare women for their domestic role, an issue of interest to the growing Syrian bourgeoisie. This program was also calculated to appeal to middle-class Egyptians and to defuse Syrian-Egyptian tensions. These writers made a great effort to show that theirs was an indigenous solution and continuously condemned thoughtless copying of the West. Perhaps they can best be seen as a group caught between the East and the West, who never felt fully at home in Egypt but had difficulty settling elsewhere.

Syrians saw themselves as pioneers of the women's awakening. They achieved this distinction mainly because they had received schooling earlier than most other women in the region and had formed some of the first women's associations. In Egypt they helped to open new professions to women and started women's journals, which were central to their program for progress. Yet the exodus of female intellectuals from Syria meant that the center of the awakening had shifted. Although the second Arabic women's journal, *al-Mar'a,* had been founded in Hama in 1893 by Nadima al-Sabuni, it was not until after the 1908 Young Turk revolution had loosened press constraints that subsequent ones were started in Syrian cities. [22] Syria under the Ottomans was simply not as hospitable to discussions of the rights of woman and social reform as Egypt under the British, and it was not as ready for change. With the help of

Syrian immigrants, Egyptians began to take the lead. Female intellectuals in Beirut and elsewhere in the Arab world started to look to Egypt for signals.[23]

COPTS AND SECULARIZATION

Copts tended to be more socially conservative than Syrian Christians. At the beginning of the twentieth century, Coptic women still veiled and practiced segregation. The male Coptic writer Salama Musa recounted in his memoirs, "I do not know that during all my life in Egypt, before travelling to France [in 1908], I ever had a conversation with a young lady, or sat and talked with a married one, or even saw the face of one." Musa encountered different social relations in Europe. "The strongest influence upon my social consciousness was certainly the freedom of women in the western world." This created a "burning flame" which "gave birth to my revolt against Egyptian traditions, with which I could have no more patience." Musa became a strong advocate of secularism, seeing this as the best option for Christians to participate fully in society and for raising women's status. Upon his return to Egypt, he followed the path of another Copt, Marqus Fahmi, who in 1894 had critiqued women's role in Egyptian society in the play *al-Mar'a fi'l-Sharq* (The woman in the East). Musa became caught up in the debates of the day— "the English occupation, and Qasim Amin's movement for the liberation of women"—and contributed to Malaka Sa'd's *al-Jins al-Latif*.[24]

Female intellectuals such as Malaka Sa'd did not take the European courses of study or tours that their male counterparts found so stimulating. Yet they witnessed a variety of changes in their own community: Coptic girls entered schools in growing numbers, women started to unveil, and men and women began to meet before marriage.[25] Malaka Sa'd encouraged this modernizing trend. But unlike Syrian Christians, Malaka Sa'd could not be labeled an alien, and she had less hesitation than Syrian writers to speak out. "Egyptian women used to study science, speak from pulpits, and govern the empire when women in other countries were still in a state of slavery and misery," she wrote of the

Pharaonic past. With the arrival of Christianity, Egyptian woman "did not lose a thing of freedom for the Christian religion did not decrease her due and did not prevent her from learning." The downfall came, she contended, when the Arabs conquered Egypt and the Islamic government "enforced the rule of the veil on the Egyptian woman" and kept her indoors. From that time on, she argued, women's position had eroded.[26] Malaka's view, aired in 1908 in the midst of growing Coptic-Muslim hostility, expressed a perspective that was often left unsaid. Still, while she rejected aspects of the Arabo-Islamic past, Malaka did not embrace the West. She warned against blindly copying European ways and looked instead for other models. A contributor to her journal pointed to the Japanese, who by their 1905 defeat of the Russians showed that an Eastern power could defeat a Western one, and suggested that they could provide Egyptians with a model.[27]

The question that Copts as a community faced (whether to maintain their autonomous status and "protections") and that women as a sex faced (whether to retain their seclusion and "privileges") was in many ways quite similar. Should they remain segregated or push for greater integration in society? Would relinquishing certain exemptions enhance or hurt their position? Malaka opted for religious integration and envisioned a wider role for women in Egyptian society. She looked forward to the day when women could be judges and lawyers and considered it necessary that they plant this idea now "so that it will ripen in the future."[28]

In identifying the root causes of women's low status—an essential first step before they could articulate solutions—writers gave various historical explanations. Only a few targeted the Arabs, accusing them of introducing practices that undermined women's position in Egyptian society. Such an attitude was not meant to win friends in Muslim circles and was muted when Coptic-Muslim relations improved, culminating in the cooperation of the 1919 revolution. Most writers blamed the British and Western customs for eroding morality, and with it women's stature, or looked further back and faulted the Turks for introducing foreign practices into Islam.

The Rights of Woman
❦

EGYPTIAN MODERNISTS

Egyptian Muslim women wrote mainly as modernists or Islamists before 1919, although the line between the two positions seemed somewhat blurred at times. Both groups argued within the context of Islam, with the intention of revitalizing and strengthening religion, and both condemned certain Western influences and excesses. Indeed, modernist and Islamist positions often differed more in emphasis than in substance. Modernists sought expansion in the realm of education and reform in marriage and divorce laws. Islamists, on the other hand, sought enforcement of Islamic laws, including women's right to education, but encouraged women to learn the law to know their rights, not to modify them. If ideological positions sometimes seemed close, political alliances showed sharper distinctions. Islamists were associated with the popular pro-Ottoman Watani party, whereas modernists tended to be linked with the liberal Umma party.

Muhammad 'Abduh, who died in 1905 before the founding of these nationalist parties, was the leading religious reformer of the period. A graduate of al-Azhar, 'Abduh taught there and at Dar al-'Ulum (a school to train Arabic teachers), edited the official Egyptian gazette *al-Waqa'i' al-Misriyya,* and worked as a government censor. Following the 'Urabi revolt, he was exiled from Egypt. He joined the pan-Islamist Jamal al-Din al-Afghani in Paris to produce the periodical *al-'Urwa al-Wuthqa* and then moved on to Beirut where he wrote and taught. He returned to Egypt after being granted amnesty by Khedive Tawfiq in the late 1880s, and became mufti of Egypt with Lord Cromer's support in 1899. It is said that he wrote parts of Qasim Amin's *Tahrir al-Mar'a,* which appeared that year.[29] 'Abduh strove to strengthen Islam by improving the quality of the religious courts, revising the curriculum at al-Azhar, and providing innovative *fatwas* (legal opinions) on marriage, divorce, and polygamy. Yet he encountered stiff opposition from Khedive 'Abbas Hilmi II and conservatives at al-Azhar, who together tried to block many of his reforms. Mustafa Kamil also criticized 'Abduh for focusing on social reform rather than political independence.[30]

Abduh's interest in reforming family law and improving women's position in society probably arose from his own domestic experience. His mother had been forced to leave the two children from her first marriage in the care of their grandparents when she moved to the natal village of her second husband. 'Abduh was the only child of this second marriage, and 'Abduh's father subsequently took a second wife, with whom he had other children. The future reformer grew up in a home with children of different mothers and probably sensed his mother's anguish at separation from some of her children. At a young age he married a girl from the village; their only son died in infancy, but they had several daughters. After his first wife's death and when in exile in Beirut, he married again and had another daughter.[31] 'Abduh had seen the strains of Egyptian family life and understood some of the obstacles women faced. This may have made him more sympathetic to the situation of women in general in Egyptian society. In his decisions on court cases, in responses to legal questions, and in his writings, 'Abduh sought to improve women's status. He argued that men and women be allowed to meet before marriage, that multiple marriage was not countenanced by the Qur'an except in extenuating circumstances, and that men not divorce their wives impulsively.

'Abduh linked two groups: those educated in Western schools trying to keep some cultural ties to the past and those educated in al-Azhar and elsewhere with an Islamic orientation espousing religious reform. The first group was typified by men like Qasim Amin and Ahmad Lutfi al-Sayyid and called for a separation of religious and political affairs. The second group was best represented by Muhammad Rashid Rida, a Syrian disciple of 'Abduh who founded the journal *al-Manar* in 1898 to publicize his teacher's views. The latter group pursued a religious revival, which became known as the *Salafi* movement. The schools that 'Abduh linked in his lifetime as a modernist splintered and moved apart toward secularism and Islamism after his death.

Modernists wanted to rid Islam of "backward" popular female practices such as the *zar* (a dance ceremony to exorcise spirits from the body), the visitation of tombs, and wailing at funerals.[32] Yet they did not want to replace them with Western habits. Sa'diyya Sa'd al-Din ("Sha-

jarat al-Durr") was one of the earliest Muslim women writers to reflect
the thinking of this school. She promoted marriage as a conjugal partnership and criticized easy male divorce, but she did not advocate the
banning of divorce altogether.[33] Muslim women writers generally preferred the slow reform of Malak Hifni Nasif to the secularism of Qasim
Amin.[34] Malak, who was one of the best known modernist writers, spoke
out against multiple marriage (she was a second wife), called for reforms
in family law, and pushed for girls' education in state schools. She also
demanded an increase in the Islamic component in schools and refrained
from challenging the veil and segregation.[35] Many of the writers in *al-
'Afaf* in the 1910s shared similar views. The editor and staff supported
reform of marriage and divorce laws, and the newspaper carried stories
depicting the hardships women encountered as victims of multiple marriage and unilateral male divorce. At the same time, the newspaper
upheld modesty and segregation and attacked women for copying European customs. This seemed to have been a case of middle-class writers
attacking the upper classes for decadent (by which they meant West-
ernizing) practices and condemning the lower classes for retrograde (or
popular) ones.[36]

EARLY ISLAMISTS

Modernists were not the only Egyptian Muslims claiming to champion
women's cause. An Islamist position emerged in reaction to modernist
and secularist trends. "Isn't it astonishing that now in the twentieth century a group of women wants to advance forward . . . while [another]
group wants to return to the seventh century," wrote Fatima Rashid in
an article on woman and her rights in Islam.[37] Fatima acknowledged
dissenting views among women seeking to improve their position in
society. She was one of those looking back to the time of the Prophet
and supported an Islamist approach that modeled relations on those of
early Islam. With a circle of like-minded women, she founded Jam'iyyat
Tarqiyat al-Mar'a in 1908 to bring women back to religion. The group in
turn started a journal to publicize its views.

Did they select this Islamist posture out of fear of the chaos that might result from the erosion of traditional values and the destruction of a system they knew how to manipulate? Deniz Kandiyoti has theorized about a choice in which some women tacitly agreed to a family pattern of subordination as young brides in return for later benefits, an accommodation she calls a "patriarchal bargain." As classical patriarchy breaks down in the modern period, some women (and perhaps those of Jam'iyyat Tarqiyat al-Mar'a) continue to cling to the system, fearing a loss of limited power.[38] Or was it an ingenious defense of indigenous cultural values under attack by the West, a "radical neo-traditionalism"?[39] Were these women reactionaries or radicals?

According to the Islamists, God and his Prophet had given women rights "that grant us equality with man in all things."[40] Muslim women had the right to inherit, to buy and sell property, and to support—all rights for which European women still struggled. Yet adherence to the Sunna and Qur'an had lapsed in the centuries after the Prophet and the Rightly Guided Caliphs, they argued, until women had reached their current state. The problem was the ignorance of Islam and lack of application of its laws; the solution was a return to "true Islam" through religious instruction.[41] Like other female thinkers, Islamists looked for historical models to show that women's progress was an indigenous idea. But their context was Islamic, not Eastern (Arab) or Egyptian (Pharaonic). They stressed the early days of Islam, glorifying Khadija, 'A'isha, Fatima, and al-Sayyida Nafisa. Biographies of notable Muslim women filled columns in *al-Rayhana, Tarqiyat al-Mar'a, Fatat al-Nil,* and similarly oriented journals. In idealizing the past, Islamists hoped for the recreation of a more glorious era.

For women such as Fatima Rashid and Sarah al-Mihiyya, self-worth came through following traditions of modesty and piety. Islamists attacked the trend of unveiling, for it implied an end to segregation. "This veil is not a disease that holds us back," wrote Fatima Rashid, "rather it is the cause of our happiness." She urged women to guard the "symbol of our Muslim grandmothers," which prevented mixing with men.[42] Still, urban women began to unveil in the early 1900s, to the alarm of Sarah al-Mihiyya. She argued that this was not the path to women's progress and derided women for wearing light veils or none at all. "Where are these women who are sauntering in the streets coming from?" she asked in 1910. "Did they fall from the sky or emerge from under the earth? Have they no family?" And she called on men to make the women in their families veil.[43] True advance came not through undermining Islamic practice, this group stressed, but in perfecting it.

Islamists attacked those who followed the ways of Western women thinking that they had greater freedom.[44] They abhorred the influx of Western goods and ideas into Egypt and argued that Westernization eroded women's position by feeding materialism and undermining morality.[45] Some blamed Qasim Amin for weakening the social system. "If the hopes of Qasim are realized, modesty will disappear, the loss of which will destroy religion," wrote one.[46] Modesty was not merely a tenet of religion but a cornerstone, giving those who veiled and practiced seclusion a strong sense of purpose. Remove it and the edifice would collapse, or so Islamists believed.

In spite of their views, Islamists did not appease religious conservatives. They challenged the status quo by forming associations, starting journals, writing in the nationalist press, and linking themselves to a political party. The posture of these Islamists, moreover, proved attractive to many and reflected a certain understanding of the limited options, for the British occupation of Egypt had narrowed the range of possible responses by Egyptian Muslims to the woman question. The issue of women's role in society henceforth became inseparable from the struggle for national independence and rhetoric about imperialism, even when the occupation itself had receded. Women writers understood that harsh criticism of their heritage would have caused a negative reaction to their cause and led to charges of treachery. The "issue of cultural betrayal"[47] steered them toward indigenous solutions, which to some observers seemed like no solution at all. Ironically, the accommodation of modernists with Islam seemed more politic, a means toward an end, than that of the Islamists, whose end was a return to Islam. The writings of the latter showed that modernists and secularists did not have a monopoly on championing the rights of woman.

GENDER, CLASS, AND IDEOLOGY

Was there a clear correlation between socioeconomic status and ideological positions on the woman question? Juan Cole has argued that the upper middle class favored women's rights, whereas the lower middle class or petite bourgeoisie opposed reforms, particularly those that challenged segregation and might have brought women into the workplace. The argument is based mostly on two participants in the debate: Qasim Amin and Talat Harb.[48] But the evidence on Harb is inconclusive, for his socioeconomic status was changing; and the motives ascribed to the lower middle class do not hold up either. Women were not calling for broad economic rights and did not threaten men in their jobs in turn-of-the-century Egypt. Moreover, the addition of female intellectuals to the picture does not support the argument or adequately explain differences in ideological positions that are more complex than dichotomized pro- and anti-woman tendencies. Sarah al-Mihiyya, for example, was probably from a wealthy family (Cole's upper middle class) but was Islamist—opposing certain reforms—rather than modernist or secularist in her views. Dissent among women writers generally reflected a middle-class intelligentsia in search of a new ideology. Their differences probably had more to do with their attitudes toward Islam and the British occupation than their exact ranking in the middle class. In fact, female intellectuals never made explicit distinctions among different ranks of the middle class.

The writers spoke mostly to urban middle- and upper-class readers, not to the overwhelmingly illiterate lower classes. Yet sometimes in discussing such concerns as seclusion, wet-nursing, or managing servants, they exposed their attitudes toward class relations and illuminated the work conditions of the lower classes. They also acknowledged that lower-class women had their own priorities. When Malaka Sa'd encouraged women to sew, for instance, she explained that for the wealthier woman "the needle is her companion," but for the poorer one "it is an even more faithful friend in times of need."[49] Writers seemed to feel that as a result of their education and privilege, they had a special responsibility to guide the lower classes, an outlook that was not untypical of intellectuals of the time.[50] These writers called upon educators to teach useful skills to women who needed to work for wages, and they founded and joined benevolent societies to help the poor. But they rarely connected the low status of women in society with economic dependence, unequal pay, or lack of job opportunities. Nor did they link women's situation to the transformation of the economy to a capitalist system, which gave rise to the new middle class.

Intellectuals tended to stress the similarity of experiences of women of different strata. They argued that all women faced prescriptions in dress, mobility, and mixing with men (although the expressions of this varied), for the ideology of modesty and ideas about honor transcended class. Marriage and divorce laws, furthermore, applied to women of the same religion regardless of class. The vision of women's domestic roles also remained unchanged whatever their background. All women had the same chores and responsibilities, wrote Labiba Hashim, for as wives and mothers they had to raise children, sew clothes, attend to their husbands, and perform other tasks that differed only in detail.[51] Women, in the words of another writer, practically formed one class (*tabaqa wahida*).[52] In short, whatever their views, female intellectuals tended to see class difference as mostly irrelevant to the question of the rights of woman.

Further evidence of their sense of female unity is that throughout this period writers used the singular *al-mar'a* (woman) much more often than the plural *al-nisa'* (women). In addition to grammatical considerations, this word choice reflected an ideological preference, signifying a perception that women constituted a group in spite of class and other differences. Writers claimed to speak for rich and poor, Egyptian and Syrian, and Muslim and Christian. Fatima Rashid, the president of Jam'iyyat Tarqiyat al-Mar'a, said she spoke on behalf of all women in Egypt, for she "personified the Egyptian woman."[53] One, the singular, could represent all. In other contexts writers spoke of "we" and used the plural to place themselves in the company of a larger group. Alexandra Avierino identified her circle as "we who struggle for the emancipation of the woman in the East," although a more conservative thinker would probably have referred to reform, not emancipation.[54] The writers stressed shared goals and formed a fragile alliance around areas of consensus.

Calls for the rights of woman, by which some meant Islamic rights and others meant something else, did not in any case imply equal rights with men. Although women writers blurred class boundaries, they re-affirmed basic gender differences. Female intellectuals seemed disturbed by suggestions that women should assume male roles and generally endorsed complementary gender roles instead. Gender lines were to be kept clear and the male-female division of labor maintained almost intact. A story related by Labiba Hashim expresses this view. Upon the occasion of a doctor's visit, Labiba was asked by her five-year-old son why she had not studied medicine. Labiba explained that it took a long time and great exertion, and if she had trained as a doctor, "I would not have been able to devote my attention to you, look after you, make beautiful clothes for you, and do all that is needed for your soul and happiness."[55] Since woman's primary role was as wife and mother, the best way to improve her situation was to educate her for a domestic vocation. The rights of woman usually implied social reforms that would enhance women's position in the home. The debate on the woman question thus basically centered on issues such as education, domesticity, and marital relations. Economic rights, particularly for those in need, received some attention, but political rights drew scant support before the 1920s.

Writers nonetheless affirmed that women were men's equal in intellectual abilities, arguing against those who claimed that women were mentally inferior. As proof of women's intelligence, they pointed to female scientists and inventors.[56] They claimed that lack of opportunity, not want of ability, had impeded their progress. Malak Hifni Nasif told an audience that had she ridden a ship with Christopher Columbus, she too would have discovered America.[57] Female intellectuals targeted education as the means to correct the imbalance. They also perceived of themselves as educators and claimed to have started their journals to instruct women. Sarah al-Mihiyya launched *Fatat al-Nil* as a "school for girls and ladies," Alexandra Avierino labelled a journal "a traveling school," and Labiba Hashim saw the press as "the greatest educator of the nation."[58]

Women's fight for expanded roles was not depicted as a class struggle, with women at war with one another or at war as an underclass. Nor was their campaign transformed into a battle of the sexes. Although some women writers accused Egyptian men of blocking them—Fatima al-Kafrawiyya argued that men prevented women from advancing and Malak Hifni Nasif spoke of men's "strangling us"[59]—such attacks did not characterize their writings. Many educated women had received strong support from individual men and recognized that they made better allies than enemies. Their comments were more often rebukes of delinquent partners, who were needed to help improve women's situation, than salvos aimed at opponents. When Amina Z. challenged *al-Sufur* for writing about "what a woman must do and what are her responsibilities," without mentioning "what a man must do and what are his responsibilities," she exhorted men to cooperate more in the current battle.[60] Women's appeals to men for assistance may have reaffirmed gender hierarchies, but they also reflected a certain pragmatism. Among other things, men controlled the financing of education, promulgation of family laws, and many women's daily movements.

Sustained attacks against men would also have been considered traitorous in a country trying to expel a foreign power. As a result, cultural and national ties often overshadowed class divisions and gender difference. Concerned about the image of Muslim women and acutely sensitive to criticism of their society, intellectuals often defended practices in front of a Western audience that they might not have supported otherwise. When Cromer attacked Islam's failure as a social system primarily for keeping "women in a position of marked inferiority,"[61] refutations came from many directions. Alexandra Avierino, probably one of the most Westernized of the writers, defended Islam, as did others.[62] Muslim women also denounced the fantasies that some Western travelers had concocted about them.[63] In reacting to such assaults, intellectuals often let foreigners shape the terms of their debate and moved away from substantive internal critiques toward discussions of images. This partially explains the defensive postures taken and lines of battle drawn.

On another front, these writers wrestled with their own self-images. Although they started journals at a time when "intellectual" and "journalist" were nearly synonymous and the press was the main vehicle for transmitting ideas, they did not see themselves as intellectuals. Having internalized cultural values about women's proper place, they experienced a tension between their literary and domestic lives. For most women writers, family life took precedence. Some stopped writing when they married and others gave it up when they had children; those who continued assured readers that they had not neglected domestic duties. An exchange between Hind Nawfal and Labiba Hashim captures the self-image of one writer. After publishing a biographical sketch on Hind's mother (Maryam al-Nahhas), Labiba announced that she would print a piece on Hind and her sister Sarah.[64] But Hind quickly sent Labiba a polite letter asking her to please "refrain from that which you have promised the readers of your journal to write on us," explaining that they were not "people of knowledge." Labiba pointed to Hind's earlier journal (*al-Fatah*) as evidence of her wide knowledge but honored her request nonetheless.[65]

Was this a real sentiment or false modesty? I suspect it was something more. That Hind Nawfal did not see herself as an intellectual in 1892 when she started her journal, or sixteen years later when Labiba tried to publish a profile on her, was not surprising. To do so would have meant that she had broken with deeply ingrained perceptions about gender and knowledge. It reflected an underlying issue in the debates about roles and an inability to cross certain lines, or to admit that they had been crossed. Hind's reaction pointed to the inconsistencies of intellectuals, whose actions had often gone further than their words. Yet for female intellectuals, the woman question was never an abstraction. It was always about real concerns, choices, and costs, and the battle started at home.

Women's advocates tended to be lumped together regardless of distinctions in positions based on ideological, political, and strategic considerations. For example, Fatima Rashid's activities as the founder of a women's organization and editor of its journal caused some to identify her as a partisan of Qasim Amin.[66] But she had little sympathy for his views, unlike many other female intellectuals. Women writers did not speak in a unified voice in part because they did not agree on the proper solution—or even the exact nature—of the problem. Differences of opinion surfaced on the boundary lines of segregation, on waged work, and on other issues. Stances varied according to an intellectual's background and outlook and in response to circumstances and audiences, as well as over time.

Among the range of positions that female intellectuals chose, three stood out. The first option was to try to restrict religion to private life and to emphasize religiously neutral subjects such as education and domesticity. This secularizing strategy was attractive to religious minorities (Copts) and immigrants (Syrians). A second option was to work within a religious (Islamic) framework, slowly assimilating acceptable modern influences and reforming Islamic law through innovative interpretations. A third option, one which challenged secularists, modernists, and religious conservatives alike, was to work for an Islamic revival that purged foreign influences and religious accretions.

Intellectuals, nevertheless, agreed on the importance of writing in the press to disseminate their views in order to generate change, and certain themes ran through their writings. At a time when the main opponent was a Western power, they did not conceptualize their struggle as one against men, and they diligently searched for local roots and an indigenous path to women's progress. They spoke of women as a collective, blurring class, regional, and religious divides, but they considered male and female roles to be quite different. Rather than radically redraw gender boundaries, they sought to improve women's half of the bargain. They focused on areas of consensus and above all campaigned for girls' education.

6

CAMPAIGNING
FOR EDUCATION

One of the central concerns of the women's press, and an important rationale for its creation, was the education of girls. Almost all the women writers promoted education of one form or another—at the very least in the home—as a necessary first step, or full step, toward women's progress. Their discussions were part of a national debate about education under occupation. Nationalists attacked the British policy on education and in particular state funding; during the first twenty years of the British occupation less than 1 percent of the state budget went to schooling. Although this was increased slightly in subsequent years, other policies (tuition at formerly free schools and English rather than Arabic instruction) also drew criticism. The debate reflected a struggle to control culture and shape national identity.[1]

Education had a special meaning for those trying to raise the status of women in Egyptian society. Many felt ignorance was women's basic problem, identified education as the cure, and attributed to it magical transforming powers. There were also practical reasons for focusing on education as a way to raise women's status. The issue unified across religious and political lines and promised results without disturbing the social order. The public appeal of education could be widened, moreover, by linking it to the nationalist struggle.

The women's press featured many articles on girls' education—arguing for more schools, reporting on state and private ventures, and critiquing their programs. Female intellectuals tried both to build a consensus for girls' education and to influence the content of that education. They also documented the expansion of girls' schooling during this period, as well as the change in attitudes. The position of women writers was increasingly popular, in part because of their persuasiveness, and their perspectives can therefore be taken as representative of a larger group. They aired views that government officials heard, and thus helped to shape programming in some of the new schools. Setting the intellectuals' essays on education against the backdrop of reforms in this area shows the range of their interests and the reach of their words.

CREATING DEMAND

The same year that Hind Nawfal started her *al-Fatah* (1892), Ya'qub Artin, an Egyptian Armenian serving as undersecretary for the Ministry of Education, conducted a "quasi-public" investigation to determine demand for girls' education. He spoke for the most part with administrators, teachers, and parents in Cairo to ascertain their opinions, admitting, "Never has one studied at depth a question so complex and so delicate as the education of young girls in a country like Egypt."[2] Artin found that the rich supported the idea of girls' learning but still preferred private instruction in the home to sending their daughters to schools. Middle-class men—whom he identified as employees of the state, doctors, judges, professionals, and merchants—proved most interested in girls' schools, as did their wives, who had had little or no education themselves. Those of the middle class who favored education for their daughters asked for state schools in which the girls would start at ages six to eight and finish at age twelve or thirteen. They wanted a program similar to that of boys, with foreign languages like Turkish optional and subjects like dressmaking, sewing, and music added. They did not oppose tuition, for they did not want their daughters to mix with girls from the lower classes.[3]

Artin found fear and hostility toward girls' education among the lower classes. He traced this in part to the experiences of some with the first state primary school for girls, al-Suyufiyya, which had been started in

1873. The earliest graduates felt "disoriented" upon returning to their families and "superior" to the men they married, according to Artin, and several of these girls "turned out poorly." These educated women probably had difficulty respecting the authority of uneducated husbands or parents, which caused great familial stress. Lower-class parents, in any case, generally preferred that their daughters work with them rather than go to school.[4]

Support for girls' education grew as certain strata began to see education as an important asset and came to see schools, rather than the home, as the milieu in which to train their daughters. Writers in the women's press argued this most forcefully, helping to build consensus on the need for girls' schools. These writers had all been educated in one way or another: a few had been tutored at home, some were products of the American and British missionary schools or French convent schools, and others were the earliest graduates of the new state schools. Many had also worked as teachers or school administrators. They opened their journals to students, teachers, parents, and school directors, sometimes setting aside special columns. They provided a picture not only of the variety of new schools but of the rituals surrounding them, reporting the openings of new schools, appointments of staff members, celebrations of graduations, lists of graduates, speeches at ceremonies, and donations to schools.

These intellectuals first focused on the right of girls to education. Educating girls was not in itself new in the modern period. Girls had sometimes attended the village Qur'anic school (*kuttab*), studied with a *shaykha* or an old *shaykh,* and upon occasion followed the path to al-Azhar.[5] Wealthy families often hired tutors to teach their daughters the Qur'an, Arabic, and Turkish, as well as embroidery and needlework, at home.[6] Late nineteenth-century advocates called for innovations that broke with the patterns of the past. They sought to institutionalize learning in schools modeled on European lines, making the course of study more uniform and extending the opportunity to study to the middle and the lower classes.

In calling for girls' education, advocates never suggested that girls enter male institutions, in spite of the fact that some girls had previously studied with boys in kuttabs. When considering girls' education on a much larger scale, a parallel system—not integration—was their goal. This was an important point, for Muslims had to be convinced that girls' education was not a Christian idea. Writers in *Tarqiyat al-Mar'a* and *Fatat al-Nil* drew on *hadith* and the opinions of Muslim scholars to stress that girls' education was not forbidden by Islam. To the contrary, it was encouraged so that a woman could learn her Islamic rights and responsibilities. The press also kept a close watch on schoolgirls to make sure that they comported themselves properly. Salma Muhammad Ridawiyya was among those who tried to dispel the thinking that coupled ignorance and chastity and attempted to create a new link between learning and piety. She invited women to raise their voices and demand education for the sake of the women's awakening and the Egyptian nation.[7]

In order to legitimize the demand and give it greater appeal, writers coupled the need for girls' education with the nationalist struggle.[8] The argument was simple: Egypt could not develop the educated male population essential for its progress without educating those who cared for the infant and child in his first years. "If we say teach girls and instruct them," wrote Regina 'Awwad, "that is because they are the mothers of tomorrow."[9] Another writer reminded readers that *al-umm wa'l-umma* (the mother and the nation) were linked in letter and spirit.[10] Others drew on the findings of modern science to emphasize the importance of the mother in shaping the infant's character and maintaining his health. Writers also pointed out that an educated woman would make a better companion for her husband. In an article entitled "Woman and the Necessity of Educating Her," Najiya Mahmud wrote that the happiness of the family, society, and humanity depended on the wife and mother.[11]

Linked to the welfare of the nation and given religious endorsement (justifications that were later used to shape the programs of the schools), the idea of girls' education took hold. Annual reports by British officials chronicled the growth of public support. Cromer wrote in 1898 that although progress was slow, "the complete apathy which prevailed in this subject only a few years ago no longer exists."[12] Two years later he noted, "The change which has come over Egyptian public opinion during the last few years in the matter of female education is certainly remarkable," and found that prejudices against female education had been "greatly shaken."[13] By 1904 he concluded that public opinion had undergone a "complete transformation."[14]

Gorst, who succeeded Cromer in 1907, wrote that year, "A strong desire to have girls properly educated now exists."[15] In his next report he stressed that this idea "gains ground yearly."[16] Kitchener, after becoming consul general in 1911, wrote, "There is probably nothing more remarkable in the social history of Egypt during the last dozen years than the growth of opinion among all classes of Egyptians in favour of the education of their daughters."[17] Two years later, "Opposition to and even apathy concerning the education of girls have now almost entirely disappeared."[18]

Whereas Artin had located strong support for girls' schools only among some segments of the middle class in 1892, British officials sketched a broadening of support to other sectors of the population in the following decades. This matches the picture of the growing demand for girls' education that emerges from the women's press. Although Cromer and his successors liked to take credit for this shift in public opinion, they had done little to cultivate it. Education advocates had used the press and other vehicles to campaign for girls' schools and proved much more active than colonial officials in generating support. Furthermore, the British were unwilling to keep pace with the demand. This caused many critics at the time and later to argue that they hindered, rather than helped, the campaign for girls' education.[19]

THE STATE SCHOOL SYSTEM

In the early nineteenth century, the Egyptian state began to establish European-style schools. This policy of developing modern secular schools received varying degrees of support from successive khedives. Traditional schools were left for the most part under the jurisdiction of the religious authorities through the century. The British decided to bring these latter lower schools under state control, but rather than blend the more traditional schools with modern ones, they kept them separate to segregate the socioeconomic classes. The British strategy regarding girls' education in Egypt was therefore to nurture a two-tiered system: kuttabs or elementary vernacular schools for daughters of the lower classes and primary schools for daughters of the middle and upper classes.

The kuttabs, traditional Qur'anic schools, were generally attached to mosques in the villages and towns of Egypt. Instruction was less formal than that associated with European schools and was based on the transmission, or memorization, of the Qur'an. Basic training might also include reading, writing, and some arithmetic.[20] Boys could go from the kuttab to an Islamic *madrasa* like al-Azhar, but girls rarely followed this path. Funded by religious endowments (*waqfs*), many kuttabs came under the control of the Waqf Administration, which was responsible to the khedive rather than to the Ministry of Education. That ministry sought to bring these kuttabs under their control or inspection beginning in the late 1890s in order to establish a more uniform system of basic education and simultaneously to erode khedivial authority. The incentive for the schools was a grant tied to the number of students in attendance. The ministry counted one girl as two boys to increase the number of girls in the schools, presenting an interesting switch from Islamic law, which counts the testimony of two women as equal to that of one man. At the same time, segregated kuttabs for girls were also established.[21]

As these schools came under state control or inspection, they began to draw on a small but growing pool of teachers trained at the Bulaq Normal School. This school was set up in 1903 specifically to provide a trained female staff for girls' kuttabs. The vernacular elementary schools prepared girls from the lower classes predominantly for paid or unpaid domestic work. The only higher education offered on this track was teaching, although in the past girls from such a background might have entered the School of Hakimas (female health practitioners) founded in 1832.[22] The kuttabs educated the largest segment of the population in school, as the number of girls in kuttabs under government inspection jumped from 1,640 in 1900 to 17,000 in 1908 and continued to grow. Enrollment climbed by a few thousand a year in spite of the fact that these schools gradually eliminated free tuition; in 1907, for example, only 31 percent of those boys and girls in the government kuttabs attended for free.[23] Yet the figures showed, according to Gorst, "that the movement in favour of female education is not restricted to the upper classes."[24]

The second of the two tracks overseen by the state were primary schools. With the exception of the School of Hakimas, only two state primary schools for girls existed until the 1910s. Cheshmat Hanim, the third wife of Khedive Isma'il, sponsored the oldest of these (al-Suyufiyya) in 1873 to educate the slaves and daughters of royal and official families. This school attracted over three hundred girls as boarders and day students, teaching Arabic, Turkish, religion, drawing, piano, and needlework. With the suppression of the slave trade in 1877, the school lost its main clientele; and after the deposition of Isma'il in 1879, Cheshmat Hanim was forced to withdraw her patronage. Al-Suyufiyya was then taken over by the Waqf Administration, which closed a second girls' school (al-Karabiyya) and merged the two. The new school was eventually renamed al-Saniyya.[25]

The mandate of the school seemed unclear. At one point a professional school was attached to train poorer girls as domestic servants to replace slaves; this section was kept separate from that which daughters of the elite attended. Artin's assessment of the school's program in 1891 proved harsh: "Everything in this institution is vague and complicated; its program, pompous in theory and on paper, produces nothing or almost nothing in practice upon which one could base the hope of a normal development of female education in Egypt."[26] The school's curriculum was flawed, but it nonetheless remained the centerpiece of the state's program for girls' education. After his accession, the new khedive 'Abbas Hilmi II even visited it to hear speeches in French and piano playing.[27]

A second girls' school, 'Abbas I, joined al-Saniyya. Both were located in Cairo and together could hold nearly five hundred students. As enrollments climbed toward that capacity, free tuition was eliminated. By 1904, all students at al-Saniyya paid fees, which were roughly five Egyptian pounds, a price affordable only to middle- and upper-class families. Moreover, officials measured the success of these schools by the increase in number of paying students, not by the increase in numbers of students enrolled.[28]

The institutionalization of girls' education and the shift from home tutoring to state schooling led to the introduction of certification. Female students sat for the first time for the primary certificate exam in 1900, taking the same test as boys but in different locations. Five of the seventeen girls who presented themselves passed, one ranking seventeenth out of the 712 who registered passing scores. Four of the five went on to the teachers' training department attached to al-Saniyya, which was established to prepare students who had earned a primary certificate to teach in state and private primary schools. The School of Hakimas (to which nursing had been added) also stipulated that a primary certificate was needed for entry and now charged tuition fees. The revisions in that school's policies effectively blocked poorer women from obtaining training as health professionals.[29]

The problems of lack of space in schools and lack of opportunity for continuing education became more acute over time. Some girls who had finished the first level in the kuttabs were too young for training schools like Bulaq Normal School but did not want to leave school altogether. Officials created superior elementary schools in 1916 for girls over twelve who had passed a special exam. The three-year program included science, history, geography, religion, Arabic, writing, sport, drawing, accounting, household finance, health, and housekeeping.[30] Yet further education for graduates of the kuttabs that was not geared toward teaching was almost nonexistent.

This paralleled the situation of female graduates of the primary schools, for no state secondary schools existed for them in Egypt at this time. A small number of girls who wanted higher education but did not want to train as teachers were accepted at al-Saniyya in an experimental program for secondary education in 1909.[31] But the first state secondary school for girls was not opened until 1920. In spite of the calls for higher education, the state did not respond; and until the 1920s, the only Egyptian woman to take the secondary certificate exam was Nabawiyya Musa (1890–1951). Her experience demonstrates the difficulty women encountered in continuing their educations. The daughter of an Egyptian army officer who had died before she was born, Nabawiyya graduated from al-Saniyya and studied on her own for the secondary degree. At the age of sixteen or so and in the face of administrative obstacles (apparently erected by Douglas Dunlop, the British adviser to the Ministry of Education),[32] she presented herself for the exam. She sat in the last bench of the hall, seat number 1087, and passed, becoming the first Egyptian women to earn a secondary degree certificate, and the last for some time.[33] The fact that the pay scale in government posts was tied to certificates rather than positions may have been a consideration for Nabawiyya, who never married and was no doubt dependent on her own income for support. She took a post as assistant mistress at the 'Abbas I girls' school and rose in the Ministry of Education until she resigned in a dispute. As a teacher, administrator, journal editor, and writer, she promoted women's education and right to work throughout her life.[34]

One of the major obstacles to the expansion of girls' education from the start was the lack of female teachers. Acknowledging this in 1892, Ya'qub Artin queried parents on their attitudes toward male teachers. Many opposed them, forcing him to consider other solutions, including the preparation of orphans or Christian and Jewish girls for teaching in Muslim schools. Yet he foresaw that this would delay girls' education for up to a decade.[35] Until the first coterie of Egyptian girls came through the schools, Syrian and other women helped to fill the void. The headmistresses at the first two girls' schools were Syrian, and a Turkish woman was later considered for the post of director of one government school.[36] European teachers also held appointments but were considered by some parents and critics less satisfactory because they generally spoke little or no Arabic.[37]

Two separate schools had been established to train Egyptian women as teachers for the two school systems. Students at Bulaq Normal School went on to teach in the kuttabs, and those at al-Saniyya Training College prepared for work in state and private primary schools. Each school drew women from different class backgrounds. Whereas recruiting candidates for Bulaq Normal School and subsequent teaching posts in the kuttabs proved easy—applications exceeded openings as lower-class women pursued a new career path—the training college associated with al-Saniyya had a harder time finding candidates. Upper-class parents were reluctant to allow their daughters to train for teaching in primary schools, yielding the terrain and the profession to middle-class women. The teachers trained at Bulaq and al-Saniyya took up posts throughout Egypt.[38]

Elizabeth Cooper, who traveled in Egypt before World War I, wrote that according to the minister of education, teachers received good salaries, were provided with comfortable homes within the school complexes, and had more freedom than they would have had within the walls of their own homes. Yet in spite of these benefits, the minister admitted that it was impossible to keep Egyptian women teachers for more than a few years after graduation, for they left after two or three years of teaching to marry.[39] Malak Hifni Nasif's career followed this pattern. She graduated from al-Saniyya and earned the primary certificate in 1900, finished teacher's training in 1903, and taught for a few years before marrying in 1907.[40]

There were other programs to increase the pool and quality of teachers. In 1901, nearly a century after the first male education missions to Europe had been initiated, the state sent women abroad for teacher training. Women had gone abroad to study in the past (a Muntahan al-Shafi'i traveled to Europe with her brother in the 1860s to study French and earn a teacher's license),[41] but these were the first women to receive state funding for their studies. Selected from among those who had excelled in the primary certificate exam and had parental consent, they went to England chaperoned by an English woman. There they attended the Stockwell Training College in London, the Homerton Training College in Cambridge, and other English schools for two- or three-year courses of study. Most prepared to be teachers and administrators at girls' schools. Yet they found themselves to be the objects of a "special control" as well as the center of a public controversy.[42]

Conservatives opposed the idea of sending Muslim women to Christian countries for higher education and attacked state sponsorship of these missions. The presence of Asma' al-Mahdi, the daughter of Shaykh al-'Abbasi al-Mahdi of al-Azhar, on a mission in 1907 did little to quiet the protest and seemed to have exacerbated it instead. Those who joined her in studying in England included Fatima Jum'a, Zaynab Labib, Amina Hasan Shukrallah, and Hanim Hamid.[43] A debate over sending these women abroad flared in the press. In an article entitled "A Great Danger," one critic wrote that the girls who went to Europe returned with more baseness than knowledge. Another writer countered that the girls maintained their honor and piety, prayed regularly, fasted on Ramadan, and only went out with their female supervisor. In short, they "do not mix with men as people imagine."[44] Nonetheless, the government cut back the missions, and in 1911 it sent a Greek, an Armenian, a Bulgarian, and a Jew rather than Muslims. This pleased the editor of *al-'Afaf*, who was thankful that the Ministry of Education had guarded the principles of the religion of the land as well as its financial resources.[45]

These protests coincided with opposition to the women's program at the newly founded Egyptian University. Employing rhetoric similar to that used against female missions abroad, male students forced the closing of the women's section at the university in 1912. The university then used the extra funds to send three more male students abroad.[46] Opposition to advanced levels of women's education was about allocations of money and resources as well as ideology. Not surprisingly, these setbacks to women's education came at the height of Muslim-Coptic tensions and amidst a strong swell of pro-Ottoman Islamic fervor fueled by the Italian invasion of Ottoman Tripoli.

Muslim women later rejoined the study missions abroad, and in the first three decades of the twentieth century, over one hundred women took advantage of state-sponsored foreign education. Women returned from these missions to take up posts in kindergartens, primary schools, and teacher training institutions.[47] These missions supplemented the teacher training schools in Egypt and helped to carve out a new profession for women. By 1925 teachers had begun to agitate for improved work conditions, showing a certain level of professional consciousness. Their complaints of long hours, low pay, too many classes, and maltreatment by supervisors also suggest that work conditions may not have been as rosy as earlier descriptions had implied.[48] Teaching proved to be one of the least prestigious professions, which may explain in part why it was one of the few opened to women. Women's entry into the profession, and the difficult work conditions that some encountered, may have further eroded the image of teaching and its social standing.[49]

Colonial officials interpreted the statistics on the numbers of students turned away from girls' schools and the long waiting lists as signs of their success. Egyptians, in contrast, read these signs as further proof of the poor record of the British on education. Yet British officials were not the only ones to hinder the improvement and expansion of girls' education. Advocates fought a rearguard action against Muslim conservatives who opposed female education, particularly at higher levels. Support for girls' education was neither unanimous nor unlimited, and initiatives tended to fold in the face of hostile pressure. Fortunately, Egyptian girls were not entirely dependent on state programs, for the private sector offered an array of educational alternatives.

PRIVATE EDUCATION

The British did not believe that education should be a monopoly of the state in Egypt or, phrased differently, that providing education was an obligation of the state. Religious minorities, community groups, private individuals, and foreigners sponsored a variety of schools, most of which were countenanced but not in any way supervised by the state. These groups provided a good portion of girls' education in Egypt, especially in the early years and at the higher levels. In attempting to fill the vacuum left by the state, they also sought to advance their own agendas.

Religious minorities had generally handled the education of their own youth in schools that paralleled the Muslim kuttabs and madrasas. The Copts began to build girls' schools in the middle of the nineteenth century in an effort to head off the inroads of Christian missionaries, some of whom had set out to convert Copts. The Coptic church established a girls' school in Azbakiyya, Cairo, in 1853. A second school was built in Harat al-Saqiyin, also in Cairo, under the administration of Patriarch Cyril IV (1854–1861), known as "Abu al-Islah" (the father of reform).[50] Other Coptic schools were sponsored by communal efforts. In Tanta, for example, a school for girls was opened in the 1890s, and private Coptic groups started free schools elsewhere.[51] The net result of attendance at these and other schools was that the percentage of literate female Copts far surpassed the percentage of literate female Muslims in the early 1900s.[52]

The Jewish community of Egypt also maintained its own system of schools. It was probably not until 1840, when a French Jewish statesman by the name of Adolphe Crémieux opened several schools in Cairo and Alexandria, that girls had an opportunity to attend school in numbers. Though these institutions soon closed, the community sponsored a girls' school in Alexandria in 1862. Girls studied fewer languages and academic subjects there than boys and learned handicrafts instead. Another push for girls' education came in the 1890s when the Alliance Israélite Universelle, a French Jewish philanthropic foundation, opened schools that were mostly coeducational in Cairo, Alexandria, and Tanta, in part to halt the flow of Jews to non-Jewish schools. Although the curriculum and method of these schools was inspired by the French, Egyptian history, geography, and Arabic were taught, and girls received instruction in handicrafts.[53]

There were continuous efforts on the part of Muslims, Christians, and Jews at school-building to counter foreign endeavors or augment state ones. Jam'iyyat Ta'lim al-Banat al-Islamiyya (the Islamic society for girls' education), for instance, was founded in 1901 by a group of men and offered free education to girls at a time when state schools had begun to charge tuition. Modeled after institutions in Istanbul, the society's schools stressed Arabic, Turkish, and Islamic instruction.[54] Throughout the country, provincial councils and local groups also started an array of schools at various levels. To give a sampling: a local committee established a girls' primary school in the town of Fayyum in 1898; funds were raised in Zaqaziq, a town in the Delta, to open a girls' school in 1904; and a charity sponsored six girls' schools in the region of Minya, a town in central Egypt, in the early 1910s.[55] Community groups raised money in appeals in the press, through speeches, and at fairs, taking education into their own hands.

A few schools were started as individual undertakings. A woman who gave her name in official correspondence only as "Zahra" opened a school for girls in the 1890s to teach reading, writing, and handiwork. In an appeal to the Ministry of Education for funding, she emphasized the rarity of girls' schools in Egypt and explained that several of her students were orphans. The appeal must have struck a chord, for she received a grant of sixty Egyptian pounds.[56] Other women started sewing schools and similar ventures to teach poorer women skills so that they could support themselves or supplement the family income. In the face of growing demands for education, Egyptians individually and collectively created a network of schools. Their efforts at school-building show that this was not an enterprise left entirely to the whim of state officials and their inertia, or to foreign missionaries and their zeal.

French Catholic, British Anglican, and American Presbyterian, as well as other missionary groups, began to expand their activities in Egypt in the second half of the nineteenth century. Whereas some churches recognized the Coptic church, others tried to convert Copts as well as Jews and Muslims (though missionizing among the latter was illegal). The missionaries built churches, hospitals, orphanages, and schools to spread their influence. Perceiving that the key to the family and its salvation was through its women, some focused their energy on female education. The American Presbyterian church, for example, sent "harem workers" to visit and instruct thousands of women in their homes.[57] The Americans built girls' schools, in the words of the Presbyterian missionary Charles Watson, "that Egypt's womanhood may be redeemed from the thralldom of ignorance, superstition, and sin, in the generation to come if not in this."[58]

Since the state was unwilling to meet the growing demand for girls' education, the Christian missionaries found a ready market for their schools, and for a time they taught a larger number of girls than any other institution in Egypt. In 1892 Christian missionaries had 360 teachers in over fifty schools teaching roughly 9,000 girls. At the same time, other nonstate schools had almost 200 teachers in forty schools teaching over 4,000 girls. The state, by comparison, had ten teachers in three schools teaching 242 students.[59] Moreover, the student mix in these schools began to change. Through the early 1890s it was rare to find a Muslim girl in a missionary school, and the schools initially catered almost exclusively to Christians. Yet two decades later close to 30 percent of the female students in missionary schools were Muslim. Interestingly, Muslim parents were more willing, or compelled due to lack of alternatives, to send their daughters than their sons to such schools. The percentage of Muslim girls who attended missionary schools was higher than that of Muslim boys as a result.[60]

Foreign schools multiplied in Egypt in the early 1900s. Elizabeth Cooper reported being amazed at the number of girls' schools of all types—French, English, and Italian—found along the streets of Cairo. Egypt, she observed, seemed to have become a "haven for the private-school teacher."[61] Not surprisingly, the schools pushed their own sectarian interests and national agendas. Competition was keenest in the rivalry between the French and the British. "The wide and powerful influence exercised by the French Convent Schools throughout Egypt upon the daughters of Mohammedans even of the highest standing should not be lost sight of," warned Douglas Dunlop in a note to British officials.[62] Girls studied in such French schools as the Soeurs de Sacré Coeur, Mère de Dieu, and Notre Dame de Sion. The French thus kept the edge in girls' education that they had lost in boys' education, in part because girls did not have the goal of government employment as an incentive to learn English. In 1914–1915, there were 2,624 Egyptian girls in French schools, 2,491 Egyptian girls in American schools, 893 in British schools, and 780 in Italian schools. Nine-tenths of these foreign schools were run by missionaries, making foreign efforts almost synonymous with missionary activity.[63]

Missionaries also opened one of the first girls' "colleges" in Egypt. In a letter setting out his vision for the school, Andrew Watson, a missionary and father of Charles Watson, explained that the girls would receive instruction that would prepare them to work as school mistresses or to manage their homes and raise their children properly in a program that was akin to a secondary degree.[64] The American College for Girls opened in Cairo in 1909 with twenty-nine students, seventeen of whom were Muslim, and the number of enrollees quickly grew. As a sign of support for this school and as a general encouragement for private initiative in the field of girls' education, the Egyptian government sent state officials to attend annual college ceremonies.[65]

Private schools rather than state ones provided the bulk of girls' education in Egypt, particularly before the state began administering the "vernacular elementary schools" or kuttabs. This was especially true at the upper levels, where state secondary schools were noticeably lacking. Many took advantage of the opportunities that private schools offered, including several of the founders of the women's press, who also taught in some of these schools. Yet education advocates did not hesitate to critique their programs and those of the state schools.

CURRICULUM, CULTURE, AND IDENTITY

The first wave of writing on education in the women's press attempted to mold public opinion in its favor and pushed for the opening of girls' schools. This was fairly successful as new private and state schools opened and the number of female students increased. It was time, Regina 'Awwad among others argued, to consider in greater depth the question of what girls were taught.[66] In a second wave of writing on this subject, intellectuals began to examine the programs of the new schools. Realizing that it was not enough to build schools and fill them, they attempted to shape a curriculum that would improve the position of women in Egyptian society. Their suggestions generally reflected their original justifications for girls' education. Having called for education to prepare girls to be better wives, mothers, and believers, they demanded a curriculum that would serve this purpose. Their programs were based on the strategy of increasing women's power in the home rather than dismantling the boundaries of that home. Their discussions about education thus transcended the schoolroom and touched on questions of cultural identity, gender roles, and class expectations.

Language of instruction proved to be one of the most hotly contested issues in respect to Egyptian education. As the British anglicized state education and foreign schools pushed their own languages, those in favor of more Arabic instruction fought back. From the late 1890s, writers condemned the superficiality of the current language training and neglect of Arabic. Najiya Rashid noted that Muslim girls emerged from foreign schools having been taught to despise their mother tongue; as a result their knowledge of Arabic was very weak.[67] Rosa Antun condemned the fashion of speaking with interjections of foreign phrases, so that a woman was unable to express her ideas either in Arabic or in a foreign language.[68] The girls coming out of the state and private schools were often anglicized or francophied and preferred foreign styles and customs. Observers complained that they mimicked outer forms, for they had only a superficial knowledge of things foreign and no insight whatsoever into their own language and culture.[69]

Recognizing the importance of language in the construction of cultural identity and in strengthening a national movement, Egyptian and Syrian writers pushed for more Arabic education. The call by Syrians for Arabic instruction also reflected an attempt to stress their common linguistic bond with Egyptians. Yet there were probably practical reasons as well as ideological ones for promoting instruction in Arabic. The greatest edge Egyptians and Syrians held over British and other foreigners competing for teaching appointments was their knowledge of Arabic. Stressing Arabic education would preserve their advantage in girls' schools and, of course, make Arabic women's journals more marketable.

The debate over language instruction flared at the outset of Sa'd Zaghlul's tenure as minister of education (1906–1910). Cromer agreed before leaving Egypt in 1907 that all possible subjects in the primary schools would be taught in Arabic. Reversing the government's policy of anglicization opened new employment opportunities for Arabic speakers and hindered some of those who did not know Arabic well. The new regulations may explain the resignations of three English teachers from state primary girls' schools in 1907.[70] Graduates of al-Saniyya Training College gradually replaced some of the foreign instructors, though foreign administrators and teachers remained in many schools. Cromer's successor, Gorst, made some concessions on Arabic instruction in the secondary schools, but as there were no state secondary schools for girls, these concessions did not affect them.[71]

Critics proved less successful in pressuring private schools to alter their stress on foreign languages and culture. Fatima 'Asim, president of Jam'iyyat al-Nahda al-Nisa'iyya (the society for women's awakening), founded in 1916, summed up the growing sense of disillusionment with this sort of schooling. Speaking to mothers about daughters educated at great expense, she noted, "You see them speaking in several languages and in their hands are diplomas. But when they gather, they speak only of dresses, dressmakers, silk, laces, and the wonder of modern fashions."[72] Advocates of girls' education found a curriculum that turned out graduates with such values inherently flawed. They had not campaigned arduously for a program that transformed women for the worse and did nothing to advance the cause of women.

A second issue of contention in education debates was the amount of religious instruction offered in Egyptian schools. As long as Muslims and Christians had maintained separate educational systems financed by private endowments, there had been no quarrel over religious instruction. Each community had autonomy and could carry on with the task of transmission of sacred texts. But once the state had become more involved in the business of education and created mixed Muslim and Christian schools, policy on religious instruction was bound to displease one group or another. Some Muslims called for more Islamic education in the secularized state schools, and Zaghlul responded in 1907 by increasing the Islamic component at the primary level.[73] Elizabeth Cooper described this sort of instruction after visiting a government school several years later. She entered a room "where there were perhaps fifty little girls of about eleven to twelve years of age all crooning in a sing-song voice verses from the Koran. The teacher for this branch of instruction was an old blind woman who knew the Koran by heart, and she commenced a surah or chapter and allowed the children to finish it."[74]

Yet Zaghlul's decision to increase the Islamic component in state schools created resentment on the part of some Copts. Communal leaders petitioned the government in 1910, demanding the right to offer Coptic instruction in every public school and ensuring that those religious instructors be paid by the state.[75] Cooper found Coptic mothers who protested that the Qur'an but not the Bible was taught in government schools.[76] State policy decreed that Coptic religion be taught only at schools with fifteen or more Christian students. There was only 1 Christian out of 217 students at al-Saniyya and 12 Christians out of 120 students at 'Abbas I Girls' School in 1907.[77] Yet numbers of Coptic girls in state primary schools may have been low because their religion was not taught at a time when other options were available for schooling in the private sector.

The issue of religious instruction proved controversial in private schools as well. Critics agreed on the need to give girls moral guidance but wanted them to be exposed to their own religion. In this case, some Muslims strongly opposed Christian instruction. Najiya Rashid addressed her coreligionists on "The Danger of Foreign Schools" in a speech published in *Tarqiyat al-Mar'a*. She warned parents that foreign schools strove "to mislead the minds of youth" and "to nurture their souls with Christian learning." Najiya asked her audience how they could send their daughters to these schools after having learned their aims. She worried that if these girls, who would one day be mothers raising sons, became Christian, the nation would become Christian. She concluded that a simple kuttab or ignorance was preferable to such an education.[78]

What language and how much religion remained contested issues. Most writers agreed, however, on the need to emphasize domestic instruction in girls' education. Advocates argued that girls should learn useful skills in addition to basics in reading, writing, math, geography, history, and religion. "Do our schools teach our daughters anything of cooking, housekeeping, and childraising?" asked Regina 'Awwad.[79] Initially they did not. When the first seventeen girls sat for the primary certificate exam in 1900, they found the same questions that male candidates found, for the subjects taught to boys and girls in primary schools were almost exactly the same. One of the girls taking that exam was among those who later argued for teaching girls practical subjects. Malak Hifni Nasif called for instruction in household management, hygiene, emergency medical care, and childraising.[80] Like others, she saw no point in instructing boys and girls in the same subjects when their roles in life differed. By elevating the tasks that women performed or managed in the home and turning them into the special science of home economics at a time when sciences had a great prestige, intellectuals hoped to elevate the status of women.

With its stress on foreign languages and little or no domestic instruction, the current curriculum was considered particularly irrelevant for girls from families of lesser means. Writers denounced the fact that the daughter of the merchant and the daughter of the worker received the same education. It was as if, one male Muslim critic noted, all were prepared to marry a judge or a banker.[81] Most writers agreed that girls of the middle and lower classes needed to acquire practical skills in order to contribute to the household economy. Poorer women, Regina 'Awwad argued, did not have the same safety net as wealthier women and might need to support themselves in case of divorce or the death of a husband.[82] Writers called for instruction in subjects that would prepare women for jobs in handicraft industries, domestic service, and similar fields, but not necessarily for higher-skilled and higher-paying jobs.

State officials responded to calls for more practical training by modifying the curriculum in girls' schools. Instruction in domestic science was pushed on both tracks of the state school system for girls of different socioeconomic backgrounds. At elementary schools, courses in cookery, laundry, hygiene, and needlework were instituted in 1910; and at the same time at al-Saniyya primary school, a special room was set aside for lessons in domestic economy and cooking.[83] Two years later the School of Domestic Economy at Qubba, which trained girls as school mistresses and domestic science teachers, was enlarged, and similar schools were opened elsewhere. The Bulaq Normal School also added a new section to train teachers in household management.[84] When girls presented themselves for the primary certificate exam in 1913, they found a new test designed specifically for them. It included a practical part in cooking, laundry, and needlework plus written questions on hygiene and housewifery.[85]

Gorst reported in 1910 that the introduction of more domestic instruction in state schools was a response to "a demand for a more practical education for girls."[86] Listing similar additions to the curriculum two years later, Kitchener wrote that these developments "show that the movement in favour of training Egyptian girls in household work is taking a practical form."[87] The British are blamed for imposing domestic instruction on girls' schools and not preparing women to be productive workers or professionals.[88] Yet they seemed to be responding to public demands for this sort of education sounded in the women's press and elsewhere. Writers had argued that the domestic work of a wife and mother was productive, and they tried to professionalize housework through the introduction of special courses of study in domestic science. In this they were no doubt influenced by the foreign home economics movement, and they endorsed a vision of gender roles approved by the government and appropriate for the new middle class.

Education preoccupied writers in the press and often took center stage. Female intellectuals initially justified girls' education on the grounds that the nation would advance if mothers and wives were better prepared for their religious and domestic roles. They then argued for a curriculum that included household management to prepare women for their domestic vocations. By improving women's position in the home, they hoped to raise women's status in society. The change in curriculum in state schools indicates that the women's press successfully influenced government policy, or at least accurately reflected the public opinion of a certain segment of urban society pushing for that policy. The British did not impose this sort of education. Rather, it fit neatly with the middle-class values of the female intellectuals who demanded it.

Nor did the British invent and then force gender segregated schooling on an unwilling population.[89] Education advocates never called for coeducation, for it would have proven highly unpopular and undermined their efforts to increase support for girls' schooling. Although early nineteenth-century kuttabs had occasionally been mixed, with the odd girl attending lessons, educated women had mostly been tutored in the privacy of the home. Institutionalizing education meant extending that privacy and segregation into the classroom by building separate schools, replicating dominant social ideals about segregation.

Writers agreed that state schools offered the best opportunity for girls' instruction, and they called for more state schools through higher levels.

Although the British claimed to favor girls' education, their enthusiasm was not translated into resources. Few state primary or elementary schools existed for girls; those that existed charged tuition and could not accommodate the growing demand for places. Under the occupation, private girls' schools provided a good portion of the available education, which was problematic in the eyes of many female intellectuals since these schools pushed their own sectarian and national interests. Writers pointed this out to encourage the expansion of state-sponsored girls' education.

Although the overwhelming majority of Egyptian girls did not attend school of any sort—state or private—public support for girls' education grew from the 1890s, particularly among the middle and upper classes. But as long as the British set ceilings on state spending, real expansion of education remained blocked. It was only with nominal independence that Egyptians gained greater control over this domain. The new government set education as a national priority, and the state later endorsed compulsory and free elementary education for boys and girls. While literacy rates remained very low and education continued to be beyond the reach of most for many years, the state had acknowledged girls' right to education. This was a great victory for those intellectuals who had campaigned for girls' education.

7

RETHINKING WORK
AND THE FAMILY

Debates on girls' education led directly to discussions of women's work roles. The two subjects were inextricably linked, for most advocates agreed that education should prepare girls for their role in life and most pushed for a practical training. The central issue was not, however, whether women should work, but whether they should enter the wage labor force in numbers or work at home. In Egypt, and throughout the Arab world, women have not entered the labor force on a regular or permanent basis in large numbers, and as a result the region has one of the lowest wage labor participation rates for women in the world.[1] This has often been associated with Islamic ideology and its strict injunctions on veiling and seclusion. Yet Muslim women in Africa have had a much higher labor force participation rate than women in the Arab world, who in this regard are more akin to non-Muslim women in India.[2] Depending on what traditions are tapped, Islam provides legitimization for a number of patterns, from complete seclusion to creation of a parallel work force of women (as in Saudi Arabia) to greater integration in the work place. The stipulations in Islamic law that a man support his wife and children probably influenced work patterns as much or more than those on veiling and seclusion.

Rather than look at Islam as the cause of the gender division of labor in the region and of low female wage labor participation, some scholars

144

have focused on socioeconomic changes. As Egypt was drawn into the world market in the nineteenth century, Egyptian agriculture was transformed from subsistence into a cash crop monoculture, with agricultural workers increasingly turned into wage laborers. By the end of the century, craft and trade guilds had also broken down, replaced by wage labor. Over the first few decades of the twentieth century, a working class emerged, and after World War I, the indigenous bourgeoisie crystallized as industries expanded.[3] One view argues that Egypt's entry into the world market as a supplier of raw cotton and importer of European finished goods eroded its domestic crafts and industries, undermining women's economic production and channeling women into service occupations.[4] But this does not seem to have been the pattern for other parts of the Ottoman Empire. Although male guild labor eroded in the nineteenth century, women's wage labor activities in textiles and other industries picked up and were carried out in factories, workshops, and at home. By accepting lower wages than male workers, female workers were able to produce goods that could compete with cheap European imports.[5]

By the late nineteenth and early twentieth centuries, and with the growth of wage labor, the numbers of women in the work force in Egypt seemed to be slowly increasing. This in turn sparked a debate in the press on proper work roles for men and women. The debate was also inspired by transformations in the domestic sphere and shifts in the household economy. Domestic slaves from Ethiopia and the Sudan had not been beyond the reach of ordinary Egyptian households through the 1870s, with reports that during certain periods even peasants purchased slaves. The signing of the Anglo-Egyptian Convention of 1877 banning the slave trade and legislation mandating manumission, along with various other factors, led to the disappearance of slavery.[6] The demise of domestic slavery and concubinage contributed to a reassessment of productive and reproductive roles in the home. Servants stepped in to fill some of the functions of domestic slaves, and wives gained ground with the elimination of a group of rivals. The homes of the middle and upper classes also enjoyed a variety of technological innovations, which encouraged a reconsideration of household tasks.

Female intellectuals debating women's work roles articulated a new domestic ideology. Most subscribed to an ideal in which male members of the family earned an income and supported female members of the family, who in turn provided household services. The transition to fixed wages or salaries probably meant that many men worked longer and more regular hours away from home. This may have left a vacuum of authority in the home, into which women willingly stepped. By elaborating woman's role as manager of the home and as wife and mother, intellectuals did not see themselves as reaffirming a customary gender division of labor prescribed by religion. They sought to revalue women's domestic work and invest it with greater meaning. At the same time, they strove to restructure family roles and relations, placing the couple at the center of the family, shifting some authority from the husband to the wife, and turning more attention to childhood. Although their vision exposed their urban and class biases—these were mostly women who did not have to work outside the home—they set an agenda for reforms in family law which transcended class. Their domestic ideology arose from specific socioeconomic circumstances and cultural considerations and may help explain the choices that women made about work.

A THIRD SEX

Writers who discussed women's work in essays in women's journals and elsewhere expressed a variety of views. On this issue they were generally unwilling to follow the path set by Western women, as the following exchange illustrates. When the visiting secretary of a French women's organization asked to meet some Egyptian women, the head of the Watani party sent her to Fatima Rashid, the president of Jam'iyyat Tarqiyat al-Mar'a, who provided a record of that 1908 meeting. The French woman explained that women in her country were fighting for the right to control their own property and wealth. Fatima asked why, if they could not manage their own incomes, women worked "like men," and wondered who ran a woman's house and raised her children if she worked outside the home. The French woman told her that women were compelled to work and that the schools looked after the children. Fatima informed her visitor that a Muslim woman, by contrast, could own and control property, had guaranteed support from her family or husband, and, failing that, could turn to the state for support. She could therefore devote herself to her family.[7]

Fatima considered a woman who earned wages outside the home to be like a man, disturbing the sexual order. She wrote about a "third sex"—not men and not women—that was developing in Europe in large numbers. As some Egyptian women attempted to follow the path of Western women, Fatima wondered what freedom there was in "coming and going, working with man shoulder-to-shoulder." Women's mixing with men in their work would only lead to "disgrace and difficulty" for them and "misery and misfortune" for the family. Fatima realized that some women in Europe had to work because their families would not provide for them. But in Egypt the family or state had to take care of women, and if Muslim women had to work, it meant that both the family and the state had neglected their duty.[8]

Rather than point to stipulations about veiling and seclusion, Fatima emphasized the support guaranteed women under law as the principle behind the gender division of labor. Many women actively pursued this right to support in court in nineteenth-century Egypt.[9] Still, Fatima weighed the pros and cons of work as an optional activity rather than a necessary one for many women. Sarah al-Mihiyya also saw no benefit in women's work for wages, at least for elite women. Working women had to go out "under the full light of a burning sun" and "among oppressive crowds," anathemas to those who could afford to be sheltered from the elements and the lower classes.[10] In short, a good job was far from being a sign of status for privileged women.

Not only were there no benefits to women's work, it also generated an array of problems. In an article entitled "Women and Work," Sarah al-Mihiyya showed the danger of gender role reversal by sketching a picture of the home life of a foreign female lawyer. "Her work interested her more than the crying of her son, discarded on the floor in front of her almost bursting from weeping and wailing." But the mother sat at her desk writing and showed "no mercy or compassion." And as she rushed to leave, she ignored her husband's request to change her son's diaper, "giving him a scornful look and a shrug of her shoulders" as she left.[11] To those who believed that a woman's first commitment was to her husband and child, the scene was alarming. This was an example of Fatima Rashid's "third sex"—an unnatural, unfeminine woman—and the resulting role reversal upset the natural order and gender relations. Writers like Sarah al-Mihiyya and Fatima Rashid decried the erosion of the family and explosion of individualism in Europe and considered the collective good of the family more important than individual rights.

Yet many Egyptian women had to work, as most writers were aware. Malak Hifni Nasif and others defended women's right to work in certain circumstances: some women were single or barren and had no children to care for; others were widowed or divorced and did not have families to help them; and still others were married and had husbands who needed their assistance. Malak argued that these women should not have to work at "lowly occupations" but should be able to become doctors or teachers. Those professions in which women served other women—health and education—were encouraged and the first to open up. Malak also pointed to the proliferation of foreign women in Egypt who offered essential services that Egyptian women should be able to provide for themselves. Invoking nationalist pride, she suggested that Egyptian women be trained for these jobs. She also found no divine edict for the current gender division of labor: "Had Adam chosen cooking and washing, and Eve to work to provide support," she postulated, "then that would have been the system followed today."[12]

Intellectuals' views on women's work ranged on a continuum. Most saw women's work for wages outside the home as threatening to gender relations and the social order, and they saw no point to it if women were supported, as they should be, by their families or had income from land or other investments to support themselves. They depicted Western working women as defeminized to discourage Egyptian women from pressing for jobs outside the home. The presence of foreign women working in Egypt nonetheless provided a rationale for some to enlist nationalist arguments and to call for the training of Egyptian women to replace these foreigners, and a few encouraged openings in the more prestigious professions.

Female intellectuals generally paid more attention to the abstract issue of women's work and the concerns of their class than to the concrete circumstances of lower-class women's work. Although some started sewing and needlework schools to teach women skills so that they could work in millinery and other trades, these writers rarely looked into workshops and factories to examine work conditions. Almost the only women workers they had contact with were those in service occupations. As a result, a gap existed between their ideal and the reality of work roles for women in Egypt. And the attacks against women's waged work may have been an indication that such work was on the rise.

LABOR PARTICIPATION AND WORK CONDITIONS

In spite of prevailing norms about support and seclusion, many Egyptian women worked in some capacity outside their homes in the late nineteenth and early twentieth centuries. The extent of this labor, waged and unwaged, is difficult to assess. How reliable were censuses when it came to measuring the number of women workers? Census takers throughout this period were men who questioned male heads of household about the activities of family members.[13] The latter often concealed women's work for a number of reasons, including mistrust of government officials, a disregard for seasonal or temporary employment, and a sense that women's work did not conform to a social ideal. Hence, in many cases women's work was hidden from official view, and the figures we have are probably a baseline. This is particularly so for agriculture, where seasonal or occasional women laborers or family workers were not counted. The censuses not only tended to underenumerate women's waged work, they initially ignored unwaged work altogether.[14]

According to the 1897 census, roughly 2 percent of the native female population over ten worked (63,731 of 3,152,404), about half of them as domestic servants.[15] Although the 1907 census did not distinguish between Egyptian and foreign workers, it acknowledged more women workers in a greater variety of jobs. These included 57,144 women in agriculture, a group not covered in the previous census and over half of whom were cultivating their own land; 19,916 in manufacturing;

7,565 in trade; and at least 25,359 in domestic service. Family members (married women, and so on) engaged in domestic work made up a new category, in which 2,265,820 or about 50 percent of adult women were included. Another 2,007,461 women were listed as persons without occupation.[16]

The 1917 census, taken in the midst of the war, shows an attempt to document the work roles of men and women more precisely. In contrast to the previous census, which listed over 2 million women without occupation, this one had less than 1,000 in that category. The higher percentage of women workers was due in part to the special circumstances of wartime and in part to census strategies. The forced recruitment of over 100,000 Egyptian males for labor in the British army that year (and similar numbers in previous years) brought more women into the work force, especially as some women were left with no support when their husbands were taken away.[17] But clearer recognition of women's agricultural activities made the difference. The 1917 census shows 1,621,717 women engaged in agriculture, including close to 50,000 working for wages; 200,000 cultivating their own land; and over 1 million working family land. Numbers in manufacturing (which did not develop significantly until after the war) are lower, with 68,152 women listed in this category, one-quarter of whom were in textile production and one-half in clothes manufacture. Three-quarters of those 38,565 women in commerce were engaged in selling foodstuffs, and about 75,000 women were domestic servants.[18] (Women selling produce in the market and working in private homes as servants were the female laborers that travelers often mentioned.)[19] The 1917 census also enumerated 450,174 female family members engaged in domestic work. Those who prepared the census inferred from their data that close to 2 million other women fit into this category.[20] Do these latter figures tell us that a new consciousness about housewifery had arisen in Egypt? Although Egyptians collected the data, British officials had probably selected the census categories. Still, nearly 500,000 affirmative responses to that category suggests that it had some meaning, reflecting social perceptions of women's economic roles.

Produced under different directors and teams, these three censuses varied enormously in tabulating women's work, and thus it is almost impossible to track trends. We cannot know for certain whether more women were working at waged or unwaged labor, or whether the census takers simply became more attuned to female labor. The censuses should be read for what they can tell us—that many women worked in a variety of capacities, from fishing and sailing to iron-making and grave digging—rather than what they cannot tell us.

Statistics do not tell us, in any case, about the conditions under which women worked in the late nineteenth and early twentieth centuries. Most women faced employers in an unregulated labor market without some of the protections of earlier periods. Lists of women's guilds from the nineteenth century—cotton workers, greengrocers, milk sellers, bakers, pastry cooks, soothsayers, domestic servants, and midwives—show that some urban tradeswomen and craftswomen had been organized collectively.[21] The guilds served a variety of functions: supplying labor, setting wages, fixing taxes and prices, limiting access to certain trades, and policing members. Most of these guilds had disappeared, however, by the 1880s and 1890s. Their decline, along with that of male guilds, coincided with the drift toward a capitalist economy. The state took over many of the administrative functions of guild shaykhs, new sources of labor undermined the guilds' monopoly on labor, and European goods challenged guild monopolies on production of traditional crafts.[22] By turn of the century, female and male workers were no longer organized in collective associations, nor were they yet protected by labor legislation.

Conditions of work varied depending on employer and occupation. Handicraft workshops and textile factories, many of which were foreign owned, often tapped female labor. Some of the jobs may have been extensions of tasks women had earlier performed in the home, but female labor was probably targeted for textile industries because it was cheaper than male labor. At Amiriyya, in the Western Desert, a workshop employed bedouin women refugees from the Sanussi campaign. Under the direction of a female overseer, women spun wool and wove carpets in traditional patterns. The workshop was set in a complex containing a dyeworks plant, a shop, and a school, with education programs that included instruction in infant care. Nina Baird, a British national, supervised the project, which was probably unique in its concern for the needs of workers.[23]

Women were generally unskilled workers at the bottom of the pay scale in this sort of enterprise. In cotton-ginning factories throughout Egypt, young girls were hired to feed the gins with seed cotton. The machines sorted the seeds and pod from the cotton before it was packed in bales and shipped to England to be woven into cloth, some of which made its way back to the Egyptian villages and towns where it had originated. In a season that lasted from late September through February or March, young girls worked up to sixteen hours a day. Throughout the day they had short breaks and were occasionally relieved by their mothers or other family members. Wages varied from factory to factory and village to town, with girls at the lowest end of the scale. In Mansura, for example, girls received three piasters per day and boys four piasters in the early 1900s. The average ages at factories also varied. At Bani Suwayf, where three-fifths of the workers were girls, they averaged ages nine to ten but some were as young as seven.[24]

The employment of children in the factories alarmed some observers, leading to the passage of Child Labor laws in 1909. These prohibited cotton ginning factories from employing children under nine altogether and children from nine to thirteen for more than eight hours a day or at night. Yet because most of the factories were foreign owned (79 of 129 in the interior), instituting stringent penalties was impossible under the capitulations, which protected foreigners from Egyptian law. This rendered the legislation impossible to enforce and therefore practically ineffective.[25]

In a study of women's work undertaken in 1918, a committee made up mostly of foreign women looked at three factories around Cairo that employed women, including one clothing factory and one cigarette factory (where women sorted leaves according to grade). The committee reported that the overcrowding evident in European industrial centers did not seem apparent, nor did women work with dangerous machinery or chemicals. But in the large number of small workrooms connected with dressmaking and millinery trades, conditions were often bad, with no proper sanitation facilities for the workers. The study found most posts poorly paid, below what they considered a minimum level needed for support, with long hours—up to fifty a week—often without a day off. Long summer breaks hurt employees, who usually did not have savings. The committee called for the formation of female trade unions. They also called for protective legislation setting standards for hygiene and sanitary facilities, limiting the number of work hours and mandating overtime pay, stipulating a day and a half off a week, and instituting inspection by female government officials of all places where female labor was employed.[26] However, protective legislation for women and the formation of female trade unions responsive to women's concerns, both of which might have helped ameliorate some of the more severe labor abuses of the time, were a couple of decades away. A labor law establishing a nine-hour working day for women, restricting their night work, requiring a weekly day of rest, and excluding them from certain dangerous industries was passed in 1933. Only after another decade was one of the first unions of women workers, Rabitat al-'Amilat al-Misriyya (the League of Egyptian Women Workers), founded by Hikmat al-Ghazali, a textile worker from Shubra al-Khayma.[27]

Lack of protections was apparent in one of the most widely practiced occupations of women—domestic service. With the end of slavery, domestic servants gradually replaced slaves as household laborers, with some freed slaves becoming servants.[28] According to the 1897 census, over 35,000 women, or 50 percent of those Egyptian women listed as working for pay outside the home, were servants. The 1917 census showed a doubling of that figure, still a significant proportion of wage earners but no longer half.[29] Some shortages of domestic workers seemed to have ensued in the transition from slave to waged household labor, which may have been one of the incentives for middle-class writers to promote domestic training in schools and a domestic ideology for women. That more Egyptian women were employed as domestic servants than in any other capacity in the late nineteenth and early twentieth centuries suggests that, paid or unpaid, most women worked in the domestic sphere.

The conditions of work and treatment of servants no doubt had a great deal to do with the family who employed them. In replacing slaves who had sometimes served as both domestic workers and concubines, some servants were apparently forced to submit to sexual demands. The Egyptian novelist Najib Mahfuz describes two such encounters in *Bayn al-Qasrayn,* a book set in Cairo around the 1919 revolution and which is considered an important social document. In one scene, the father of the family depicted in the novel condemns his son for "raping the most humble servant in his family's home."[30] Newspapers and court records also contain stories of the seduction, rape, and forced marriages of some servants. Working in close private quarters away from the public eye and distant from their own families, servants often had little protection from male advances and little recourse in law. The editor of *al-'Afaf* protested when an Egyptian pharmacist who had raped his servant was imprisoned for only one month and then released. Another man married a servant his wife had taken in, much to the chagrin of that first wife.[31]

Defining the roles of servants and learning to manage them better were of concern to women writers. Yet rigid class boundaries barring informal interaction between servant and mistress did not seem to exist in Egypt. Elizabeth Cooper noted that in comparison with women in Western countries, Egyptian women were much more familiar with their servants, who came in and out of rooms without knocking and participated readily in conversations.[32] In this sense servants might have been seen by their employers as part of the family, as some slaves had been.

Nonetheless, the routine of the servant was not easy. Malaka Sa'd proposed that a servant's schedule start at six in the morning and last until ten in the evening, with one hour for rest in the late afternoon and one day off a week.[33] With such schedules most servants must have eaten at the homes of their employers and slept there as well, although not always in the best conditions according to the 1918 study mentioned above. Also according to that report, the monthly salary of housekeepers in Cairo ranged from 2 to 5.50 Egyptian pounds a month, and that of cooks, maids, and general servants 1 to 5 Egyptian pounds a month.[34] Sarah al-Mihiyya had suggested three years earlier that a servant be paid six Egyptian pounds per month, which was above average and certainly better than the wages of a female factory worker, who received about one pound per month.[35] Other writers pleaded with readers to treat servants humanely, a call that was stepped up after reports that a young servant girl had fallen while cleaning a window.[36]

Writers were especially concerned about the servant's role in the family. Noting that compared to the slave in the nineteenth century, "the servant has become the mistress in the house" in the twentieth century, Rosa Antun tried to foster respect between servants and their employers.[37] Critics complained that many women yielded control of the housework to servants and then disclaimed responsibility for the results. Women blamed servants for an array of problems, according to Regina 'Awwad, from children's dirty clothes and general disorder to poorly prepared food.[38] Others condemned the morals of servants, suggesting that they were a bad influence on the children.[39] Writers urged women to reclaim domestic tasks, directly or through better management, to raise the status of domesticity and the stature of the housewife.

MISTRESS OF THE HOUSE

Many writers saw waged working women as the exception to a domestic rule. Rather than focus on improving the work conditions of waged women, female intellectuals turned their energies to improving the domestic environment. Enhancing this sphere was seen as the best strategy for raising women's status, and the outpouring of domestic literature instructing the wife, mother, and "mistress of the house" showed pursuit of this goal. Starting with Hind Nawfal's al-Fatah, women's journals carried columns and articles on this subject.[40] They all devoted large sections to instructions on housekeeping. The journals elevated a domestic ideal and then offered readers training in how to live up to it.[41] Numerous books were published on this topic.

The new domestic ideology grew out of socioeconomic and technological changes. In the more affluent parts of Cairo and Alexandria, housework was transformed in the late nineteenth and early twentieth centuries with the introduction of gas, water, and electricity, and the appearance of new appliances like the oven and sewing machine. Young girls had to be formally instructed in an age of science to run a home properly and raise children well, tasks that were no longer meant to be entrusted to others. Domestic work became professionalized with its own schools, texts, journals, and a jargon. Phrases like *tadbir al-manzil* (household management) and *rabbat al-dar* (mistress of the house) frequently appeared in the press. Both were titles of popular works: Francis Mikha'il's widely circulated *Tadbir al-Manzil* and Malaka Sa'd's oft-reprinted schooltext *Rabbat al-Dar*.[42] Job descriptions suggested that the new woman should be "a wise diplomat in directing the affairs of her house, a doctor capable of caring for her children's health, a seamstress, a nurse, a teacher, and a guide."[43] As men of the middle class became lawyers, doctors, engineers, and bureaucrats, women developed their own profession.

The texts and teachers took scattered chores performed in the home and gathered them together, attempting to rationalize them. Housewives were put at the helm, overseeing the servants and managing the system. Good management meant that a woman should know how to perform all the tasks and then delegate some. The target of much of this literature—the middle-class housewife—had fewer servants and performed more of the housework than her upper-class counterparts, while lower-class women performed it entirely on their own, in their own homes as well as in the homes of others.

Malaka Sa'd's manual *Rabbat al-Dar* was one of the most detailed works presenting the principles of housekeeping to an Arabic-reading audience. It provided explicit instructions on cleaning, sewing, and cooking in an attempt to professionalize the work of the housewife and modernize the Egyptian household. The ideal "mistress of the house" was to dedicate herself to making her home clean and attractive. Charged with furnishing the rooms, she was also instructed to add decorative items, including pictures, photographs, and flowers. Malaka gave precise details on cleaning, a task that a housewife must direct or do herself. Turning scattered chores into a profession was part of an effort to transform attitudes both toward housework and toward those who were associated with this work. Cooking, for example, was a responsibility that was meant to fill the housewife with pride. Although some women felt that cooking degraded them, Malaka argued that there was no shame in it, and women were encouraged to learn how to cook so at the very least they could supervise the kitchen properly. Housewives were also charged with setting the menu, insuring that provisions were purchased, organizing the table, and overseeing the preparation and preservation of food.[44]

Household management placed a special stress on productivity. "The time of long sleeps, of sitting and languishing has passed," Malaka told her audience. "We are now in a time of diligence, activity, and thinking about the usefulness of work."[45] Rationalizing housework meant measuring it by placing clocks and calendars throughout the home. The new attention to time also meant scheduling activities. One future housewife recorded her program on a day off from school: She awoke at 6 A.M., dressed in her house clothes, made breakfast, and then arranged her desk, clothes closet, and bed. She swept the room and tidied the reception area. At 9:30 A.M. she went into the kitchen to help the cook and to learn how to prepare some dishes. She changed for lunch, ate, and rested until 3 P.M. She then took a bath and prepared herself for two hours of visiting. After 5:45 P.M. she went to a cinema, theater, or club, returning home at 9:30 to eat something and be in bed by 10 P.M.[46]

The new emphasis placed on productivity and order was linked to "real savings" in the household budget. Although their work in the home went unremunerated, it had economic value in the eyes of the authors, some of whom suggested that the housewife be paid a monthly allowance.[47] Housewives managed money; urged to be careful in spending, they wanted concrete advice on budgeting. Malaka Sa'd and Sarah al-Mihiyya both gave guidelines in response to the queries of readers. Monthly allotments included 25 to 40 percent for food, 15 to 20 percent for rent or mortgage, 8 to 15 percent for savings and insurance, and 7 to 12 percent for clothes, plus money for tuition, printed materials, medicine, charity, servants' salaries, and infants' needs.[48] Economizing was a particular imperative for the middle class, especially after the 1907 recession, and writers suggested a number of ways of keeping expenses down, including buying items in bulk and shopping in person rather than dispatching a servant.[49] Huda Sha'rawi and her mother learned the advantages of going themselves to the new department stores recently established in the larger cities. "Not only was there a wide range of goods to choose from," she remembered, "but there was money to be saved through wise spending."[50]

Sewing children's and women's clothing proved another way of economizing and was made easier by the introduction of the sewing machine at the end of the century. Journals advertised Singer machines, which were available to all women and presented a means of livelihood for some. Elizabeth Cooper reported that one day she opened her door in Cairo to an itinerant seamstress carrying a machine who offered to do her sewing.[51] Women's periodicals also ran pictures of clothing, included patterns, and gave tips on sewing. The journal *al-A'mal al-Yadawiyya li'l-Sayyidat* focused almost exclusively on this sort of handiwork instruction. Malaka Sa'd also provided extensive advice on sewing and embroidery, encouraging a woman to learn these skills, for, she argued, "the needle is the badge that makes her proud."[52]

The preoccupation of intellectuals with domesticity may have been a response to the upheaval in the world around them. In the face of disruptions—colonial occupation, migration, urbanization, and booms and busts—Egyptians sought stability. The home depicted in this literature was a retreat away from the outside world: "a small kingdom," in the words of one, "the empire of the woman," according to another.[53] The values associated with the ideology of domesticity—greater efficiency and economy in the home—would have been most appealing to a middle class trying to carve a space for itself in Egyptian society. By focusing on the skills involved in housekeeping and stressing that these required the instruction taught in the new schools, writers hoped to raise the value of housework and by implication the value of women in the eyes of society.

RESHAPING THE FAMILY

The new ideology of domesticity called for reshaping the family. Writers elaborated on aspects of this in the women's press, discussing women's maternal responsibilities, childhood development, and marital relations. Much of the medieval Islamic literature that dealt with issues of childhood was addressed to the father not the mother. As the primary parental authority, the father, and his relationship with his son, proved paramount in these texts and treatises.[54] This literature mirrored a legal reality—children belonged to the father, who was responsible for their support, while the mother cared for the child up to a certain age. In the case of divorce, the father got custody of the children, and in case of the father's death, the father's family retained guardianship of them.

The literature from the late nineteenth century showed a decided shift in focus and audience from the father to the mother as the central figure in shaping the child. As Najiya Mahmud wrote, when the child is born, his first glance falls upon his mother, and she must be prepared with proper instruction for her crucial role.[55] Authors churned out books, articles, and speeches for mothers and mothers-to-be. These included translations such as *Tadbir Sihhat al-Hamil wa'l-Nafsa' wa'l-Tifl* (Healthcare of the pregnant, the confined, and the infant) and *Nasa'ih li'l-Ummahat* (Advice for mothers), purchased by schools to teach "mothers of the future," plus scores of original works.[56] The mother was no longer just a vessel for bringing an infant into the world but a critical influence on the child's early life. The new literature also focused more on the female child than had earlier literature.

Great attention was paid to pregnancy and the first years of childhood in medical and developmental literature that was now available in Arabic print. The new literature tried to lower the number of deaths in childbirth and to reduce infant mortality. Deaths of women during delivery were estimated to be as high as 3 percent among urban women at the turn of the century.[57] Some of these deaths were connected to a hesitancy to call in doctors—who were invariably men—when there were complications. When one woman labored for three days before she died, her infant unborn, a writer in *al-Rayhana* criticized an attitude that had led to a senseless death.[58] Yet the cost of a doctor would have been prohibitive for most Egyptians, although some specialists in women's diseases apparently offered their services free to the poor.[59]

Women writers pushed for the reform of the School of Hakimas as well as the creation of a medical school for women in order to improve women's health care, especially during maternity and childbirth. Apart from those few cases of labor attended by male doctors, over 90 percent of births in Egypt were attended by midwives, who were responsible for registering those births. Midwives numbered over 4,000 in the 1907 census, which included women with foreign diplomas, *dayas* (who practiced mostly in villages and some towns), and hakimas (whose training fell somewhere in between a full medical course and a speciality in midwifery and who were graduates of the School of Hakimas).[60] Several of the latter contributed articles to the women's press to educate readers and to respond to their questions. Women also began to go abroad to train as doctors, and by 1914 a few women seemed to be training in Egypt.[61] Gender segregation was used both to bar women from medical education and to legitimize the need for it.

The tremendously high infant mortality rate in Egypt alarmed observers. Elizabeth Cooper was told before the war that 65 percent of children born in Cairo died before they reached the age of four.[62] Infant mortality throughout Egypt after the war was estimated at 37 percent, causing one doctor to remark that "the women give birth uselessly one time in every three."[63] But the state did very little to provide basic health care, leaving initiative in private hands. After a high wave of infant mortality in 1909, volunteers established dispensaries to instruct new mothers in infant care; these clinics received thousands of visitors.[64] For their part, writers instructed their readers on good health practices after delivery, criticized practices like celebrating immediately following childbirth, and emphasized the need for rest. They also directed mothers to call a doctor when their baby became ill, presuming their readers would have been able to afford a doctor's services.[65]

In the days before bottles were available, giving the child to a wet nurse was a common practice among different strata and widespread among the wealthy.[66] According to Islamic law, breastfeeding created bonds of kinship between the infant and wet nurse. Those who had breastfed from the same woman could not marry, and the tie between infant and wet nurse was legally a lifelong one. But wet nurses also became associated with a high incidence of accidental death. When one woman who had given birth to twins—a boy and a girl—did not have sufficient milk to breastfeed the two, her mother-in-law advised her, "Do not give her [the wet nurse] the boy. . . . Give her the girl. . . . Girls are stronger." The suggestion implied that the girl should be able to survive what was possibly risky care, and that the mother-in-law was more concerned with the fate of the boy. A month later the girl died of suffocation when the wet nurse rolled on top of her while both were sleeping.[67]

Writers in the women's press condemned the practice of giving infants to a wet nurse. Although some mothers "brag about not nursing their children themselves," Rosa Antun argued, "there is nothing in this custom that calls for boasting."[68] Female intellectuals stressed that wet-nursing weakened mother-child bonds at a time when they were trying to fortify them. Since some women had problems with nursing, writers suggested various remedies.[69] Middle-class intellectuals may have argued against the practice of hiring a wet nurse as an economizing measure as well as a modernizing one, for wet nurses may have been hard to find at the turn of the century and costly.[70] But calls for mothers to breastfeed their own infants also grew out of efforts to redefine maternal responsibilities and to invest them with greater importance. They further coincided with a greater interest in child development.

These writers sought to celebrate motherhood and strengthen mother-child bonds, but they were reticent when it came to the issue of family size. Since there was almost no discussion of sex or of birth control in the press, it is difficult to ascertain to what extent women tried to control or plan pregnancies.[71] There is evidence that women in Egypt had abortions. In 1917, for example, 104 abortions were performed at seven provincial maternity homes.[72] There is no indication under what circumstances these operations were performed, however, or who the women were. Nor do we really know how many abortions were carried out at a time when surreptitious ones would usually have gone unreported. That these occurred is clear; al-'Afaf reported that a six-month-old fetus was discovered outside the home of a Cairene pasha, whose unmarried daughter became the target of a police investigation.[73]

The extent to which women terminated pregnancies is uncertain. What seems uncontested was the centrality of pregnancy and nursing in many women's lives. Sa'diyya Sa'd al-Din ("Shajarat al-Durr") gave a rather bleak portrayal of the female life cycle in turn-of-the-century Egypt. She wrote that a girl lived until the age of fifteen "in the frivolity of childhood" and spent the years after forty "in the troubles of old age." She broke down the interim twenty-five years as follows: "9 years pregnant, 1 year, 4 months in confinement, 6 years breastfeeding, 4 years, 2 months, and possibly 20 days in sickness. The unceasing discomforts of the body and soul last 20 years, 6 months, 20 days. There remain to her from all the days of strength and vigorous life 4 years, five months, and 10 days, if she is always physically and mentally healthy."[74] Sa'diyya added that only half of the twelve children the average woman bore survived, a figure that may not have been that far off considering infant mortality was estimated at 37 percent twenty years later. Malaka Sa'd also arrived at an ideal family consisting of six children (or at least that is how many she set the table for in her manual on household management).[75]

Average family size is hard to determine when at any given moment families were at different stages in the family life cycle and women at different points in their childbearing years. In the 1917 census, 73 percent of families in Cairo were of one to five persons and 23 percent of six to ten persons; in Alexandria, the figures were 72 percent and 25 percent, respectively.[76] According to these figures, a Cairene and Alexandrian household would average six to seven people at most. Presuming two parents and possibly other adults in the household would leave a high average of four or five children. Urban family size would seem to have been smaller than popularly imagined by observers.[77]

These statistics do not reflect the number of miscarriages, pregnancies, and live births a woman might have had, however. Relatively high rates of fertility help to explain women's low rate of participation in the wage labor force. Bearing and nursing children was a full-time job, and a tiring one at that. As one observer noted, many thirty-year-old women looked as though they were fifty, struggling with four or five young children under their care.[78] Yet in the view of most of these writers, motherhood was ultimately rewarding. The importance of the endeavor was the theme taken up by the new *tarbiya* literature, which instructed women on raising and socializing their children. Notable among these works was Labiba Hashim's *Kitab fi'l-Tarbiya* (A book on childraising), based on a series of ten lectures delivered at the women's section of the new Egyptian University in 1911.[79]

Taken together the new literature argued that childraising was no longer a job to be delegated to servants or relatives. Mothers were directed to spend more time with their children, closely supervising their health and development.[80] The press was full of medical advice, ranging from writers' home cures to doctors' recommendations. Concerned mothers wrote inquiring about their children's illnesses; their letters and a response from a specialist were printed in the journal.[81] Women were alerted to epidemics, instructed on the transmission and prevention of diseases, and encouraged to inoculate their children.[82] In some homes, cupboards were set up for medical supplies readily available in pharmacies, a few of which advertised in the women's press. The journals suggested games and stories for children, and physical exercise was stressed.[83] Labiba Hashim gave tips on how to guide young children in a series of conversations with her five-year-old son; Rosa Antun argued that mothers should not favor boys over girls, a prevalent pattern in Egyptian society; and Sarah al-Mihiyya instructed mothers on what to do for their daughters during menstruation, providing background information on the menstrual cycle.[84]

The new approach to mothering reflected a changing notion of the concept of childhood among certain classes. This was evident in the movement to raise the minimum age of marriage. Edward Lane found that brides were as young as twelve or thirteen and few more than sixteen in urban Egypt in the 1830s.[85] As a result of the growing awareness of the physical and psychological harm of early marriages—Malak Hifni Nasif observed that many of those girls who married at a young age developed "diseases of the nerves (hysteria)"[86]—late nineteenth- and early twentieth-century reformers tried to prevent them. A bill introduced into the Legislative Assembly by a Muslim deputy in 1914 attempted to fix the marriage age at sixteen but was defeated. Administrators amended the penal code a few years later to treat consummation of marriage to a child under twelve as rape, although the marriage itself was still considered valid.[87] Then, under the 1923 Egyptian Code of Organization and

Procedure for Shari'a Courts, all marriages had to be registered in order to make legal claims, and the courts would not hear claims of marriage if the bride's age was less than sixteen and the groom's less than eighteen at the time of the contract. Furthermore, officials would not conclude or register a marriage contract between couples who had not reached these ages.[88]

The attempt to raise the legal age for marriage, and by implication extend childhood, mirrored a trend already underway. The 1907 and 1917 censuses show that most girls married between the ages of twenty and twenty-nine, and the number of girls who married at a younger age—the overwhelming majority of whom were fifteen to nineteen—was less than 10 percent of the female population.[89] A few delayed marriage because of schooling, the spread of which also reflected a changing notion of childhood.

By professionalizing household management and increasing the importance of maternal responsibilities, writers hoped to raise the status of women. They also strove to reform marital relations. Compared to the emphasis on women's managerial and maternal roles, there was less discussion of a woman's wifely duties and almost none at all of her sexual role. But implicit in the domestic vision was a provider—a husband—without whom the whole vision failed to materialize and even with whom the vision sometimes faded and disappeared. Marriage stirred an intense debate as writers questioned the way marriages were arranged and dissolved, and the way they impinged on childhood. Writers strove to reform attitudes and laws on marriage and divorce and, in the process, reshape the family.[90]

The ideal of marriage in nineteenth-century Egypt was an arranged one between a young man (or an old one) and a young woman, who—unless they were related—did not meet before the ceremony. Women occasionally had to share their spouses with other wives and concubines and had little opportunity to initiate an end to unhappy alliances. On the other hand, wives were sometimes the victims of easy male divorce. It was an arrangement tilted heavily in favor of the man, placing him at the center of the family and giving him almost unlimited control. Advocates of the new ideology of domesticity, which strove to give women greater authority in the home, proposed a new marital ideal to accompany it. Writers like Sa'diyya Sa'd al-Din argued that marriage should be based on love, not economic considerations, and a couple should be able to meet before marriage to determine affinity.[91] Child marriages were condemned as were large gaps in ages between spouses. *Al-'Afaf* carried the story of the forced marriage of a twenty-year-old educated Cairene woman, past secretary of a women's organization, to a wealthy man of eighty. The editor used the story of this woman, and her attempted suicide, to illustrate the injustice of marrying a young girl or woman to an older man—or any man—against her will.[92]

Writers maintained that marriages should remain monogamous. Although for the most part they did—the 1907 census reported 6 percent more married women than men, which was roughly taken as the rate of polygamy[93]—women had little say in the matter. The possibility of polygamy and the threat of divorce hung over the head of women married to Muslim men. Sa'diyya Sa'd al-Din discussed the feelings of mistrust the fear of divorce engendered in a woman, forcing her "to use deceit, lies, and cheating" to please her husband.[94] If the marriage faltered or a husband took a second wife, the woman had no recourse to ending the union. Reformers argued that women should have a way to leave an unwanted marriage. Their arguments were backed by stories in the press and reports of suicides and murders by women who felt trapped in marriage. At the same time, men were warned against hasty and frequent pronouncements of divorce.[95]

Some success came toward legally enshrining the new ideal of marriage in the 1920s. In addition to setting minimum ages for marriage, women's grounds for divorce were expanded and men's grounds slightly curtailed. A law enacted in 1920 and supplemented in 1929 recognized four principles upon which a woman could apply to the court for dissolution of a marriage: if the husband had a chronic or incurable disease, failed to provide maintenance, deserted her, or maltreated her. The 1929 law also stipulated that divorces under compulsion or intoxication (but not in jest) were invalid; so, too, were oaths or utterances not intended to lead to divorce; and, finally, almost all pronouncements of divorce were considered single and revocable.[96] A new ideal of marriage—a partnership founded on affection—emerged in Egypt as part of the reshaping of the family and redefinition of gender roles linked to the shift toward capitalism and the rise of nationalism.

Writers in the women's press debated the advantages and disadvantages of women's work. Most saw the question as an abstract one, for they were not compelled to work for wages. For those single, divorced, widowed, and married women who had to work, writers called for job training, particularly in professions related to health and education which supported the domestic dream. Yet for the most part, female intellectuals considered women's place to be in the home, and they sought to elevate this sphere by investing it with greater importance and turning the scattered chores of the housewife into a profession. The promoters of the ideology of domesticity also focused on maternal responsibilities, providing instruction on childbearing and childrearing and in the process attempting to change attitudes toward childhood. A harmonious home depended upon a healthy marriage, and therefore women writers pushed for reforms in marriage and divorce.

The new ideology of domesticity gave women greater responsibility in the home without challenging its boundaries. Not all were enamored with the vision. A writer named 'Aliya argued in *al-Sufur* that whereas people called a woman the "mistress of the house," she was actually a "prisoner" whose influence did not extend beyond the borders of her home.[97] The path taken to advance the cause of women was posited on a gender division of labor in which men worked outside the home in the labor force and women worked in the home. However, this ideal did not correspond to the real situation of many women, who worked in agriculture, industry, commerce, and service jobs, and may have inadvertently depressed the conditions of that work. A few writers such as 'Aliya pushed for the greater integration of women into the economy beyond the household, recognizing the situation of many women workers, particularly young, temporary, and unorganized ones. That some women were forced to work at certain times in their lives eventually eroded the opposition of female intellectuals to women working for wages outside the home. Nabawiyya Musa, one of the best known advocates of women's education and work, outlined her arguments in a book published in 1920, *al-Mar'a wa'l-'Amal* (The woman and work).[98] In the 1920s and 1930s women began to enter legal, medical, and other professions and continued to work in agriculture, industry, commerce, and service. Eventually some protective legislation was enacted and unions organized to push for improved work conditions.

When writers in the early women's press articulated a domestic ideology, were they merely echoing a colonial discourse? To suggest this would be to ignore the critique of Western women's work roles by Egyptian writers and to simplify the debates and changes occurring in Egypt and in European countries. The adoption of a domestic ideology by female intellectuals in Egypt was in part a strategic decision. By emphasizing the complementary nature of gender roles and a gender division of labor, women did not threaten men, who already felt challenged by foreign competition. Instead of taking on the controversial issue of women's work for wages outside the home, writers focused on a package of domestic reforms. These reforms aimed to give women greater authority and status within the family. At the same time, they left the door open to women's entry into the wage labor force by arguing for women's work at specific jobs in cases of need. While considering further explanations for the perpetuation of the gender division of labor in Egypt, perhaps we should take the words of some of these writers at face value: they simply saw no advantage and no prestige in working for wages outside the home when they did not have to and when the jobs available were unattractive. They preferred to devote themselves to their families and to explore other activities, such as the foundation of associations.

8

THE ADVENT OF
ASSOCIATIONS

In the late nineteenth century, charitable organizations, learned societies, and other types of associations began to emerge in Egypt. Like older indigenous forms of collectivity such as sufi orders and guilds, they were generally constituted along religious and gender lines and had important social dimensions.[1] But they were founded for new purposes and often patterned after European institutions. In developing their rituals and activities, these associations made important contributions to Egyptian culture and society. They also set the stage for political parties and served as a springboard to public activism. During this period women as well as men started associations, building on informal gatherings and drawing on skills learned in managing large households.[2]

Associational life moved forward even as women foreswore politics—although they construed the meaning of politics narrowly.[3] Hind Nawfal had promised that her journal had "no goal in the realm of politics," and many writers followed her lead.[4] At a time when European and American suffragettes called for the vote, Egyptian women did not have similar aspirations. In fact, voting had little significance in Egypt under the British occupation. The vote was restricted to men of property, and very few people voted, in part because semi-parliamentary forms had little real power. Of 134,000 male adults entitled to vote in Cairo in 1908, only 34,000 registered and only 1,500 voted, that is, only 1.1 percent of the possible voters.[5] In such a context, calls for the right to vote would have been premature. Nor did women press for inclusion in the early political parties, congresses, or assemblies. The male elite dominated the realm of politics, and elite women continued to adhere more or less to the rules of segregation.[6]

Meaningful participation in politics remained limited until women began to dismantle the barriers to public activity. They started by establishing their own associations. These associations helped women move toward greater integration in Egyptian society by widening their sphere of social activities and by opening the door to new professions. Through this work they also perfected skills that served them in nationalist, feminist, and Islamist struggles. Associations thus prepared the ground for women's greater political participation. The women's press proved central in this endeavor; it provided a forum for women to work out their positions and programs. The press also became a record of the meetings of these groups, publicizing and promoting their activities. In establishing a network of associations with varying agendas, women found a public voice and a new arena for activism.

RUNNING CHARITABLE ORGANIZATIONS

A flurry of charitable organizations appeared in Egypt in the late nineteenth and early twentieth centuries. They incorporated religious traditions of giving alms (*zakat*) to the poor and establishing endowments (*waqfs*) for their benefit. Under Islamic law, fixed property or assets could be set aside in perpetuity as inviolable trusts for specific charitable purposes. The earned income of that property could go to maintain a mosque, a school, a fountain, an orphanage, or another cause stipulated by the founder. The system of charitable trusts helped to provide for the social welfare needs of the poor, orphans, and widows, as well as to supply a steady source of income to the overseer of the trust.

In spite of Muhammad 'Ali's confiscation of trusts at the beginning of the nineteenth century, wealthy benefactors continued to establish waqfs into the twentieth century. Weaknesses in this system, however, were apparent. Waqfs frequently tied up large tracts of land in the hands of a few families and often discouraged the productive use of that land. Moreover, the instructions of founders often proved untenable: authorities considered the fountains endowed in earlier periods a source of disease and found the school curricula stipulated in some waqfs outdated. As a centralizing measure, the khedives wrested control of the waqfs from the ulama; the state, in turn, battled with the khedives in order to get access to the lucrative source of income tied up in the endowments.[7]

Yet the state expanded health, education, and welfare services slowly. New sorts of charitable organizations arose in the late nineteenth century due to the dearth of social programs. They also emerged as a way for secular leaders to challenge clerical authority. By raising their own funds, lay leaders had the autonomy to create agencies to help the poor in an attempt to win their allegiance. For example, Syrian immigrants who contended with communal clerics for control of resources and for leadership of the community started charities to advance their own goals.[8] Similarly, Butrus Ghali helped form the Coptic Charitable Society in 1881, and Sa'd Zaghlul, Muhammad 'Abduh, and others founded the Muslim Benevolent Society in 1892.[9] Welfare societies thus helped to undermine the traditional religious leadership within various communities and played an important role in advancing alternative sets of leaders with new political agendas.

The emergence of indigenous welfare societies was also a reaction against foreign inroads in the field of social welfare. The wives of British officials erected the Lady Cromer's Refuge in memory of Cromer's first wife in 1898 and later opened other dispensaries.[10] Princess 'Ayn al-Hayat, founder of Mabarrat Muhammad 'Ali (the Muhammad 'Ali Charity), confessed, "It is, indeed, shameful that we in Egypt do not undertake such projects, ourselves."[11] Elite women sought to regain control of the social welfare movement in the early 1900s by starting charitable organizations. Voluntarism became an outlet for them and gave them a legitimate excuse to work outside the home to help the poor and, as they argued, to help the nation advance.[12]

Since women were often the ones in distress when the family broke down, it was only fitting that privileged women help them: indigent mothers needed assistance in caring for small children and deserted women with no place to turn to needed support. Women came to dominate the social welfare movement in Egypt for the decades that followed. Just as the Muslim Brothers would do later in the century, elite women identified social welfare as a neglected field and fertile ground for building a power base and pushing toward the center of politics.

Women's charitable organizations continued a long tradition of female giving. Muslim women inherited by law, held property in their own names, and often founded waqfs. Many projects endowed in this way, including quite a few from the Mamluk period, were named for their female benefactors.[13] This form of giving continued into the early 1900s: when the School for the Blind in Zaytun near Cairo called for public support in 1906, "a charitable Lady" gave a portion of her landed estate in trust for the benefit of the school; another wealthy benefactor set aside over six hundred feddans for the Muslim Benevolent Society and al-Azhar; and the Egyptian University, as we shall see, relied heavily on a grant from a woman.[14] Although women of means frequently established waqfs, they administered endowments less frequently and often had agents represent their interests in court and elsewhere.[15] Early twentieth-century charitable organizations gave women a more active role in philanthropy and provided them with an opportunity to oversee their own projects.

A number of charitable networks flourished throughout Egypt. Most were local or regional endeavors formed along religious lines. Egyptian and Syrian Christians further organized along sectarian lines, with Copts, Greek Catholics, Greek Orthodox, Maronites, and others often forming separate societies. In the early 1900s they started such voluntary associations as the Maronite Ladies' Charitable Society, the Women's Helping Hand Charitable Society, the Women's Charitable Society of Alexandria, the Syrian Ladies' Charitable Society of Tanta, and the Coptic Women's Society in Fayyum. Education of the poor, care of orphans, and support for young girls were some of the activities carried out by these groups.[16]

Each community, however small, tended to form its own welfare societies. Jewish women in Alexandria founded a society in 1905 that gave clothing, shoes, and other items to the poor. Another Jewish group gave pregnant women money and dispensed milk to nursing women and supplied diapers for their babies. Similar societies surfaced in Cairo and in provincial centers: sixty Jewish women in Tanta, for example, founded an association in 1911 that provided poor children with clothes and started a school to teach girls dressmaking.[17]

One of the first charities established by Muslim women was Jam'iyyat al-Shafaqa bi'l-Atfal (the Society of Compassion for Children). Founded in 1908 by Zaynab Anis, a member of Jam'iyyat Tarqiyat al-Mar'a and the wife of a doctor, the group planned to establish an orphanage. The over fifty members identified themselves as daughters of effendis and beys and were thus from middle- and upper-class families. They received letters of support from women of notable families and planned a bazaar and other activities to raise funds. They also sought publicity in the press, recognizing that theirs was one of the first such endeavors by Muslim women in Egypt.[18]

A similar charity was founded shortly thereafter. It was in the wake of a high wave of infant mortality in the 1909 epidemic that Princess 'Ayn al-Hayat organized Mabarrat Muhammad 'Ali to instruct new mothers in infant care.[19] The group crafted and sold cards to raise money for their cause. Princess Nazli Halim took over as president upon Princess 'Ayn al-Hayat's death, and Huda Sha'rawi, future founder of al-Ittihad al-Nisa'i al-Misri (the Egyptian Feminist Union), also played a prominent role. The group opened its first dispensary in 'Abdin in 1913, and Mabarrat Muhammad 'Ali continued to flourish for decades.[20]

Another society with longevity, Jam'iyyat al-Mar'a al-Jadida (the Society of the New Woman), was formed by several hundred women in 1919 or earlier. While some sources point to a prewar origin (roughly 1911), others indicate a postwar beginning as the founding date of La Femme Nouvelle, as the group was known in French. According to one account, the society was started by middle-class Coptic women who invited Muslim women to join them, a cooperation that would have reflected alliances forged during the national struggle.[21] Amina Sidqi, wife of a doctor from the upper middle class, ran the operation; Huda Sha'rawi served as honorary president; and Princess Chevikiar acted as a sponsor. The group started training schools to instruct girls in dressmaking, embroidery, carpet weaving, and other crafts. It also opened orphanages and childcare centers.[22]

Elizabeth Cooper may have been referring to one of these groups when she noted, "a band of generous women are carrying on a home for helpless women and babies, the patronesses of which are members of the well-known and influential families of Egypt."[23] Women of the middle and upper class founded most charities, and these women in turn sought the sponsorship of notable or royal figures. A patron gave the enterprise greater legitimacy and publicity as well as some capital. It also gave the founders access to the khedivial court and other circles of power. Amina Hanim, the mother of Khedive 'Abbas Hilmi II, sponsored several projects. Within the Coptic community, the women of the Butrus Ghali family filled a similar role, supporting Coptic foundations by attending openings and fundraisers.[24] Largesse was considered an important way to enhance a family's prestige and to broaden its base of support.

Fundraising was a central activity for women engaged in welfare work, especially as many programs relied on private donations rather than endowments. One strategy was to hold a fair, offering different items for sale. At the annual charity bazaar in Cairo, Elizabeth Cooper noted that "the harem ladies of Cairo can be found in great numbers on the days set apart for them."[25] Sometimes charities held exhibitions for which organizers collected folk arts and crafts for display. The groups also collected donations through public appeals and regular dues, occasionally reporting sums received and spent in the press.

Most charities directed their energies to communal problems. Yet women also mobilized for national and international crises. When Italian forces invaded Ottoman Tripoli in 1911, a group of Cairene women responded by founding Lajnat al-Sayyidat bi'l-'Abbasiyya (the Ladies' Committee in 'Abbasiyya). They met in October of that year at the home of 'Aziza Fawzi, secretary of the committee, to raise funds for the Ottoman army. They decided to hold weekly meetings, give a membership card to each participant, present progress reports, and sponsor charity bazaars; but they postponed elections until more members were present. Along with a report of the first meeting, the names of forty-nine female contributors were published in *al-'Afaf,* an impressive showing of political concern and public action.[26] That same month two similar women's committees were formed in Asyut and Bani Suwayf; they collected hundreds of pounds for the Ottoman cause.[27] Malak Hifni Nasif founded a society to send clothes and financial aid to Tripoli during the conflict. She also started a school in her home during World War I to teach nursing, and she knit clothing for distribution to those in need, activities that other women also took up.[28]

Charities in this period mostly targeted the needs of poor urban women through a variety of projects. A few benevolent societies opened clinics, offering prenatal advice and postnatal care for mothers and infants as part of a continuous effort to lower the high infant and child mortality rates. Other associations ran orphanages for abandoned children, set aside funds for young girls to marry, and distributed food and clothing to the poor. Some groups started clubs and trade schools to teach young women technical skills such as sewing so that they could find jobs in the textile or clothing industries.[29] These projects marked an expansion in the welfare services customarily provided by mosques, sufi orders, other religious institutions, and individuals. Yet an expansion was needed, for disruptions caused by the increased landlessness of peasants, the flight of some to the towns and cities, and the beginnings of a working class probably meant that more and more Egyptians were falling through familial and communal safety nets.

It is difficult to assess the impact of these charitable endeavors on the recipients of aid, for complete records are lacking and project evaluations are absent from reports in the press. One sign of success is that Mabarrat Muhammad 'Ali and Jam'iyyat al-Mar'a al-Jadida ran programs for decades. On the eve of the 1952 revolution, the former operated two hospitals, three dispensaries, and eleven mobile units.[30] Many other charitable institutions were established over the years, including a tuberculosis clinic and similar facilities.[31] Recognizing the political importance of social services, the government nationalized many of these institutions in the 1960s.[32] Still, women continued their activism in this field, and it is not surprising that the first cabinet position held by a woman was minister of social affairs.[33]

The full story of Egyptian charities and the role of women in the social welfare movement still needs to be told.[34] It is clear, nonetheless, that early twentieth-century charities sponsored a variety of programs for the poor but without necessarily addressing the root causes of disease and poverty. Deeper analysis might have shown that their efforts were little more than a salve for profound social inequities and economic distress. But such a critical awareness was not widespread at a time when elite women's role in welfare societies paralleled elite male domination of politics, and both were paternalistic. Furthermore, the drive for national independence tended to obfuscate social and economic problems and placed reform in these areas on hold. Egyptian politicians remained preoccupied with nationalist issues and power struggles through the 1920s and 1930s and neglected meaningful relief for the poor. Until the state turned toward reform and expanded its services in health, education, and welfare, charities provided at least some badly needed assistance.

Although their impact on those whom they tried to help is hard to assess, charitable organizations had a readily discernable influence on the lives of the women who participated in them as well as on women's relationship to the public realm. Charitable work came to be seen as a legitimate outlet for women of means as they learned new skills: convening meetings, holding elections, writing reports, keeping accounts, and publicizing events. Through voluntary associations, women expanded the parameters of permissible activities and increased their mobility. Community service became a way for wealthy women to bolster their status at the same time they tried to improve the lives of poorer women. The autonomy gained in participating in charities also spilled over into other endeavors. Voluntary work served as a path to professions and an entry into the world of politics, and volunteers saw the spread of welfare societies as another sign of the awakening of women. The cooperative ventures that emerged during this period also provided a blueprint for other types of collective organizing.

LEARNED SOCIETIES AND WOMAN'S RIGHTS GROUPS

The late nineteenth and early twentieth centuries marked the appearance of a variety of women's organizations. Some grew out of informal salons, which were popular during this period. Eugénie Le Brun, the French wife of Husayn Rushdi (a government official), invited women to her home to discuss contemporary social issues.[35] Among others, Princess Nazli Fazil, Alexandra Avierino, and Mayy Ziyada hosted salons that drew men and women.[36] These gatherings of intellectuals and politicians tended toward literary, social, and political debate.

More formal groups developed at some of the new girls' schools, an early sign of student activism. One of the first female learned societies, Zahrat Misr (the Flower of Egypt), was formed at the American Girls' School in Cairo in 1889. Members met every two weeks to discuss literary and scientific topics of benefit to daughters of the East. The group modeled itself after a society in Beirut, Jam'iyyat Bakurat Suriyya (the Society of the Dawn of Syria), one of the earliest such organizations of women in the Middle East.[37] Esther Moyal, a member of the Syrian group, described their purpose as "working for the progress of Eastern woman" and invited Hind Nawfal, among others, to join.[38]

A year after the foundation of political parties in Egypt had established a new model for organizing, Fatima Rashid started a new sort of women's group. With a circle of Muslim women she founded Jam'iyyat Tarqiyat al-Mar'a (the Society for Woman's Progress) in 1908 to push for woman's rights within the context of Islam. Patterned after parties of the period, Jam'iyyat Tarqiyat al-Mar'a used similar tools, including meetings, speeches, articles in the press, and a publication. The group met in the home of Fatima, who was elected president, and selected officers and approved bylaws. They subsequently gathered every two weeks or so to hear speeches and discuss current affairs, and they sent articles to the nationalist press to publicize their positions. They also founded their own monthly journal, *Tarqiyat al-Mar'a*. Edited by Fatima, it reported the activities of members, documented their meetings, and outlined their agenda. Each member paid ten piasters a month in dues to cover the cost of the publication; any extra funds were donated to the girls' division of an Islamic charity.[39]

Dedicated to the advancement of Egyptian Muslim women, Jam'iyyat Tarqiyat al-Mar'a had a religious outlook. Members called for the enforcement of Islamic law, which they argued provided them with all the rights they needed—in particular the rights to inherit, to receive support from their husbands or the state, and to education. They looked to the seventh century as the time of true Islam, and they held up the Prophet's wives and daughters as models. In their writings they supported veiling and the segregation of men and women, and they objected to women working outside the home except in cases of need. This group accepted and defended a system that exacted certain costs at a young age but promised rewards and status later in life. Rather than renegotiate women's status—perhaps losing power and prestige in the short term—they clung to the known "patriarchal bargain."[40]

Still, the members of this women's group did not consign themselves to silence and anonymity. Their bylaws stipulated that they had to sign their names to articles and lists published in their periodical. Although some men prevented the women in their families from joining Jam'iyyat Tarqiyat al-Mar'a because of this rule, the group hoped to create a public presence for women through this device. Fatima and her colleagues championed "the signing of names," and by the end of their first year they considered the appearance of women's names in the nationalist press as one of their main achievements.[41] Jam'iyyat Tarqiyat al-Mar'a sought change by shaping public opinion and strove to increase women's influence in the public arena. In spite of the conservatism of some of their rhetoric and their endorsement of segregation, participation in Jam'iyyat Tarqiyat al-Mar'a reflected a broadening of women's roles or, in the words of Fatima Rashid, "the awakening of woman and her entering the active life."[42]

The members of this group were daughters and wives of effendis and beys, not of pashas and princes. This placed them in the middle and upper strata but not at the top. Those who gave their father's or husband's occupations listed them as doctors, lawyers, government officials, school inspectors, and writers, generally middle-class professions. This is significant because elite women are often credited with founding the first women's organizations in Egypt in the 1920s—specifically al-Ittihad al-Nisa'i al-Misri—and middle-class women are not seen to have participated widely in the Egyptian women's movement until the 1940s. This is simply not the case. Jam'iyyat Tarqiyat al-Mar'a had numerous middle-class members, some of them in important positions. In addition, the group was not confined to the Egyptian capital but drew its support from all over the country, from Port Sa'id to Manfalut, from Alexandria to Aswan. At the end of the first year membership totaled over 165.[43]

The newspaper *al-'Afaf* appeared in 1910, following a line not dissimilar from that of *Tarqiyat al-Mar'a*. At a party in May 1911 celebrating the founding of the paper, a woman identified only as Z. S. of Helwan proposed that the paper start a women's club (*nadi*). Z. S.'s proposal was presented by proxy (a *shaykh*) to the male half of the party gathered on the ground floor of the building, while over one hundred and fifty women gathered on the floors above to listen to the speeches and poems, some of which had been written by women.[44] The formation of separate men's and women's parties was approved by the men who were assembled. Within a week *al-'Afaf* announced the establishment of Hizb *al-'Afaf* al-Nashit (the Party of *al-'Afaf* for the Stronger Sex) and Hizb *al-'Afaf* al-Latif (the Party of *al-'Afaf* for the Gentle Sex). The new party was to meet in the home of "one of the ladies," and until a president could be elected, the paper's female representative, Zakiya al-Kafrawiyya, was charged with directing the affairs of the party and handling its correspondence. The daughter of a doctor, Zakiya was probably of middle-class background, as were others in the group around *al-'Afaf*.[45]

This was not an auspicious beginning for an autonomous women's organization, however. The circle of women gathered around the paper *al-'Afaf* yielded to male prerogative and awaited approval to form their own club. Meanwhile, the paper fought a rearguard action against an even more conservative opposition. Although *al-'Afaf* presented itself as the protector of women's virtue, the paper was attacked for allegedly holding a mixed reception, allowing its female representative to circulate at the celebration, and proposing to form mixed parties. The editor,

Sulayman al-Salimi, denied these charges and others launched against his staff and writers. He subsequently altered the cover of the paper, darkening the light veil draped across a woman's face and blocking out her features, to reassert the paper's claim of guarding women's chastity.[46] The male and female intellectuals gathered around *al-'Afaf* proved vulnerable to criticism by religious conservatives and acted to prove their true Islamic colors by propping up the system of strict segregation and strengthening it rather than working to dismantle it. Although the paper continued for over a decade as an important record of the ideas of this circle, the activities and fate of Hizb *al-'Afaf* al-Latif in the wake of this episode are uncertain. Elizabeth Cooper, in Egypt shortly thereafter, may have been referring to this group among others when she wrote, "A few of the more progressive ladies are trying to start women's clubs in Cairo."[47] Zakiya al-Kafrawiyya did start a more modest club at about this time to teach women sewing so that they would not be so dependent on foreign dressmakers and could save money.[48]

Tarqiyat al-Mar'a and Hizb *al-'Afaf* al-Latif were comprised of Muslim women linked to pro-Ottoman Egyptian nationalists. Two other organizations founded in 1914 had different membership profiles and programs. A group of women met in February 1914 at the Egyptian University to form Jam'iyyat Ittihad al-Nisa' al-Tahdhibi (the Women's Educational Alliance). The Egyptians were mostly wives of beys and pashas, and the group enjoyed the matronage of Amina Hanim, the khedive's mother. A few Egyptian and Syrian writers were present, including Nabawiyya Musa, Mayy Ziyada, Labiba Hashim, and Malak Hifni Nasif. The latter served as Arabic secretary, and Henriette Devonshire, a French author who was among the European women participating, acted as one of the translators of the group.[49]

The first orders of business were electing officers, forming committees, and establishing bylaws. The group opened membership to women of all nationalities over fifteen years of age and set dues at fifteen piasters. In consideration of their diverse composition, the group decided not to "accept discussions that touch on religion or politics in any form." They restricted their mandate to sponsorship of educational lectures and used a reformist agenda to advance the cause of women. Malak Hifni Nasif delivered the first lecture to the group in March at the Egyptian University. Her speech, "Woman's Influence in the World," was reported and reprinted in several journals.[50]

Two decisions of Jam'iyyat Ittihad al-Nisa' al-Tahdhibi proved consistent with resolutions of earlier societies. Their bylaws declared that all those attending meetings had to sign their names, thus preventing anonymous participation and forcing women to acknowledge their activities publicly. The group also decided to start a journal to promote its educational goals.[51] Whether or not the journal was ever published is uncertain, but it is clear that many women's organizations considered a journal an essential tool for propagating their ideas. Either they formed around a periodical already in existence or started their own publication.

A second society, called Jam'iyyat al-Ruqiyy al-Adabi li'l-Sayyidat al-Misriyyat (the Literary Promotion Society for Egyptian Ladies), was started in April 1914. Huda Sha'rawi, a member of the society founded earlier that year, proposed the idea and held the first meetings of mostly Egyptian and some Syrian women at her home. Princess Amina Halim (not to be confused with the khedive's mother Amina) served as president, and other princesses participated. Similar to Jam'iyyat Ittihad al-Nisa' al-Tahdhibi in aims and activities, this group was equally committed to a reformist agenda. The group planned a broad range of lectures and lessons in art, music, and other topics at the Egyptian University, and a French speaker—Marguerite Clement—opened the talks. But the plan stalled when war broke out and some members summering in Istanbul and Europe were caught abroad.[52]

Many of these learned societies and woman's rights groups were disbanded before or during the war.[53] Yet new associations arose to replace the old ones. Fatima 'Asim, a Muslim married to a lawyer, founded a society in January 1916 devoted to the advancement of Eastern women. The name the group chose, Jam'iyyat al-Nahda al-Nisa'iyya (the Society for Women's Awakening), captured the spirit of the age and the sense that women were emerging out of darkness into light and learning.[54] The name also reflected the optimism of the early decades of women's organizing, when the series of societies founded by women were seen as symbols of progress as well as agents of change. Observers recognized the importance of taking action. "Don't wait, gentlewomen, for what men will bestow upon you, for the wait will be long," wrote a woman who signed herself "one faithful to her nation" and who encouraged women to organize.[55]

These first societies shared certain features. They were formal associations pledged to work for women's advancement through Islamic activism or reform. In attempts to disseminate their views as widely as possible, members publicized their proceedings in the general press or published a newspaper or journal. The groups met regularly in private homes and occasionally in public halls to discuss issues, to debate, and to deliver speeches.

THE RITUAL OF PUBLIC SPEAKING

"I stand before you today, anguished by the enormous importance of the situation," began Dawlat Hanim 'Ismat, in an address to fellow members of Jam'iyyat Tarqiyat al-Mar'a. "I stammer an apology if I make mistakes, for this is the first speech my hand has written."[56] Dawlat Hanim's trepidation was well founded, for preparing a speech required a good knowledge of literary Arabic and delivering it well demanded a great deal of confidence and poise. This speech, and others like it, were later reprinted in the society's journal, *Tarqiyat al-Mar'a,* preserving a record of the speaking event.

Speech-making emerged as a central ritual of the newly constituted societies. It gave a group a reason to meet, to hear the words of a member or visitor, and to share an experience. Articulating words aloud—sometimes reading and at other times reciting a memorized text—brought them to life and gave them resonance. At the same time, it enhanced the social and intellectual bonds of the association. After oral transmission at a meeting, the speech was often circulated as a pamphlet or published in a periodical or book. Transformed into a literary text, it could be perused in private. Speeches were widely disseminated and became an important element of the new literary culture, linking oral and written traditions.

Speech-making was also meant to spark debate, giving the spoken word a political currency. In the hands of charismatic orators, speeches became effective tools for rallying support and moving listeners to action. The speech as such was an old politico-religious form, most familiar in Egypt as a Friday sermon (*khutbat al-jum'a*), an exhortation (*wa'z*), or in similar guises. While there was nothing new about the occurrence and the proliferation of speeches, the Friday sermon had become stylized and pedantic over time, with preachers often reciting prepared sermons, some of them selected from old anthologies. Criticism of the form intensified only after World War I, and gradually sermons became revitalized through simplified language and selection of timely topics.[57] The societies that sprang up in Cairo and elsewhere in Egypt from the late nineteenth century adopted the speech as a centerpiece of meetings and developed it for their own purposes. This was not exhorting from the pulpit. The form usually took a secular turn in these contexts and flourished with the multiplication of associations and periodicals. Speeches were set down and the texts printed as women and men worked at perfecting this art.

Although it is doubtful that women attended the mosque on Fridays to hear the khutba in this period (a right demanded by some)[58] or that women had religious training in preaching, women became skilled in the art of public speaking. Perhaps they learned something about oral transmission from itinerant female storytellers or learned about the art of presentation by listening to male speakers from behind screens. Some probably developed an expertise in public speaking as part of their education in the new girls' schools: the speeches of students were often reported and occasionally recorded in the press. By requiring students to take oral exams and to make public presentations at ceremonies, celebrations, and other occasions, schools cultivated oratory skill. The graduates who went on to teach had additional practice in the public speaking that became crucial to the smooth functioning of societies.

Adept at preparing literary texts, our writers also penned speeches, and a number gained recognition as public speakers in the early 1900s. The associations provided the writers with a ready audience upon whom they could test ideas and from whom they could draw responses. Through such encounters the imagined readers of the press became real and immediate listeners. The speech gave the writers an excellent vehicle to gauge public opinion. In the process of entertaining and enlightening listeners, female intellectuals also promoted their own publications. By having the speaking event reported in the press and by having their speeches recorded in print, they further enhanced their own renown.

Fatima Rashid spoke frequently before fellow members of Jam'iyyat Tarqiyat al-Mar'a and her speeches were subsequently published in that group's journal.[59] Labiba Hashim appeared in front of charities, clubs, reading circles, and schools throughout Egypt and Syria and reproduced many of her own talks in *Fatat al-Sharq*.[60] Speakers often traveled communal circuits: Malaka Sa'd and Olivia 'Abd al-Shahid both spoke to Coptic charities, societies, and schools.[61] Although Christians occasionally spoke in front of mixed audiences, Muslim women mostly spoke to female audiences. They all spoke on a variety of topics, including charity.[62]

Malak Hifni Nasif became one of the best known speakers of the day. Her husband's connections to the Umma party (he was a founder) gave her access to the party's club. She launched her speaking career there in 1909 in what was considered one of the largest public gatherings of women until that time; hundreds of women came to the club to hear her speak.[63] When Muslims responded to the Coptic congress in Asyut in March 1911 with an Egyptian congress of their own in Heliopolis one month later, Malak submitted a paper on "Progress for the Egyptian Muslim Woman" under her pen name Bahithat al-Badiya. Yet contrary to most accounts, Malak did not deliver what was probably her most famous speech at the congress. A proxy, Ahmad Mustafa, presented her fifteen-minute paper to the audience of several thousand men. That she did not read this oft-cited speech herself illustrates the reality of segregation in 1911 and places her demands in a different light.[64]

Half of the ten propositions Malak had presented to the congress dealt with education; the others were related to health, morality and security, marriage and divorce, and religious ritual and practice. In fact, they reflected ideas expressed in the women's press for almost two decades. Malak's propositions were debated on the last day of sessions along with the other proposals submitted to the congress. Her demand to allow women to enter the mosques to pray and hear sermons (with provisions that women come in through a separate entrance half an hour before men, pray on raised platforms, and leave earlier) provoked a "hot discussion," according to the minutes. But when order was restored the motion was rejected by a majority of votes. Her demand to prohibit unnecessary polygamy and unjustified divorce also generated debate. Again "the question went out of hand," and the motion was suppressed.[65] Malak's proposals on education fared better. Recommendations that female Muslim instructors teach religious morality in girls' schools and that religious instruction be made mandatory were sent to the executive committee.[66] The all-male assembly preferred propositions that strengthened Islam without challenging their own prerogatives to suggestions that they yield some space and advantages to women. The congress, in any case, had no legislative power and proved more important as a record of platforms than as an instrument of reform.

The scenario of Muslim men reading women's speeches was not uncommon in the early 1900s. At the reception of the newspaper *al-'Afaf*, for example, women listened from behind a curtain as a male proxy had read the speech Zakiya al-Kafrawiyya had prepared.[67] Muslim women's public speaking remained limited to female audiences in schools, homes, and a few other venues. Attempts to extend this sometimes met with resistance, as demonstrated by a controversy at the new Egyptian University, an institution born in contention and only after Prince (later King) Fu'ad pushed the nationalist project forward with French support. Fundraisers called on women to contribute to building the school. "If it was to be for ladies, I would help it with all that I possess," said one woman, but since it was intended for men, she felt that they had to give what they could to complete their plan.[68] Other women gave generously (though, as we shall see, women were not treated so graciously), and the Egyptian University opened in December 1908. The school offered a limited number of courses and lectures in the humanities, awarded few degrees, and had no links to the law, medical, engineering, and teachers' colleges. Students interested in professional training had to attend these other state schools.[69]

The university offered some courses for women and advertised its selection in posters. The "Ladies' Section" included Arabic and French lectures on history, health, household economy, general science, education, and morality at five piasters a piece.[70] Zakiya al-Kafrawiyya spoke on "Modesty, the Crown of Woman and How To Guard It," not needing a proxy this time as the audience—over fifty women—did not include men. Malak Hifni Nasif and Nabawiyya Musa also spoke in the Ladies' Section.[71] Labiba Hashim was appointed a professor in the program and delivered the series of talks on childrearing that were later published as the book *Kitab fi'l-Tarbiya*. As she later recollected, she also had the "good fortune" of meeting Nabawiyya Musa when they both gave Arabic lectures at the university.[72] The press carried reports and reprints of lectures, and editors encouraged women to attend the programs. Applications to hear lectures and attendance at the women's section comparable to that in other courses of study confirmed that a keen interest in the series existed.[73]

There was strong opposition to women's presence at the university, however, even in segregated settings. A group of male students demonstrated to close the Ladies' Section, blocking women from entering the building. The conflict escalated when students sent death threats to the secretary of the university, 'Abd al-'Aziz Fahmi. Confronted by such a hostile opposition, university officials closed the section sometime in 1912 or 1913.[74] Ironically, at about the same time, the university received its largest endowment from a woman, Princess Fatima Isma'il (Fu'ad's sister).[75] In spite of that support, the university officially closed its doors to women until the 1920s. Women's activities at the university went underground, with occasional lectures that were unaffiliated with the institution held on Fridays when the school was closed. Jam'iyyat al-Ruqiyy al-Adabi li'l-Sayyidat al-Misriyyat set up one such lecture series, sponsored by Princess Amina Halim. This forum, like the university itself, was a royal project.

Speech-making had become a central ritual at gatherings of intellectuals and activists. A year after Malak Hifni Nasif died, colleagues and friends from all over Egypt gathered at the university for a memorial service. Those present included Nabawiyya Musa, Huda Sha'rawi, Mayy Ziyada, and Malaka Sa'd as well as representatives from such women's societies as Jam'iyyat al-Mar'a al-Jadida and Jam'iyyat Fatat Misr al-Fatah (the Society for the Young Woman of Young Egypt). After the Qur'an was read, they dedicated a room to the memory of the "leader of the woman's movement." And, as expected, they delivered a number of speeches.[76]

In the decades leading up to and through World War I, women founded a number of associations in Egypt, only some of which are mentioned here. There are references in the press to other women's organizations about which little is known, sometimes no more than a name and an approximate date of founding. It is clear that many of the members of these associations were of middle-class background, countering claims that the women's movement in Egypt trickled down from the top. The presence of women's organizations dedicated to social welfare, education, and woman's rights also indicates that the decades before 1919 were not just ones of debating. Participation in societies equipped founders and members with an array of skills. They learned to convene meetings, establish bylaws, vote for officers, raise funds, balance accounts, publish journals, and give speeches. The spread of associations in early twentieth-century Egypt broadened the boundaries of the possible for women and allowed them to explore new activities.

Decades of organizing set the stage for women's involvement in the 1919 revolution.[77] It should come as no surprise that women were able to assemble quickly and mobilize for protests. Moreover, earlier activities had prepared the way for greater public activism. Marching in demonstrations (still veiled and segregated) was the next logical step in expanding the parameters of the permissible. The cause was that of the nation, which women writers had invoked for decades to legitimize new activities. When Huda Sha'rawi and other women founded al-Ittihad al-Nisa'i al-Misri in 1923, they drew on the groundwork of earlier activists, reviving some of the demands of Jam'iyyat Tarqiyat al-Mar'a and other societies.[78]

Female associations provided women with a platform to politics and continued to do so in the following decades. Leading female activists of all tendencies in Egypt, from Doria Shafiq (a liberal) to Inji Aflatun (a communist) to Zaynab al-Ghazali (an Islamist) had their roots in women's organizations.[79] Many more recent female politicians and parliamentarians have also emerged from segregated social organizations to work in national politics.[80] Yet women's organizations have been more than training grounds for nationalist, leftist, or Islamist politics. They have been important institutions in their own right, contributing to social welfare and enriching cultural life in Egypt.

The writers who helped pioneer charitable organizations, learned societies, and woman's rights groups served the organizations as speakers. In spite of occasional opposition, they succeeded in establishing a new tradition of female oration. Women writers met one another through these organizations, on the lecture trail, and in special gatherings and helped to move meetings out of homes and into public halls. The societies served the writers by providing them with a forum to transmit orally what they had set down in writing. In this way, the speaking event transformed readers into a live audience, which had the opportunity to respond to spoken words. Speaking and writing were thus intrinsically linked, disseminating ideas in different ways and attempting to turn ideas into action. This affirmed women's commitment to the women's awakening and reaffirmed the perception that change had indeed occurred.

CONCLUSION

The phrase the women's awakening (*al-nahda al-nisa'iyya*) ran through the women's press and appeared as the name of organizations and publications. The phrase meant different things to observers, but the women's awakening can best be seen as a movement for greater possibilities and expanded opportunities for women. Some women opposed the direction of change, the slow but perceptible breaking down of the system of segregation in the late nineteenth and early twentieth centuries. Others tried to encourage reform toward greater integration. This latter vision eventually prevailed in spite of the odds and the opposition from varied quarters. The women's awakening achieved many of its goals and set precedents and foundations for later female activism not only in Egypt but throughout the Arab world.

Although they were generally left out of history, the female intellectuals who started the women's journals that spurred the women's awakening were very much a part of it. They were quite aware of the political forces swirling around them, including the rise of nationalism, which called for a redefinition of gender relations. This diverse group of women was drawn mainly from the middle classes, a finding that challenges perceptions that the women's movement in Egypt was in its initial stages an upper-class affair. Yet the first generation of women to write and publish in Arabic in numbers overcame the obstacles to self-expression and shed their inhibitions to identify themselves only slowly. They took up the pen, exploring a variety of genres, at a propitious moment: literature and language were in the midst of transition and print culture was just taking off. By their own admission, they started journals to provide women with a place to publish and supplied them with material of special interest, developing an agreed-upon canon, so to speak. The enterprise proved a risky one, however, and required not only literary skills but business acumen. In founding their own periodicals, female editors gained control over the production of literary culture, offered women greater access to the world of print, and at the same time inaugurated a new profession. Although the number of readers remained a small percentage of the total population, female literacy became more accepted and expected in certain circles. Habits of reading and responses to the press also indicate that readers formed an active community, helping to shape periodicals, propagate their own views, and push for change.

In turning to various topics debated in the press and setting them in their social contexts, it is not surprising to find that the perspectives of female intellectuals varied. Three trends—secularist, modernist, and Islamist—stood out. The view that women shared a position on the rights of woman and that only later the consensus broke down, or that personalities rather than real ideological differences generated the splits, must be reconsidered in light of the diversity of opinions expressed in the women's press. There was agreement, nonetheless, on the need for education, and many intellectuals placed the campaign for schooling for girls at the center of their program for reform and reported achievements in this field. They called for more schools, assessed state and private options, and argued over the curriculum. The domestic education that the writers pushed for with some success matched their vision of women's work roles. The writers preferred housework to waged work and articulated a domestic ideology that strove to improve women's position by elevating their status and expanding their authority in the home. Directed mostly toward the middle classes, this ideology built on prevailing work patterns in Egypt, where paid female labor force participation proved extremely low. Although their domestic visions did not necessarily reflect the productive and reproductive realities of most women, their calls for reform in family law transcended class. A variety of charitable, learned, and woman's rights associations were formed during this period, paving the way for the greater participation of Egyptian women in the public realm. The women who wrote for the women's press often spoke at meetings of these societies, and in this way they helped to develop a new speaking tradition. Their activism brought them full circle as they translated ideas that they had set down on paper into action.

How bold was the program at the heart of the women's awakening? The lack of dramatic flourishes—street marches and the public unveiling of elite figures—should not overshadow the importance of the incremental changes that made these grander gestures possible. Although the tendency has been to look at the most explosive moments and the so-called primary thinkers and activists, the constant hum by a variety of lesser-known and sometimes unknown writers chipped away at certain conventions. Progress in advancing the cause of women was not inevitable but came from continued efforts by persistent advocates, who kept the issues alive in women's journals and other forums. Egypt's experiment with reform—slow and steady evolution—contrasted with that later adopted by Turkey, which abrogated religious law and tried to make a clean revolutionary break with the past. In Egypt there was a certain accommodation of religious sensibilities in the short term, although the goal was often to modify practices and laws.

The program of women's advocates must be seen against the historical background. In proposing a domestic ideology, the writers were not urging a return to traditional Islamic gender roles, whatever those may have been. Much had changed in the course of the nineteenth century: the shift to capitalism had sped the demise of slavery and the rise of wage labor; new classes—from large landowners to a professional middle class and an incipient working class—had emerged; urbanization had increased; and new technologies were readily available in certain quarters. The writers' endorsement of a domestic ideology sought to soften the edges of a sometimes harsh transition, and they aimed the new ideology toward the middle classes in particular. They argued for a marital ideal based on partnership and love in keeping with a bourgeois notion of family and called for greater maternal responsibility in childcare. This was an attempt to alter deeply embedded practices and beliefs. Although polygamy may have been relatively rare, frequent divorce was not. And whereas for centuries the education of the sons had been the father's concern and literature on this and other aspects of childhood directed toward him, the new ideology centered on the mother and her role in childraising.

The women's awakening was not only linked to socioeconomic change in Egypt but was tied to political developments as well, notably the rise of nationalism. The struggle for national independence, which began earlier in Egypt than elsewhere in the Arab world, called for a "reimagining" of identity and a shift in loyalty from the religious community to the territorial entity. It also implied that Egyptians reshape the family and renegotiate gender roles appropriate to a nation-state. For while the nationalist struggle provided women with an excuse to legitimize new activities, it also mobilized increasingly larger groups, women among them. The program advanced by female intellectuals meshed nicely with the nationalist agenda by stressing education, productivity, volunteerism, and similar values.

Just as theirs was not a call to return to traditional Islamic gender relations, nor was it a wholesale adoption of a Western model. The cult of domesticity had already peaked and begun to decline in the West, and gender relations had moved on to new stages. No doubt there was some borrowing, but there was also a process of sifting and discarding, for the program advanced in the pages of the women's press was mainly a response to internal dynamics. It sought to fulfill the needs of certain sectors of a society with new capitalist relations and nationalist aspirations. The proposals outlined by female intellectuals thus cannot be reduced to a dichotomy between adoption of Western values or a return to Islamic practices.

Was the women's awakening confined only to the middle classes? Or was it an awakening of wider segments of Egyptian society? The women pioneering the press and engaged in similar activities never intended to restrict themselves to a small circle. They perceived themselves as a vanguard and saw their movement as one that would touch all women: Egyptian, Muslim, and Eastern. As writers they set precedents for women to publish their works, sign their names, and produce literature. Once these hurdles had been overcome, it was no longer so painful for women to write and disseminate their ideas. In editing journals, they established a new profession for women, breaking barriers and smoothing the path for entry into other professions. The creation and spread of literary texts also helped to cultivate new habits of reading. Many of these benefits may have initially been limited to women of means, but eventually their impact spread. Some of the programs that these women championed quickly reached beyond the middle classes. Although fees were now charged in state schools, free education was occasionally available elsewhere. Volunteers opened centers for job training and provided aid to those in need through new charitable endeavors. Furthermore, family reform was meant to reach rich and poor alike. In short, although the women's awakening was mainly an urban phenomenon affecting the middle and upper classes, it created immediate ripples beyond these strata and its influence spread further over time.

The women's awakening thus had a lasting impact on Egyptian society. In the decades before the 1919 revolution writers in the women's press and female activists laid the foundations for reforms by encouraging debate on social issues and by cultivating public opinion. The fall of the Ottoman Empire and the elimination of Egyptian-Ottomanism as a nationalist option muted the voices of the Islamists and pushed forward the fortunes of those modernists and secularists who championed greater integration of women in society. Once the British awarded Egypt nominal independence, it was easier to enact certain programs that had been of central concern to reformers for decades. Had women's advocates not prepared the ground for these changes well in advance, the opportunities of a liberal decade might have been lost.

In the 1920s, the state set primary education for boys and girls as a priority (although setting up a system to provide mass education would take years), began building secondary schools for girls, and reopened the doors of the Egyptian University. Entry into the university prepared women for new careers. At the same time, labor protections lagged; they were not passed until the 1930s. But these, in fact, had not been on the agenda of the early intellectuals. Family reform legislation had been, and it was passed in the 1920s. While limited in scope, it remained the only substantive reforms on marriage and divorce for half a century. Some of the charitable organizations founded in the early 1900s continued to provide services for decades, and new ventures were launched. None of the early woman's rights groups still met, but those that arose in the postwar decades followed the ideological trajectories established earlier in the century. At the same time, some of the stricter rules on segregation were relaxed.

The women's press flourished in the interwar period. Some periodicals, notably *Fatat al-Sharq* and *al-Jins al-Latif,* simply continued production, and a variety of new Arabic women's journals entered the market. From the 1890s on, women's journals are rich in details on social life, economic conditions, cultural production, political debates, and, of course, women's issues and gender relations and provide a fertile source for the historian. They also give a glimpse into the lives of the female intellectuals who crafted them. Sarah al-Mihiyya, Fatima Rashid, Malaka Sa'd, Labiba Hashim, and the other writers introduced here did not necessarily think of themselves as intellectuals. Yet they worked in the world of ideas. Moreover, they formed the vanguard of an Arab female intellectual elite and set in motion the women's movement. The cumulative evidence presented here should certainly help lay to rest the myth that women yielded the struggle for women's rights, or the thinking about that struggle, to men.

NOTES

Introduction

1. Hind Nawfal, "Idah wa-Iltimas wa-Istismah," *al-Fatah* 1, no. 1 (1892): 3.
2. On the Egyptian women's press from 1919, see Ijlal Khalifa, *al-Sihafa al-Nisa'iyya fi Misr, 1919–1939* (M.A. thesis, University of Cairo, Faculty of Arts, 1966); idem, *al-Sihafa al-Nisa'iyya fi Misr, 1940–1965* (Ph.D. diss., University of Cairo, Faculty of Arts, 1970); idem, *al-Haraka al-Nisa'iyya al-Haditha* (Cairo: al-Matba'a al-'Arabiyya al-Haditha, 1973).
3. Martin Hartmann, *The Arabic Press of Egypt* (London: Luzac, 1899), 48.
4. For a historical overview of the Arabic press, see Ami Ayalon, "*Sihafa:* The Arab Experiment in Journalism," *Middle Eastern Studies* 28 (1992): 258–80, and his forthcoming book on this subject; Tom J. McFadden, *Daily Journalism in the Arab States* (Columbus: Ohio State University Press, 1953).
5. Gabriel Baer, *Studies in the Social History of Modern Egypt* (Chicago: University of Chicago Press, 1969), 210.
6. Judith E. Tucker, *Women in Nineteenth-Century Egypt* (Cambridge: Cambridge University Press, 1985), 194–98.
7. See, e.g., Latifa Muhammad Salim, *al-Mar'a al-Misriyya wa'l-Taghyir al-Ijtima'i, 1919–1945* (Cairo: al-Hay'a al-Misriyya al-'Amma li'l-Kitab, 1984); Amal Kamil al-Subki, *al-Haraka al-Nisa'iyya fi Misr, 1919–1952* (Cairo: al-Hay'a al-Misriyya al-'Amma li'l-Kitab, 1986).
8. Charles Vial, "Rifa'a al-Tahtawi (1801–1873) précurseur du féminisme en Egypte," *Maghreb-Machrek*, no. 87 (1980): 35–48, esp. 35.

9. Byron D. Cannon, "Nineteenth-Century Arabic Writings on Women and Society: The Interim Role of the Masonic Press in Cairo—(al-Lata'if, 1885–1895)," *International Journal of Middle East Studies* 17 (1985): 463–84.

10. Kassem-Amin (Qasim Amin), *Les Egyptiens: Réponse à M. Le Duc d'Harcourt* (Cairo: Jules Barbier, 1894); Qasim Amin, *al-A'mal al-Kamila li-Qasim Amin,* ed. Muhammad 'Imara (Beirut: al-Mu'assasa al-'Arabiyya li'l-Dirasat wa'l-Nashr, 1976); Mary Flounders Arnett, "Qasim Amin and the Beginnings of the Feminist Movement in Egypt" (D.Phil. diss., Dropsie College, 1965); Albert Hourani, *Arabic Thought in the Liberal Age, 1798–1939,* 2d ed. (Cambridge: Cambridge University Press, 1983), 164–70; Juan Ricardo Cole, "Feminism, Class, and Islam in Turn-of-the-Century Egypt," *International Journal of Middle East Studies* 13 (1981): 387–407, esp. 393.

11. Cole, "Feminism, Class, and Islam," 401.

12. Robert Tignor, *Modernization and the British Rule in Egypt, 1882–1914* (Princeton: Princeton University Press, 1966), 341.

13. Yvonne Y. Haddad, "Islam, Women and Revolution in Twentieth-Century Arab Thought," *The Muslim World* 74 (1984): 160.

14. Leila Ahmed, *Women and Gender in Islam: Historical Roots of a Modern Debate* (New Haven: Yale University Press, 1992), 162–63.

15. See Margot Badran, "Huda Sha'rawi and the Liberation of the Egyptian Woman" (D.Phil. diss., Oxford University, 1977).

16. On early feminism, see Nancy F. Cott, *The Grounding of Modern Feminism* (New Haven: Yale University Press, 1987).

17. For an alternative view on the use of the term *feminism,* see Margot Badran and Miriam Cooke, eds. *Opening the Gates: A Century of Arab Feminist Writing* (Bloomington: Indiana University Press, 1990), intro. Badran distinguishes between men's and women's feminism, arguing that women's feminism preceded men's. See her "The Origins of Feminism in Egypt," in *Current Issues in Women's History,* ed. Arina Angerman et al. (London: Routledge, 1989), 155.

18. For background, see Hourani, *Arabic Thought.*

19. Throughout this study, Syrian (*al-Suriyyun*) refers to those men and women from what were then provinces of the Ottoman Empire and what are today the states of Lebanon and Syria.

20. See, e.g., Thomas Philipp, "Feminism and Nationalist Politics in Egypt," in *Women in the Muslim World,* ed. Lois Beck and Nikki Keddie (Cambridge: Harvard University Press, 1978), 281.

21. Nadia Farag, "al-Muqtataf, 1876–1900: A Study of the Influence of Victo-

rian Thought on Modern Arabic Thought" (D.Phil. diss., Oxford University, 1969), 173–96.

Chapter 1. Pioneers of the Women's Press

1. See Benedict Anderson, *Imagined Communities: Reflections on the Origins and Spread of Nationalism,* rev. ed. (London: Verso, 1991); Beth Baron, "The Construction of National Honour in Egypt," *Gender and History* 5 (1993): 244–55.

2. For background on Syrian migration and settlement in Egypt, see Thomas Philipp, "Demographic Patterns of Syrian Immigration to Egypt in the Nineteenth Century: An Interpretation," *Asian and African Studies* 16 (1982): 171–95; idem, *The Syrians in Egypt, 1725–1975* (Stuttgart: Franz Steiner Verlag, 1985); Albert Hourani, *The Emergence of the Modern Middle East* (London: Macmillan, 1981), chap. 7.

3. Maryam Jabra'il Nasrallah al-Nahhas, *Ma'rid al-Hasna' fi Tarajim Mashahir al-Nisa'* (Alexandria: Matba'at Jaridat Misr, 1879); for biographical details on Maryam al-Nahhas, see Zaynab Fawwaz, *al-Durr al-Manthur fi Tabaqat Rabbat al-Khudur* (Cairo: al-Matba'a al-Kubra al-Amiriyya bi-Bulaq, 1312/ 1894), 515–16; Khayr al-Din al-Zirikli, *al-A'lam: Qamus Tarajim li-Ashhar al-Rijal wa'l-Nisa' min al-'Arab wa'l-Musta'ribin wa'l-Mustashriqin* (Beirut: Dar al-'Ilm, 1980), 7:210, 8:19.

4. A. Schölch, "Constitutional Development in Nineteenth Century Egypt— A Reconsideration," *Middle Eastern Studies* 10 (1974): 3–14; idem, *Egypt for the Egyptians! The Sociopolitical Crisis in Egypt, 1878–1882* (London: Ithaca, 1981); Juan R. I. Cole, "Of Crowds and Empires: Afro-Asian Riots and European Expansion, 1857–1882," *Comparative Studies in Society and History* 31 (1989): 106–33.

5. See A. Albert Kudsi-Zadeh, "The Emergence of Political Journalism in Egypt," *The Muslim World* 70 (1980): 47–55; Abbas Kelidar, "Shaykh 'Ali Yusuf: Egyptian Journalist and Islamic Nationalist," in *Intellectual Life in the Arab East, 1890–1939,* ed. Marwan R. Buheiry (Beirut: American University of Beirut Press, 1981), 10–20.

6. Philipp, *Syrians in Egypt,* 98.

7. Nadia Farag, "The Lewis Affair and the Fortunes of al-Muqtataf," *Middle Eastern Studies* 18 (1972): 73–83; idem, "al-Muqtataf, 1876–1900: A Study of the Influence of Victorian Thought on Modern Arabic Thought" (D.Phil. diss., Oxford University, 1969).

8. Nasim Nawfal, "al-I'lan," *al-Fatah* 1, no. 7 (1893): 289–90; Rosa Antun, "Jam'iyyat al-Sayyidat al-Khayriyya fi'l-Iskandriyya," *al-Sayyidat wa'l-Banat* 2, no. 8 (1906): 211–15; Labiba Hashim, "Shahirat al-Nisa'," *Fatat al-Sharq* 2, no. 3 (1907): 81–82; Philippe de Tarrazi, *Ta'rikh al-Sihafa al-'Arabiyya* (Beirut: al-Matba'a al-Adabiyya, 1914), 3:96; Ilyas Zakhura, *al-Suriyyun fi Misr* (Cairo: al-Matba'a al-'Arabiyya, 1927), 144.

9. "Al-Firdaus," *al-Hilal* 4, no. 12 (1896): 880; Martin Hartmann, *The Arabic Press of Egypt* (London: Luzac, 1899), 41, 57, 61; Tarrazi, *Ta'rikh al-Sihafa,* 1:115–16, 4:282; "Bayan," *Anis al-Jalis* 1, no. 6 (1898): 194.

10. Jurji Zaydan, "Mir'at al-Hasna'," *al-Hilal* 5, no. 6 (1896): 240; "Mir'at al-Hasna'," *al-Muqtataf* 20, no. 12 (1896): 934.

11. Salim Sarkis, "Man Hiya Anisa Maryam Mazhar?" *Majallat Sarkis* 2, no. 21 (1907): 645–51.

12. Salim Sarkis, *Kitab Ghara'ib al-Maktubji* (Cairo: Matba'at al-Salam, 1896), 58–59.

13. Sarkis, "Man Hiya?"

14. Sarkis, *Ghara'ib al-Maktubji.* For differing views on the severity of Ottoman censorship, see Donald J. Cioeta, "Ottoman Censorship in Lebanon and Syria, 1876–1908," *International Journal of Middle East Studies* 10 (1979): 167–86; Caesar Farah, "Censorship and Freedom of Expression in Ottoman Syria and Egypt," in *Nationalism in a Non-National State: The Dissolution of the Ottoman Empire,* ed. William W. Haddad and William Ochsenwald (Columbus: Ohio State University Press, 1977), 151–94.

15. Hartmann, *Arabic Press,* 41. Two years later when he was charged with personal attacks on the sultan and inciting assassination, he fled Egypt and was condemned to death in absentia (Great Britain, Public Record Office, Foreign Office (FO) 407/152, no. 17, Rodd to Salisbury, Cairo, 15 Aug. 1899, p. 20). He later returned to Egypt to edit *Majallat Sarkis* (al-Zirikli, *al-A'lam,* 3:118).

16. Information throughout this section is drawn from FO 891/18, "Enquiry Procès Verbal in the Evidence of Madam Avierino in the Suit of Crime No. 1853, Ezbakieh, July 1924" (in Arabic and English translation) and various correspondence in FO 141/521/9061, I and II.

17. Ahmad Muharram and Wali al-Din Yakan, "al-Amira Alexandra," *Fatat al-Sharq* 10, no. 1 (1915): 2–11; Fathiyya Muhammad, *Balaghat al-Nisa' fi'l-Qarn al-'Ishrin* (Cairo: Matba'at al-Sa'ada, 1925), 81–82; Imili Faris Ibrahim, *al-Haraka al-Nisa'iyya al-Lubnaniyya* (Beirut: Dar al-Thaqafa, 1966), 107–8.

18. Alexandra Avierino, "Bayan Haqiqa," *Anis al-Jalis* 9, no. 12 (1906): 360–61; Tarrazi, *Ta'rikh al-Sihafa*, 4:326–27.

19. Alexandra Avierino, "al-Nisa' wa'l-Salam," *Anis al-Jalis* 2, no. 10 (1899): 389–92; idem, "Mu'tamar al-Salam," *Anis al-Jalis* 3, no. 1 (1900): 38; Princess Wiszniewska, "Jam'iyyat al-Salam," *Anis al-Jalis* 3, no. 4 (1900): 152–54; Alexandra Avierino, "Khidmat al-Wataniyya," *Anis al-Jalis* 3, no. 9 (1900): 321–28.

20. Sandi E. Cooper, "Women's Participation in European Peace Movements: The Struggle to Prevent World War I," in *Women and Peace: Theoretical, Historical, and Practical Perspectives*, ed. Ruth Roach Pierson (London: Croom Helm, 1987), 57–58; idem, "Wiszniewska, Marie-Gabrielle-Hortense Hugot," in *Biographical Dictionary of Modern Peace Leaders*, ed. Harold Josephson et al. (Westport, Conn.: Greenwood, 1985), 1021–23.

21. Alexandra Avierino, "Bayan Amr," *Anis al-Jalis* 9, no. 11 (1906): 336.

22. Hartmann, *Arabic Press*, 49; Alexandra Avierino, "Ihda' al-Majalla," *Anis al-Jalis* 1, no. 1 (1898): 6.

23. *Le Lotus* 1, no. 11 (1902): 630; Alexandra Avierino, "Khidmatuna al-Wataniyya," *Anis al-Jalis* 6, no. 8 (1903): 1508–14; idem, "Tashrif Babawi," *Anis al-Jalis* 6, no. 8 (1903): 1535; Tarrazi, *Ta'rikh al-Sihafa*, 4:326–27; Yusuf As'ad Daghir, *Masadir al-Dirasa al-Adabiyya* (Beirut: l'Université Libanaise, 1972), 138; Zirikli, *al-A'lam*, 237–39.

24. Alexandra Avierino, "al-Sihafa al-Nisa'iyya fi Misr," *Anis al-Jalis* 3, no. 12 (1901): 461–64; *Le Lotus*, 1, no. 12 (1902); Max de Zogheb, "Causerie Retrospective," *Le Lotus* 1, no. 1 (1901): 3–6; Muhammad, *Balaghat al-Nisa'*, 87.

25. Daghir, *Masadir al-Dirasa al-Adabiyya*, 137–39.

26. 'Abbas Hilmi II Papers, Durham University, files 229/259–229/314, letters from Alexandra Avierino to 'Abbas Hilmi II.

27. FO 141/521/9061, Keown-Boyd to Anthony, Cairo, 26 June 1920.

28. See FO 891/18, "Procès Verbal."

29. FO 141/521/9061, esp. Residency Minute, Cairo, 17 Apr. 1923; Allenby to MacDonald, Cairo, 10 May 1924.

30. FO 141/521/9061, Osborne to Kerr, London, 12 Aug. 1924; see also Abblitt to Wiggin, Cairo, 29 Sept. 1925.

31. *Encyclopaedia Judaica (EJ)* (Jerusalem: Keter, 1977), s.v. "Moyal, Esther"; Jurji Niqula Baz, "Esther Azhari Moyal," *al-'Alam al-Isra'ili* 9, nos. 357–58 (12 Nisan/Apr. 1946): 10.

32. Jeanne Madeline Weimann, *The Fair Women* (Chicago: Academy of Chi-

cago, 1981), 139, 274; Hind Nawfal, "al-Qism al-Nisa'i fi Ma'rid Chicago," al-Fatah 1, no. 1 (1892): 37–38; al-Fatah 1, no. 2 (1893): 65; EJ, "Moyal, Esther"; Baz, "Esther Azhari Moyal." On Hanna Kisbani Kurani, see Labiba Hashim, "Hanna Kisbani Kurani," Fatat al-Sharq 2, no. 10 (1908): 361–66; Muhammad, Balaghat al-Nisa', 104–9; Daghir, Masadir al-Dirasa al-Adabiyya, 1091–92.

33. Zaynab Fawwaz, al-Rasa'il al-Zaynabiyya (Cairo: al-Matba'a al-Mutawassita, 1915), 31, 59–60, 64, 71–74.

34. Al-Talmud, trans. Shimon Yusuf Moyal (Cairo: Matba'at al-'Arab, 5769/ 1909). Shimon thanks Jurji Zaydan, who had apparently considered translating this text earlier (4–5). On Shimon Moyal's life, see Y. S., "Sawt al-'Uthmaniyya," al-Sharq 3, no. 9 (1973): 49–50; EJ, "Moyal, Esther"; Baz, "Esther Azhari Moyal"; Ruth Kark, Jaffa: A City in Evolution, 1799–1917 (Jerusalem: Yad Izhak Ben-Zvi, 1990), 162, 205.

35. I thank Shmuel Moreh for sharing this information.

36. Esther is presented as "the owner of the journal al-'A'ila" in the introduction to a book published in 1907. See Emile Zola, al-Mal. al-Mal. al-Mal., trans. Esther Moyal (Cairo: Matba'at al-Shuri, 1907), 1.

37. Alfred Dreyfus, a Jewish captain in the French army, was convicted of high treason in a closed trial in 1894. After he was stripped of rank and deported, evidence surfaced that challenged the initial verdict, unleashing a public debate about anti-Semitism and the state. In an open letter to the president of the French Republic entitled "J'Accuse," Emile Zola denounced the French general staff. The verdict of a new trial finding Dreyfus guilty with extenuating circumstances was annulled in 1906, and Dreyfus was reinstated into the army with decorations. For more on the Dreyfus affair, see Nicholas Halasz, Captain Dreyfus: The Story of a Mass Hysteria (New York: Simon and Schuster, 1955).

38. Esther Moyal, Ta'rikh Hayat Emile Zola (Cairo: Matba'at al-Tawfiq, 1903); K. T. Khairallah, "La Syrie," Revue du Monde Musulman 19 (Apr.-June 1912): 113; see, e.g., Zola, al-Mal.

39. Y. S., "Sawt al-'Uthmaniyya"; Kark, Jaffa, 198.

40. Shmuel Moreh, al-Matbu'at al-'Arabiyya allati Alafuha aw Nasharuha al-Udaba' wa'l-'Ulama' al-Yahud, 1863–1973 (Jerusalem: Dugma, 1973): 110; Tarrazi, Ta'rikh al-Sihafa, 4:70, 287; Baz, "Esther Azhari Moyal," 10.

41. See Introduction.

42. "Al-Hawanim," al-Manar 3, no. 8 (1900): 186–87.

43. Al-Mar'a fi'l-Islam 1, no. 1 (1901); al-Zirikli, al-A'lam, 1:39.

44. "Al-Mar'a," *Anis al-Jalis* 4, no. 7 (1901): 749.
45. Tarrazi, *Ta'rikh al-Sihafa*, 4:328; Jurji Niqula Baz, "Majallat al-Nisa'," *Fatat Lubnan* 1, no. 1 (1914): 7–10; Qistaki Ilyas 'Attara, *Ta'rikh Takwin al-Suhuf al-Misriyya* (Alexandria: Matba'at al-Taqaddum, 1928), 292.
46. With the exception of *al-Mar'a fi'l-Islam,* no copies of these journals were located.
47. The name is now popularly rendered Shajarat al-Durr rather than Shajar al-Durr.
48. "Shajarat al-Durr," *Anis al-Jalis* 4, no. 5 (1901): 677; "Shajarat al-Durr," *al-Manar* 4, no. 10 (1901): 400; for an extract, see *al-Muqtataf* 26, no. 8 (1901): 752–54.
49. Shajarat al-Durr, "Mujmal Hayat al-Nisa'," *Anis al-Jalis* 1, no. 6 (1898): 176–79; idem, "al-Talaq wa-Ta'addud al-Zawjat," *Anis al-Jalis* 1, no. 7 (1898): 203–6.
50. Al-Maqrizi, *Kitab al-Suluk li-Ma'rifat Duwal al-Muluk,* ed. M. Ziyada (Cairo: Committee on Authorship, Translation, and Publication, 1936), 1:324–44, 361–68; R. Stephen Humphreys, *From Saladin to the Mongols: The Ayyubids of Damascus, 1193–1260* (Albany: State University of New York Press, 1977), 301–4, 329–30; *Encyclopaedia of Islam* (Leiden: E. J. Brill, 1987), s.v. "Shadjar al-Durr."
51. For more on Mamluk women, see Carl F. Petry, "Class Solidarity Versus Gender Gain: Custodians of Property in Later Medieval Egypt," in *Women in Middle Eastern History: Shifting Boundaries in Sex and Gender,* ed. Nikki R. Keddie and Beth Baron (New Haven: Yale University Press, 1991), 122–42; Ahmad 'Abd Ar-Raziq, *La femme au temps des mamlouks en Égypte* (Cairo: Institut Français d'Archéologie Orientale, 1973), 292–93.
52. *Dictionary of the Middle Ages,* ed. Joseph R. Strayer (New York: Charles Scribner's Sons, 1989), s.v. "Concubinage, Islamic."
53. On slavery in nineteenth-century Egypt, see Gabriel Baer, *Studies in the Social History of Modern Egypt* (Chicago: University of Chicago Press, 1969), chap. 10; Ehud R. Toledano, *The Ottoman Slave Trade and Its Suppression* (Princeton: Princeton University Press, 1982), chap. 5; idem, "Slave Dealers, Women, Pregnancy, and Abortion: The Story of a Circassian Slavegirl in Mid-Nineteenth Century Cairo," *Slavery and Abolition* 2 (1981): 53–68; Judith E. Tucker, *Women in Nineteenth-Century Egypt* (Cambridge: Cambridge University Press, 1985), chap. 5.
54. On 'A'isha Taymuriyya, see Fawwaz, *al-Durr al-Manthur,* 303–4.
55. *Al-Muqtataf* 26, no. 8 (1901): 754.

56. Amin 'Awwad, "Istiqlal al-'Uthmaniyyin," *al-Sa'ada* 4, no. 3 (1909): 9, 11–16.

57. P. J. Vatikiotis, *The History of Egypt*, 3d ed. (London: Weidenfeld and Nicolson, 1969), 224–29; Walid Kazziha, "The Jaridah-Ummah Group and Egyptian Politics," *Middle Eastern Studies* 13 (1977): 373–85.

58. Israel Gershoni and James P. Jankowski, *Egypt, Islam, and the Arabs: The Search for Egyptian Nationhood, 1900–1930* (New York: Oxford University Press, 1986), intro.

59. Rosa Antun, "Madrasat al-Banat bi'l-Ibrahimiyya," *al-Sayyidat wa'l-Banat* 1, no. 3 (1903): 65–67; al-Zirikli, *al-A'lam*, 3:5; 5:141; 8:45–46; Daghir, *Masadir al-Dirasa al-Adabiyya*, 297; Donald M. Reid, *The Odyssey of Farah Antun: A Syrian Christian's Quest for Secularism* (Chicago: Bibliotheca Islamica, 1975).

60. Farah Antun, " 'Awdat Majallat al-Sayyidat," *al-Sayyidat wa'l-Banat* 2, no. 7 (1906): 177–80; Rosa Antun, "Faji'atuna al-Mu'lima," *al-Sayyidat wa'l-Banat* 2, no. 8 (1906): 232; Jurji Niqula Baz, "Zifaf Rasifa ila Sadiq," *al-Hasna'* 1, no. 5 (1909): 159.

61. Sasson Somekh, *The Changing Rhythm: A Study of Najib Mahfuz's Novels* (Leiden: E. J. Brill, 1973), 8; Tareq Y. Ismael and Rifa'at El-Sa'id, *The Communist Movement in Egypt, 1920–1988* (Syracuse: Syracuse University Press, 1990), 10–11, 25.

62. Reid, *Farah Antun*, 117–18; Niqula Haddad, *al-Hubb wa'l-Zawaj* (Cairo: al-Matba'a al-'Umumiyya, 1901).

63. See *al-Sayyidat* 3, no. 1 (1921): 1.

64. Rosa Antun Haddad, *Farah Antun: Hayatuhu wa-Ta'binuhu wa-Mukhtaratuhu* (Cairo: Matba'at Yusuf Kawi, 1923).

65. Daghir, *Masadir al-Dirasa al-Adabiyya*, 1365–67; Tarrazi, *Ta'rikh al-Sihafa*, 4:296–97; al-Zirikli, *al-A'lam*, 5:240.

66. Labiba Hashim, *Kitab fi'l-Tarbiya* (Cairo: Matba'at al-Ma'arif, 1911); *Fatat al-Sharq* 9, no. 1 (1914): 43–50; Tarrazi, *Ta'rikh al-Sihafa*, 4:296–97; al-Zirikli, *al-A'lam*, 5:240.

67. Labiba Hashim, "Kitab Maftuh," *Fatat al-Sharq* 3, no. 5 (1909): 170–76; for the reply, see *Fatat al-Sharq* 3, no. 10 (1909): 396.

68. Najib Madi, "al-Marhum 'Abduh Hashim," *Fatat al-Sharq* 10, no. 6 (1916): 232–33; Tarrazi, *Ta'rikh al-Sihafa*, 4:296–97; al-Zirikli, *al-A'lam*, 5:240.

69. Vatikiotis, *Egypt*, 204–6.

70. "Al-Rayhana," *Fatat al-Sharq* 1, no. 7 (1907): 215–16.

71. Ibn Yahya, "Asbab Insha' al-Rayhana al-Usbu'iyya," *al-Rayhana* 1, no. 1 (20 Mar. 1908): 1.

72. Fatima Rashid has sometimes been confused with Fatima Nimat Rashid, founder of a feminist party in the 1940s, a younger woman of different outlook. See, e.g., Ijlal Khalifa, *al-Haraka al-Nisa'iyya al-Haditha* (Cairo: al-Matba'a al-'Arabiyya al-Haditha, 1973), 32, 52–53.

73. Fatima Rashid, "Farah al-Sayyidat Misr," *Tarqiyat al-Mar'a* 1, no. 6 (1326/ 1908): 81; Najiya Rashid, "Khutba," *Tarqiyat al-Mar'a* 1, no. 8 (1326/1908): 119–22.

74. Albert Hourani, *Arabic Thought in the Liberal Age, 1798–1939*, 2d ed. (Cambridge: Cambridge University Press, 1983), 162.

75. Anwar Jundi, *Muhammad Farid Wajdi: Ra'id al-Tawfiq bayn al-'Ilm wa'l-Din* (Cairo: al-Hay'a al-Misriyya al-'Amma li'l-Kitab, 1974), 9, 38, 123–28; 'Attara, *Ta'rikh Takwin al-Suhuf*, 304; Daghir, *Masadir al-Dirasa al-Adabiyya*, 1395–98; J. Brugman, *An Introduction to the History of Modern Arabic Literature in Egypt* (Leiden: E. J. Brill, 1984), 123.

76. Egypt, Ministry of Finance, *The Census of Egypt Taken in 1907* (Cairo: National Printing Department, 1909), 117, 97; B. L. Carter, *The Copts in Egyptian Politics* (London: Croom Helm, 1986), 5.

77. Doris Behrens-Abouseif, "The Political Situation of the Copts, 1798–1923," in *Christians and Jews in the Ottoman Empire*, ed. Benjamin Braude and Bernard Lewis (New York: Holmes and Meier, 1982), 1:185–205; Subhi Labib, "The Copts in Egyptian Society and Politics, 1882–1919," in *Islam, Nationalism, and Radicalism in Egypt and the Sudan*, ed. Gabriel R. Warburg and Uri M. Kupferschmidt (New York: Praeger, 1983), 301–21; Airi Tamura, "Ethnic Consciousness and Its Transformation in the Course of Nation-Building: The Muslim and the Copt in Egypt, 1906–1919," *The Muslim World* 75 (1985): 102–14.

78. Salama Musa tried to obtain a license to start a journal in 1911 and only succeeded a few years later (FO 371/1113/12729, Moussa to Robertson, Cairo, 2 Mar. 1911; FO 371/1113/18095, Graham to Cheetham, Cairo, 29 Apr. 1911). Kyriakos Mikhail also faced difficulty in obtaining a license (FO 371/1640/57311, Mikhail to Grey, London, 19 Dec. 1913; FO 371/ 1964/4392, Kitchener to Grey, Cairo, 25 Jan. 1914; FO 371/2349/29093, Mikhail to Grey, London, 10 Mar. 1915).

79. Malaka Sa'd, *Rabbat al-Dar* (Cairo: Matba'at al-Tawfiq, 1915), 4.

80. FO 371/451/31779, Gorst, Cairo, 16 Sept. 1908, "The Press in Egypt."

81. FO 407/163, no. 4, Cromer to Lansdowne, Cairo, 26 Feb. 1904, "Annual Report of 1903," p. 33; FO 407/164, no. 82, Cromer to Lansdowne, Cairo, 15 Mar. 1905, "Annual Report of 1904," p. 116; FO 371/247/8788, Cromer to Grey, Cairo, 3 Mar. 1907, "Annual Report of 1906," p. 8.

82. FO 371/451/31779, Gorst, "The Press in Egypt," p. 1.

83. FO 371/660/6829, Gorst to Grey, Cairo, 11 Feb. 1909, "Press Law of 1881"; FO 371/892/11188, Gorst to Grey, Cairo, 26 Mar. 1910, "Annual Report of 1909," p. 2; Vatikiotis, *Egypt,* 196.

84. FO 371/660/12761, Graham to Grey, Cairo, 4 Apr. 1909.

85. Labiba Hashim, "Kalima ila al-Sayyidat," *Fatat al-Sharq* 3, no. 7 (1909): 260.

86. FO 371/895/47209, Gorst to Nicolson, Cairo, 24 Dec. 1910; FO 371/1112/14962, Cheetham to Grey, Cairo, 16 Apr. 1911; FO 371/1964/36880, Cheetham to Grey, Cairo, 1 Aug. 1914.

87. FO 371/1964/4392, Kitchener to Grey, Cairo, 25 Jan. 1914.

88. Tarrazi, *Ta'rikh al-Sihafa,* 4:302; 'Attara, *Ta'rikh Takwin al-Suhuf,* 312; *al-'A'ila al-Qibtiyya* 1, no. 2 (1909); *Fatat al-Sharq* 3, no. 7 (1909): 272; *al-Jins al-Latif* 1, no. 10 (1909): 319.

89. *Al-Manar* 11, no. 12 (1909): 927; *al-Jins al-Latif* 2, no. 3 (1909): 87; *al-Jins al-Latif* 3, no. 4 (1910): 108; *al-Jins al-Latif* 3, no. 7 (1911): 189.

90. 'Attara, *Ta'rikh Takwin al-Suhuf,* 311, 318; Tarrazi, *Ta'rikh al-Sihafa,* 4:304, 334.

91. See, e.g., "Istayqizna Ayyatuha al-Sayyidat," *al-'Afaf* 1, no. 35 (13 Oct. 1911): 6.

92. FO 371/2926/61053, Graham, Cairo, 2 Mar. 1917, "Memorandum on Future British Policy with Regard to Egypt," p. 5.

93. Jacob M. Landau, *Parliaments and Parties in Egypt* (Tel Aviv: Israel Press, 1953).

94. Ahmad Hasanayn identifies Sarah al-Mihiyya as Syrian, but Lebanese and Syrian authors do not include her on their lists; Philipp writes "Egyptian Jewish" with a question mark. From her journal it is evident that Sarah is an Egyptian Muslim. See Ahmad Tahir Hasanayn, *Dawr al-Shamiyyin al-Muhajirin ila Misr fi'l-Nahda al-Adabiyya al-Haditha* (Damascus: Dar al-Wathba, 1983), 84; Thomas Philipp, "Feminism and Nationalist Politics in Egypt," in *Women in the Muslim World,* ed. Lois Beck and Nikki Keddie (Cambridge: Harvard University Press, 1978), 280.

95. Sarah al-Mihiyya, "Bayna Fatatayn," *Fatat al-Nil* 1, no. 4 (1332/1914): 125–33.

96. See FO 371/1973/81561, Cheetham to Grey, Cairo, 30 Nov. 1914.

97. Gershoni and Jankowski, *Egypt, Islam, and the Arabs,* 34.

98. *Al-Sufur* 5, no. 202 (22 May 1919): 1.

99. FO 141/469/1616, Smith to Residency, Cairo, 18 Aug. 1917, "List of Persons (Egyptians) Executed Transported or Banished since 1914 for Political Offences"; *al-Sufur* 5, no. 211 (21 Aug. 1919): 1; on Hamdi, see Daghir, *Masadir al-Dirasa al-'Adabiyya,* 763–64.

100. For different views of women's roles in the 1919 revolution, see Khalifa, *al-Haraka al-Nisa'iyya,* chap. 1; Afaf Lutfi al-Sayyid Marsot, "The Revolutionary Gentlewomen in Egypt," in *Women in the Muslim World,* 261–76; Philipp, "Feminism and Nationalist Politics," 277–94; John D. McIntyre, Jr., *The Boycott of the Milner Mission: A Study in Egyptian Nationalism* (New York: Peter Lang, 1985), 127–55; Margot Badran, "Dual Liberation: Feminism and Nationalism in Egypt, 1870s–1925," *Feminist Issues* (Spring 1988): 15–33; Beth Baron, "Mothers, Morality, and Nationalism in Pre-1919 Egypt," in *The Origins of Arab Nationalism,* ed. Rashid Khalidi et al. (New York: Columbia University Press, 1991), 271–88.

101. Gershoni and Jankowski, *Egypt, Islam, and the Arabs,* 40–54.

102. For a listing, see Ijlal Khalifa, "al-Sihafa al-Nisa'iyya fi Misr, 1919–1939" (M.A. thesis, University of Cairo, Faculty of Arts, 1966).

103. Hisham Sharabi, *Arab Intellectuals and the West: The Formative Years, 1875–1914* (Baltimore: Johns Hopkins University Press, 1970), 3–6.

Chapter 2. Creating Literary Texts

1. See Muhammad Badr Ma'ubdi, *Adab al-Nisa' fi'l-Jahiliyya wa'l-Islam* (Cairo: Muntasim al-Tab' wa'l-Nashr, n.d.).

2. For a good summary of the issues, see J. Brugman, *An Introduction to the History of Modern Arabic Literature in Egypt* (Leiden: E. J. Brill, 1984), 8–13.

3. *Encyclopaedia of Islam,* 2d ed. (Leiden: E. J. Brill, 1965), s.v. "Djarida"; Brugman, *Modern Arabic Literature,* 11–15; Jack A. Crabbs, Jr., *The Writing of History in Nineteenth-Century Egypt: A Study in National Transformation* (Cairo: American University in Cairo Press, 1984), 200. For a history of the Bulaq Press, see Abu al-Fatuh Radwan, *Ta'rikh Matba'at Bulaq* (Cairo: al-Matba'a al-Amiriyya, 1953).

4. Khalil Sabat, *Ta'rikh al-Tiba'a fi'l-Sharq al-'Arabi* (Cairo: Dar al-Ma'arif, 1958), 234.

5. 'Aziza, "Safha li'l-Banat," *al-Jins al-Latif* 1, no. 10 (1909): 313.

6. 'Umar Rida Kahhala, *A'lam al-Nisa' fi 'Alamay al-'Arab wa'l-Islam* (Bei-

rut: Mu'assasat al-Risala, 1977), 4:294; Anwar Jundi, *Adab al-Mar'a al-'Arabiyya* (Cairo: Matba'at al-Risala, n.d.), 42.

7. See, e.g., Firdaus Tawfiq, *Khawatir wa-Sawanih* (Cairo: Matba'at Misr, 1919), 3–4; Zaynab Fawwaz, *al-Durr al-Manthur fi Tabaqat Rabbat al-Khudur* (Cairo: al-Matba'a al-Kubra al-Amiriyya bi-Bulaq, 1312/1894), 1.

8. Munira 'Atiya Suriyal, "al-Mar'a al-Misriyya," *al-Jins al-Latif* 3, no. 10 (1911): 279.

9. Fatima Kamil al-Kafrawiyya, *Siyasat al-Mar'a* (Cairo: al-Athar, 1915), 2.

10. Beth Baron, "Mothers, Morality, and Nationalism in Pre-1919 Egypt," in *The Origins of Arab Nationalism,* ed. Rashid Khalidi et al. (New York: Columbia University Press, 1991), 271–88.

11. Malaka Sa'd, *Rabbat al-Dar* (Cairo: Matba'at al-Tawfiq, 1915), 23–24.

12. FO 891/18, "Madame Avierino: Interrogation by Parquet," Cairo, 16 July 1924, p. 3; Alexandra Avierino, " 'Alat al-Kitaba," *Anis al-Jalis* 6, no. 11 (1903): 1626–28.

13. Huda Shaarawi, *Harem Years: Memoirs of an Egyptian Feminist, 1879–1924,* trans. and intro. Margot Badran (London: Virago, 1986), 42.

14. Malaka Sa'd, "al-Sa'ada al-'A'iliyya," *al-Jins al-Latif* 1, no. 3 (1908): 78–79; idem, *Rabbat al-Dar,* 6.

15. Jurji Zaydan, "Fatat al-Sharq," *al-Hilal* 15, no. 2 (1906): 125.

16. Labiba Hashim, "Shahirat al-Nisa'," *Fatat al-Sharq* 2, no. 3 (1907): 82.

17. See, e.g., "al-Khansa'," *al-Sayyidat wa'l-Banat* 1, no. 3 (1903): 76–77; "al-Khansa'," *al-'Afaf* 1, no. 12 (27 Jan. 1911). On al-Khansa' (c. 575–664), see "al-Khansa'," in *al-Munjid fi'l-'Alam,* 9th ed. (Beirut: Dar al-Mashriq, 1976), 273–74; Reynolds A. Nicholson, *A Literary History of the Arabs* (Cambridge: Cambridge University Press, 1969), 126–27; "al-Khansa'," in *Middle Eastern Muslim Women Speak,* ed. Elizabeth Warnock Fernea and Basima Qattan Bezirgan (Austin: University of Texas Press, 1977), 3–6. Among the other poets mentioned were "Najiya Bint Damdam," *al-Rayhana* 1, no. 3 (1908): 88; "Hind Qurayshiyya," *al-'Afaf* 1, no. 22 (7 Apr. 1911).

18. See, e.g., *Fatat al-Sharq* 1, no. 1 (1906): 2. On gender difference in writing, see Elaine Showalter, "Feminist Criticism in the Wilderness," *Writing and Sexual Difference,* ed. Elizabeth Abel (Chicago: University of Chicago Press, 1982), 9–35; Janet Todd, *Feminist Literary History, A Defence* (Oxford: Polity, 1988).

19. "Madam Adam," *Anis al-Jalis* 1, no. 2 (1898): 37; "Jane Austen," *al-Jins al-Latif* 11, no. 3 (1918): 33–34; "Charlotte Brontë," *al-Jins al-Latif* 11, no. 6 (1918).

20. On oral culture, see Lila Abu-Lughod, *Veiled Sentiments: Honor and Poetry in a Bedouin Society* (Berkeley: University of California Press, 1986); Pierre Cachia, *Popular Narrative Ballads of Modern Egypt* (Oxford: Clarendon, 1989).

21. Esther Moyal, "al-Sayyid 'Abd al-Khaliq al-Sadat wa-Karimatuhu," *al-'A'ila* 3, no. 11 (1904): 83–84; Ahmad Baha' al-Din, *Ayyam la-ha Ta'rikh* (Cairo: Kitab Ruz al-Yusuf, 1954), 1:47–61; Abbas Kelidar, "Shaykh 'Ali Yusuf: Egyptian Journalist and Islamic Nationalist," in *Intellectual Life in the Arab East, 1890–1939*, ed. Marwan R. Buheiry (Beirut: American University of Beirut Press, 1981), 18; FO 371/67/27566, Findlay to Grey, Alexandria, 5 Aug. 1906.

22. Donald M. Reid, "The Rise of Professions and Professional Organization in Modern Egypt," *Comparative Studies in Society and History* 16 (1974): 24–57; Robert Springbord, "Professional Syndicates in Egyptian Politics, 1952–1970," *International Journal of Middle East Studies* 9 (1978): 275–95.

23. Sasson Somekh, *The Changing Rhythym: A Study of Najib Mahfuz's Novels* (Leiden: E. J. Brill, 1973), 3.

24. Muhammad Husayn Haykal, *Zaynab: Manazir wa-Akhlaq Rifiyya* (1914; rpt., Cairo: Maktabat al-Nahda al-Misriyya, 1963), 7–12; Somekh, *Changing Rhythym*, 3; Brugman, *Modern Arabic Literature*, 238–39.

25. Salim Sarkis, "Man Hiya Anisa Maryam Mazhar?" *Majallat Sarkis* 2, no. 21 (1907): 645–51; "al-Mar'a fi'l-Islam," *al-'Afaf* 1, no. 27 (19 May 1911): 6.

26. Fatima Rashid, "Khutba Khitamiyya," *Tarqiyat al-Mar'a* 1, no. 12 (1327/ 1909): 177.

27. See, e.g., *al-'Afaf* 2, no. 65 (10 July 1914): 5.

28. "Fi Sabil al-Ruqiyy," *al-Jins al-Latif* 4, no. 4 (1911): 100; "Nahnu wa'l-Ruqiyy," *al-Jins al-Latif* 4, no. 5 (1911): 133.

29. See, e.g., "Istayqizna Ayyatuha al-Sayyidat," *al-'Afaf* 1, no. 35 (13 Oct. 1911): 6; "Ama Hana laki al-Waqt," *al-Jins al-Latif* 10, no. 9 (1918): 228.

30. Zaynab Fawwaz, *Husn al-'Awaqib* (1893; rpt., Cairo: al-Matba'a al-Hindiyya, 1899); idem, *al-Durr al-Manthur*; Alexandra Avierino, "Kutub al-Shahr wa-Jara'iduhu," *Anis al-Jalis* 2, no. 6 (1899): 236; Jundi, *Adab al-Mar'a*, 76. On Zaynab Fawwaz's life, see Labiba Hashim, "al-Sayyida Zaynab Fawwaz," *Fatat al-Sharq* 1, no. 8 (1907): 225–28; Fathiyya Muhammad, *Balaghat al-Nisa' fi'l-Qarn al-'Ishrin* (Cairo: Matba'at al-Sa'ada, 1925), 122; Kahhala, *A'lam al-Nisa'*, 2:82; Khayr al-Din al-Zirikli, *al-A'lam: Qamus Tarajim li-Ashhar al-Rijal wa'l-Nisa' min al-'Arab wa'l-Musta'ribin wa'l-Mustashriqin* (Beirut: Dar al-'Ilm, 1980), 3:67.

31. Yusuf As'ad Daghir, *Mu'jam al-Asma' al-Musta'ara wa-Ashbahuha* (Beirut: Maktabat Lubnan, 1982), 74.

32. Shajarat al-Durr, "Mujmal Hayat al-Nisa'," *Anis al-Jalis* 1, no. 6 (1898): 176–79; Fatat al-Nil, "al-Malika Hatshepsut," *al-Jins al-Latif* 6, no. 3 (1913): 69–74; Rashid Rida, "Fatat al-Nil," *al-Manar* 17, no. 5 (1914): 392.

33. On Malak Hifni Nasif's life, see Labiba Hashim, "Bahithat al-Badiya," *Fatat al-Sharq* 13, no. 3 (1918): 81–83; al-Zirikli, *al-A'lam*, 2:265, 5:279, 7:287–88; Kahhala, *A'lam al-Nisa'*, 5:74–101; Mayy [Mary Ziyada], *Bahithat al-Badiya* (Cairo: Matba'at al-Muqtataf, 1920); Malak Hifni Nasif, *Athar Bahithat al-Badiya*, ed. Majid al-Din Hifni Nasif and intro. Suhayr al-Qalamawi (Cairo: al-Mu'assasa al-Misriyya al-'Amma, 1962); Charles C. Adams, *Islam and Modernism in Egypt: A Study of the Modern Reform Movement Inaugurated by Muhammad 'Abduh* (London: Oxford University Press, 1933), 212, 235; Evelyn Aleene Early, "Bahithat al-Badiya: Cairo Viewed from the Fayyum Oasis," *Journal of Near Eastern Studies* 40 (1981): 339–41.

34. Beth Baron, "Unveiling in Early Twentieth Century Egypt: Practical and Symbolic Considerations," *Middle Eastern Studies* 25 (1989): 375.

35. Malaka Sa'd, "al-Zahra," *al-Jins al-Latif* 10, no. 8 (1917): 213; Jundi, *Adab al-Mar'a*, 85.

36. Labiba Hashim, "al-Amira Nazli Hanim," *Fatat al-Sharq* 8, no. 4 (1914): 151.

37. Gabriel Baer, *Population and Society in the Arab East* (London: Routledge and Kegan Paul, 1964), 42.

38. Hind Iskandar 'Ammun, *Ta'rikh Misr* (Cairo: Matba'at al-Ma'arif, 1913); S. M. Zwemer, "A Woman as Historian of Egypt," *The Moslem World* 6 (1916): 198. Three years earlier officials at the Egyptian University had barred Jurji Zaydan from teaching Islamic history because he was not Muslim (Donald Malcolm Reid, *Cairo University and the Making of Modern Egypt* [Cambridge: Cambridge University Press, 1990], 35–37).

39. Amina Z., "Bab al-Ibar," *al-Sufur* 1, no. 44 (31 Mar. 1916): 5.

40. Sulayman al-Salimi, "al-Tazwir al-Barid," *al-'Afaf* 1, no. 27 (19 May 1911): 15.

41. Ibid.; Alexandra Avierino, "Huquq al-Mar'a al-Muslima," *Anis al-Jalis* 1, no. 6 (1898): 161.

42. *Al-Mu'ayyad* (3 Feb. 1898), 3, quoted in Martin Hartmann, *The Arabic Press of Egypt* (London: Luzac, 1899), 49. On a similar charge in another context, see Fedwa Malti-Douglas, *Woman's Body, Woman's Word: Gender and Discourse in Arabo-Islamic Writing* (Princeton: Princeton University Press, 1991), 168–69.

43. *Sayyidat wa'l-Banat* 1, no. 1 (1903): 1; Farah Antun, "Majallat al-Sayyidat" and "'Awda Majallat al-Sayyidat," *al-Sayyidat wa'l-Banat* 2, no. 7 (1906): 177–80; Donald M. Reid, "The Odyssey of Farah Antun: A Syrian Christian's Quest for Secularism" (Ph.D. diss., Princeton University, 1968), 101.

44. FO 891/18, "Enquiry Procès Verbal in the Evidence of Madam Avierino in the Suit of Crime No. 1853, Ezbakieh, July 1924."

45. "Al-Mar'a Didduha wa-La-ha," *al-'Afaf* 1, no. 31 (25 June 1911): 2; Malak Amin, "Ila al-Katib Didd al-Mar'a," *al-'Afaf* 1, no. 34 (4 Aug. 1911): 8–9; *al-'Afaf* 1, no. 35 (13 Oct. 1911): 8.

46. Fatima Rashid, "Khutba Khitamiyya," 177; "al-Qanun," *Tarqiyat al-Mar'a* 1, no. 1 (1326/1908): 4; Najiya Rashid, "Khutba," *Tarqiyat al-Mar'a* 1, no. 8 (1326/1908): 121.

47. Labiba Hashim, "al-Nahda al-Nisa'iyya fi Misr," *Fatat al-Sharq* 8, no. 5 (1914): 185.

48. For more on the debate *al-hijab* (veiling) versus *al-sufur* (unveiling), see Baron, "Unveiling in Egypt," 370–86.

49. Ibid., 374–76.

50. On 'A'isha al-Taymuriyya and Warda al-Yaziji, see Marilyn Booth, "Biography and Feminist Rhetoric in Early Twentieth-Century Egypt: Mayy Ziyada's Studies of Three Women's Lives," *Journal of Women's History* 3 (1991): 38–64; see also Fawwaz, *al-Durr al-Manthur,* 303–4.

51. Maryam Jabra'il Nasrallah al-Nahhas, *Ma'rid al-Hasna' fi Tarajim Mashahir al-Nisa'* (Alexandria: Matba'at Jaridat Misr, 1879); Fawwaz, *al-Durr al-Manthur.*

52. Anwar Jundi, *al-Nathr al-'Arabi al-Mu'asir fi Mi'a 'Am* (Cairo: Maktabat al-Nahda al-Misriyya, 1961), 304.

53. See, e.g., Rosa Antun Haddad, *Farah Antun: Hayatuhu wa-Ta'binuhu wa-Mukhtaratuhu* (Cairo: Matba'at Yusuf Kawa, 1923); on Mayy Ziyada's biographical output, see Booth, "Biography and Feminist Rhetoric."

54. Jurji Niqula Baz, "Esther Azhari Moyal," *al-'Alam al-Isra'ili* 9, nos. 357–58 (12 Nisan/Apr. 1946): 10; Emile Zola, *al-Mal. al-Mal. al-Mal.,* trans. Esther Moyal (Cairo: Matba'at al-Shuri, 1907), preface.

55. Brugman, *Modern Arabic Literature,* 213.

56. Brugman, *Modern Arabic Literature,* 212–13; John A. Haywood, *Modern Arabic Literature, 1800–1970* (London: Lund Humphries, 1971), 126; Sarah al-Mihiyya, "Thurayya," *Fatat al-Nil* 1, no. 3 (1332/1914): 115–19 and in subsequent issues.

57. Brugman, *Modern Arabic Literature,* 210–11.

58. Hanna Sarkis, "Qalb al-Rajul," *Anis al-Jalis* 7, no. 4 (1904): 1792; Labiba Hashim, *Qalb al-Rajul* (Cairo: Matba'at al-Ma'arif, n.d.), preface.

59. Jundi, *Adab al-Mar'a*, 75–77; Haywood, *Modern Arabic Literature,* 125; Yusuf As'ad Daghir, *Masadir al-Dirasa al-Adabiyya* (Beirut: l'Université Libanaise, 1972), 137–39.

60. Jacques Tajir, *Harakat al-Tarjama bi-Misr khilal al-Qarn al-Tas'i 'Ashara* (Cairo: Dar al-Ma'arif, 1945), 106; "al-Sihha fi'l-Jins al-Latif," *al-Fatah* 1, no. 5 (1893): 216–18; *al-'Afaf* 1, no. 2 (11 Nov. 1910): 3; see also "al-Bab al-Tibbi," *al-Jins al-Latif* 3, no. 4 (1910): 102–3.

61. Labiba Hashim, *Kitab fi'l-Tarbiya* (Cairo: Matba'at al-Ma'arif, 1911).

62. "Al-'A'ila al-Misriyya," *al-Jins al-Latif* 5, no. 1 (1912): 28. See also "al-Ijtima'iyyat," *Fatat al-Sharq* 9, no. 5 (1915): 195; " 'Ala Masrah al-'Awatif," *al-Sufur* 1, no. 35 (28 Jan. 1916): 3–4; "Kitab Rasa'il ila al-Fatayat," *al-Sufur* 3, no. 137 (3 Jan. 1918): 1, 4.

63. Sa'd, *Rabbat al-Dar;* idem, "Thamarat al-Adab," *al-Jins al-Latif* 8, no. 1 (1915): 33.

64. Nabawiyya Musa, *al-Mutala'a al-'Arabiyya li-Madaris al-Banat* (Cairo: al-Matba'a al-Amiriyya, 1911); Zaynab Mursi, *al-Ayat al-Bayyinat fi Tarbiyat al-Banat* (Cairo: Matba'at Karara, 1912). For a study that looks at more recent Egyptian school texts, see Avner Giladi, "Some Aspects of Social and National Contents in Egyptian Curricula and Textbooks," *Asian and African Studies* 19 (1985): 157–86, esp. 172–75.

65. Louis Awad, ed. *The Literature of Ideas in Egypt* (Atlanta: Scholars Press, 1986), intro.

66. Zaynab Fawwaz, *al-Rasa'il al-Zaynabiyya* (1906; rpt., Cairo: al-Matba'a al-Mutawassita, 1915).

67. Bahithat al-Badiya [Malak Hifni Nasif], *al-Nisa'iyyat* (Cairo: Matba'at al-Jarida, 1910).

68. See, e.g., 'Abd al-Hamid Hamdi, "Kitab Fatah," *al-Sufur* 2, no. 70 (6 Oct. 1916): 5–6.

69. On the development of Arabic autobiography, see Thomas Philipp, "The Autobiography in Modern Arab Literature and Culture," *Poetics Today* 14 (1993, in press); Malti-Douglas, *Woman's Body,* 145–46, 162–63.

70. For studies charting language change from different disciplinary perspectives, see Ami Ayalon, *Language and Change in the Arab Middle East* (New York: Oxford University Press, 1987); Jaroslav Stetkevych, *The Modern Arabic Literary Language: Lexical and Stylistic Developments* (Chicago: University of Chicago Press, 1970).

71. Labiba Hashim, "al-Mar'a al-Sharqiyya," *Anis al-Jalis* 1, no. 5 (1898): 149.

72. Alexandra Avierino, "al-Mu'ayyad al-Jadid," *Anis al-Jalis* 9, no. 7 (1906): 277.

73. Rashid Rida, "al-Nisa'iyyat," *al-Manar* 14, no. 1 (1911): 73, 71.

74. Some Middle Eastern writers—male and female—still use pseudonyms today; they are often motivated by security concerns.

Chapter 3. The Making of a Journal

1. FO 141/464/1263, Delaney, "Reuter's Service in Egypt," Cairo, 18 May 1920.

2. *All About Postal Matters* (Florence: Landi, 1898), 20–23.

3. *Al-Sayyidat wa'l-Banat* 1, no. 12 (1904): 383; Robert L. Tignor, "The Introduction of Modern Banking into Egypt," *Asian and African Studies* 15 (1981): 103–22.

4. Carl F. Petry, "Class Solidarity versus Gender Gain: Custodians of Property in Later Medieval Egypt," in *Women in Middle Eastern History: Shifting Boundaries in Sex and Gender,* ed. Nikki R. Keddie and Beth Baron (New Haven: Yale University Press, 1991), 122–42.

5. Judith E. Tucker, *Women in Nineteenth-Century Egypt* (Cambridge: Cambridge University Press, 1985), 81–101.

6. Nadia Farag, "al-Muqtataf, 1876–1900: A Study of the Influence of Victorian Thought on Modern Arabic Thought" (D.Phil. diss., Oxford University, 1969), 21–22, 49–50; Byron D. Cannon, "Nineteenth-Century Arabic Writings on Women and Society: The Interim Role of the Masonic Press in Cairo—(al-Lata'if, 1885–1895)," *International Journal of Middle East Studies* 17 (1985): 473–79.

7. Ilyas Zakhura, *al-Suriyyun fi Misr* (Cairo: al-Matba'a al-'Arabiyya, 1927), 165–73; Helen Kitchen, "Al-Ahram—The Times of the Arab World," *Middle East Journal* 4 (1950): 157–58.

8. Hind Nawfal, "Idah wa-Iltimas wa-Istismah," *al-Fatah* 1, no. 1 (1892): 1–6.

9. *Anis al-Jalis* 1, no. 1 (1898): 5.

10. Nawfal, "Idah," 4–6; Rosa Antun, "Muqaddima," *al-Sayyidat wa'l-Banat* 1, no. 1 (1903): 3.

11. Kathryn Shevelow, *Women and Print Culture: The Construction of Femininity in the Early Periodical* (London: Routledge, 1989), 151, quote from p. 190.

12. Pamela Frances Stent Langlois, "The Feminine Press in England and France, 1875–1900" (Ph.D. diss., University of Massachusetts, 1979).

13. Fatima Rashid, "Latafat al-A'da'," *Tarqiyat al-Mar'a* 1, no. 3 (1326/ 1908): 47.

14. "Un Journal féminin de Constantinople," *Revue du Monde Musulman* 2, no. 10 (1908): 337–38; "Une Revue féminine de Constantinople," *Revue du Monde Musulman* 3, nos. 7–8 (1909): 501–5; Jurji Niqula Baz, "al-Majallat al-Nisa'iyya al-'Arabiyya," *al-Hasna'* 1, no. 1 (1909): 14–15; Saint Nihal Singh, "The New Woman in the Mohammedan World," *The American Review of Reviews* 46 (1912): 716–20; "The Feminist Movement in Turkey," *The Moslem World* 4 (1914): 422–23; Tezer Taşkiran, *Women in Turkey,* trans. Nida Tektaş (Istanbul: Redhouse, 1976), 34–35; Ahmed Emin, "The Development of Modern Turkey as Measured by Its Press," *Studies in History, Economics, and Public Law* 59 (1914): 115.

15. Emin, "Development of Modern Turkey," 110.

16. Nükhet Sirman, "Feminism in Turkey: A Short History," *New Perspectives on Turkey* 3 (1989): 8.

17. Frontispieces of *al-'Afaf* 1, no. 26 (12 May 1911) and *al-'Afaf* 1, no. 29 (9 June 1911).

18. FO 371/660/6829, Gorst to Grey, "Press Law of 1881," Cairo, 11 Feb. 1909.

19. Sarah al-Mihiyya, "Min Dars Ustadh," *al-'Afaf* 1, no. 3 (18 Nov. 1910): 1; idem, "al-Muqaddima," *Fatat al-Nil* 1, no. 1 (1332/1913): 5.

20. Hind Nawfal, "Idah," 3; *Fatat al-Sharq* 1, no. 1 (1906): 1–2.

21. Sarah al-Mihiyya, "Taharrush al-Dubbat bi'l-Sayyidat," *al-'Afaf* 1, no. 23 (14 Apr. 1911): 3.

22. Rosa Antun, "al-Muqaddima," 1; idem, "Maqallat al-Rijal wa'l-Majalla," *al-Sayyidat wa'l-Banat* 1, no. 4 (1903): 114.

23. Sulayman al-Salimi, "Hawadith Mahalliyyat al-'Afaf," *al-'Afaf* 1, no. 24 (21 Apr. 1911): 4.

24. *Fatat al-Sharq* 8, no. 7 (1914): 281.

25. See, e.g., Labiba Hashim, "Fatat al-Sharq fi Sanatiha al-Thamina," *Fatat al-Sharq* 8, no. 1 (1913): 3.

26. Alexandra Avierino, "al-Sariqa al-Adabiyya," *Anis al-Jalis* 8, nos. 3–4 (1905): 120.

27. Fatima Rashid, "al-I'tidhar," *Tarqiyat al-Mar'a* 1, no. 1 (1326/1908): 16.

28. Donald M. Reid, "The Odyssey of Farah Antun: A Syrian Christian's Quest for Secularism" (Ph.D. diss., Princeton University, 1968), 127; Arthur Goldschmidt, Jr., "The Egyptian Nationalist Party: 1892–1919," in *Political and Social Change in Modern Egypt,* ed. P. M. Holt (London: Oxford University

Press, 1968), 323 n.3. Due to the similarity in values of the English and Egyptian pounds (one English pound equaled 97.5 Egyptian piasters in 1915), there was often confusion about which was meant (FO 371/2351/96908, McMahon to Grey, Cairo, 5 July 1915, "Report on Egyptian Coinage"). This ambiguity faces readers of British documents today as well. As the difference was minimal and prices often represented approximations anyway, I have taken Egyptian and English pounds to be practically interchangeable.

29. FO 141/680/9527, Badr El Din, "The Waez Printing Office," Cairo, 25 July 1919.

30. FO 141/817/4379, "Report on Moslem Propaganda," Cairo, 11 Feb. 1917, p. 3.

31. FO 633/5, no. 220, Baring to Pauncefote, Cairo, 6 Nov. 1887, pp. 162–63.

32. FO 407/114, no. 1, Cromer to Salisbury, Cairo, 1 July 1892, p. 1; FO 371/1639/23658, Kitchener to Grey, Cairo, 16 May 1913; FO 371/1640/44106, Kyriacopoulo to Grey, Zeitun, 18 Sept. 1913.

33. Ijlal Khalifa, "al-Sihafa al-Nisa'iyya fi Misr, 1919–1939" (M.A. thesis, University of Cairo, Faculty of Arts, 1966), 29.

34. *Fatat al-Nil* 1, no. 3 (1332/1914): 100; *Fatat al-Sharq* 2, no. 2 (1907): 67.

35. FO 371/894/27119, Graham to Cheetham, Cairo, 10 July 1910.

36. FO 371/67/27566, Findlay to Grey, Alexandria, 5 Aug. 1906, p. 1.

37. Ibid., p. 4.

38. Alexandra Avierino, "al-Fawa'id al-Muhmala," *Anis al-Jalis* 6, no. 12 (1903): 1636–39, esp. 1637. On the decline of guilds, see Gabriel Baer, *Egyptian Guilds in Modern Times* (Jerusalem: Israel Oriental Society, 1964).

39. *Al-Jins al-Latif* 8, no. 6 (1915): 223; *al-'Afaf* 2, no. 63 (9 June 1914): 7.

40. Muhammad Hilmi, "Hadrat Mushtariki al-'Afaf," *al-'Afaf* 1, no. 10 (13 Jan. 1911): 4.

41. *Anis al-Jalis* 10, no. 1 (1908): 27.

42. E. R. J. Owen, "The Attitudes of British Officials to the Development of the Egyptian Economy, 1882–1922," in *Studies in the Economic History of the Middle East*, ed. M. A. Cook (London: Oxford University Press, 1970), 490; Robert Tignor, *Modernization and the British Rule in Egypt, 1882–1914* (Princeton: Princeton University Press, 1966), 370; idem, *State, Private Enterprise, and Economic Change in Egypt, 1918–1952* (Princeton: Princeton University Press, 1984), 40–41.

43. FO 369/926/183200, Alban, Cairo, 31 Aug. 1917.

44. Labiba Hashim, "Muqaddimat al-Sana al-Thalitha," *Fatat al-Sharq* 3, no. 1 (1908): 2; idem, "Khitam al-Sana al-'Ashira," *Fatat al-Sharq* 10, no. 10 (1916): 395; idem, "Tanbih," *Fatat al-Sharq* 11, no. 3 (1916): 136.

45. *Al-Jins al-Latif* 8, no. 7 (1916): 256; *al-Jins al-Latif* 8, no. 10 (1916): 362; *al-Jins al-Latif* 10, no. 5 (1917): 167.

46. Labiba Hashim, "Kayfa Uharriru Majallati!!!" *Fatat al-Sharq* 9, no. 7 (1915): 243–48.

47. Charles C. Adams, *Islam and Modernism in Egypt: A Study of the Modern Reform Movement Inaugurated by Muhammad 'Abduh* (London: Oxford University Press, 1933), 180.

48. See "I'lan" in *al-Jins al-Latif* 3, no. 10 (1911): 288; *al-Jins al-Latif* 5, no. 8 (1913): 285; *al-Jins al-Latif* 8, no. 9 (1916): 234.

49. FO 407/151, no. 42, Cromer to Salisbury, Cairo, 17 Apr. 1899, p. 31.

50. See notices under "Tadbir al-Manzil," in *al-Manar* 1, no. 13 (1898): 235, and in *Fatat al-Sharq* 5, no. 4 (1911): 149.

51. Hind Nawfal, "Durr al-Manthur fi Tarajim [sic] Rabbat-al-Khudur," *al-Fatah* 1, no. 7 (1893): 328–29.

52. Egypt, Dar al-Watha'iq al-Qawmiyya (National Archives, DW), Majlis al-Wuzara' (MW), al-Busta 50, Mazlum to the Council of Ministers, 22 Nov. 1900; DW/MW, al-Busta 43, "Résumé du texte du rapport postal sur l'exercice," 1913, pp. 1–2; FO 407/100, no. 41, Baring to Salisbury, Cairo, 15 May 1890; FO 371/249/26131, Graham to Grey, Cairo, 26 July 1907; FO 371/1112/11940, "Post Offices," 31 Dec. 1910, p. 23; *All About Postal Matters,* 20–23; Egypt, Ministry of Finance, *Postal Traffic in Egypt, 1880–1906* (Cairo: National Printing Department, 1907).

53. Rashid Rida, "al-Barid al-Misri," *al-Manar* 1, no. 48 (1899): 936.

54. Sulayman al-Salimi, "Ila Mudir al-Busta al-'Amm," *al-'Afaf* 1, no. 29 (29 June 1911): 5.

55. Jurji Zaydan, "Maslahat al-Busta al-Misriyya," *al-Hilal* 2, no. 2 (1893): 60; Labiba Hashim, "Rijal al-Fadl," *Fatat al-Sharq* 1, no. 6 (1906): 178.

56. Labiba Hashim, "Hadiyat al-'Id," *Fatat al-Sharq* 3, no. 4 (1909): 127–28.

57. Juan Ricardo Cole, "Feminism, Class, and Islam in Turn-of-the-Century Egypt," *International Journal of Middle East Studies* 13 (1981): 393.

58. Hilmi, "Hadrat Mushtariki al-'Afaf."

59. Alexandra Avierino, "Shaqa' al-Ummahat," *Anis al-Jalis* 3, no. 11 (1900): 434.

60. FO 371/1964/4392, Kitchener to Grey, Cairo, 25 Jan. 1914.

61. Alexandra Avierino, "al-Sihafa al-'Arabiyya," *Anis al-Jalis* 7, no. 2 (1904): 1698.

62. FO 371/3726/90308, Egypforce to Military Intelligence, Cairo, 11 May 1919; FO 371/3726/134972, Minutes, Sept. 1919.

63. Esther Moyal, *Ta'rikh Hayat Emile Zola* (Cairo: Matba'at al-Tawfiq, 1897), title page; Malaka Sa'd, *Rabbat al-Dar* (Cairo: Matba'at al-Tawfiq, 1915), 6; *Anis al-Jalis* 2, no. 11 (1899): photograph following p. 444.

64. See, e.g., Malaka Sa'd, "al-Nisa' al-'Amilat," *al-Jins al-Latif* 8, no. 4 (1915): 141.

65. On women in health care, see Laverne Kuhnke, "The 'Doctoress' on a Donkey: Women Health Officers in Nineteenth Century Egypt," *Clio Medica* 9 (1974): 193–205. On women teachers, see chap. 6.

66. Labiba Hashim, "Ayna al-Sa'ada," *Fatat al-Sharq* 13, no. 7 (1919): 274; *Fatat al-Sharq* 1, no. 1 (1906): 1–2.

67. Malaka Sa'd, "Fatihat al-'Am al-Sadis," *al-Jins al-Latif* 6, no. 1 (1913): 2.

68. Alexandra Avierino, "Shajarat al-Durr," *Anis al-Jalis* 4, no. 5 (1901): 677.

69. Labiba Hashim, "al-Jins al-Latif," *Fatat al-Sharq* 2, no. 10 (1908): 398.

70. Ibn Yahya, "Asbab Insha' al-Rayhana al-Usbu'iyya," *al-Rayhana* 1, no. 1 (20 Mar. 1908): 1.

71. 'Abd al-Hamid Hamdi, "al-Sufur," *al-Sufur* 1, no. 1 (21 May 1915): 1.

72. "Al-Fatah," *al-Muqtataf* 17, no. 3 (1892): 209–10.

73. Jurji Zaydan, "al-Fatah," *al-Hilal* 1, no. 4 (1892): 190; see, e.g., idem, "Firdaus," *al-Hilal* 4, no. 12 (1896): 880.

74. Rashid Rida, "al-Hawanim," *al-Manar* 3, no. 8 (1900): 186–87.

75. Khayr al-Din al-Zirikli, *al-A'lam: Qamus Tarajim li-Ashhar al-Rijal wa'l-Nisa' min al-'Arab wa'l-Musta'ribin wa'l-Mustashriqin* (Beirut: Dar al-'Ilm, 1980), 2:118; K. T. Khairallah, "La Syrie," *Revue du Monde Musulman* 19 (1912): 116–17; Mayy Ziyada, "Warda al-Yaziji," *Opening the Gates: A Century of Arab Feminist Writing*, ed. Margot Badran and Miriam Cooke (Bloomington: Indiana University Press, 1990), 241.

76. Yusuf Daghir, *Masadir al-Dirasa al-Adabiyya* (Beirut: l'Université Libanaise, 1972), 160.

77. Jurji Niqula Baz, "Majallat al-Nisa'," *Fatat Lubnan* 1, no. 1 (1914): 7–10; see also idem, "al-Majallat al-Nisa'iyya," *Fatat al-Sharq* 2, no. 6 (1908): 212–15; idem, "al-Majallat al-Nisa'iyya al-'Arabiyya," *al-Hasna'* 1, no. 1 (1909): 12–15.

78. FO 141/521/9061, no. 5, Avierino, Cairo, 23 June 1920; FO 141/521/9061,

no. 23, Avierino to Allenby, London, 27 Mar. 1923; Philippe de Tarrazi, *Ta'rikh al-Sihafa al-'Arabiyya* (Beirut: al-Matba'a al-Amirikaniyya, 1933), 4:327.

79. Fatima Rashid, "I'lan," *Tarqiyat al-Mar'a* 1, no. 12 (1327/1909): 187–88.

80. Nasim Nawfal, "al-I'lan," *al-Fatah* 1, no. 7 (1893): 289–90; Farah Antun, " 'Awdat Majallat al-Sayyidat," *al-Sayyidat wa'l-Banat* 2, no. 7 (1906): 177–80.

Chapter 4. The Community of Readers

1. Jonathan P. Berkey, "Women and Islamic Education in the Mamluk Period," in *Women in Middle Eastern History: Shifting Boundaries in Sex and Gender,* ed. Nikki R. Keddie and Beth Baron (New Haven: Yale University Press, 1991), 143–57.

2. Edward William Lane, *An Account of the Manners and Customs of the Modern Egyptians* (3d ed., 1842; rpt., London: Ward and Lock, 1890), 51.

3. Lucie Duff Gordon, *Letters from Egypt* (1869; rpt., London: Virago, 1983), 125.

4. Gabriel Baer, *Studies in the Social History of Modern Egypt* (Chicago: University of Chicago Press, 1969), 168.

5. See, e.g., Riya Salima [Eugénie Le Brun], *Harems et musulmanes d'Egypte (lettres)* (Paris: Felix Juven, n.d.), 10; FO 141/745/8900, Mohamed Djemaleddin to Allenby, 26 Nov. 1920.

6. Suhayr al-Qalamawi, *Ahadith Jaddati* (Cairo: Lajnat al-Ta'lif wa'l-Tarjama wa'l-Nashr, 1935), 62, quoted in Soha Abdel Kader, *Egyptian Women in a Changing Society, 1899–1987* (Boulder, Colo.: Lynne Rienner, 1987), 101.

7. On the history of reading, see the works of Robert Darnton, "Reading, Writing, and Publishing in Eighteenth-Century France: A Case Study in the Sociology of Literature," in *Historical Studies Today,* ed. Felix Gilbert and Stephen R. Graubard (New York: W. W. Norton, 1972), 238–80; idem, "Readers Respond to Rousseau: The Fabrication of Romantic Sensitivity," in *The Great Cat Massacre and Other Episodes in French Cultural History* (New York: Vintage, 1985), 215–56; and idem, "First Steps Toward a History of Reading," in *The Kiss of Lamourette: Reflections in Cultural History* (New York: W. W. Norton, 1990), 154–87. Among other works that proved useful here are Susan R. Suleiman and Inge Crosman, ed. *The Reader in the Text: Essays on Audience and Interpretation* (Princeton: Princeton University

Press, 1980), esp. Suleiman's introduction; Annette Kolodny, "A Map for Rereading: Gender and Interpretation of Literary Texts," in *The New Feminist Criticism: Essays on Women, Literature, and Theory*, ed. Elaine Showalter (New York: Pantheon, 1985), 46–62; Elizabeth A. Flynn and Patrocinio P. Schweickart, ed. *Gender and Reading: Essays on Readers, Texts, and Contexts* (Baltimore: Johns Hopkins University Press, 1986).

8. Egypt, Nizarat al-Maliyya, *Ta'dad Sukkan al-Qutr al-Misri, 1897* (hereafter *Census of 1897*) (Cairo: al-Matba'a al-Kubra al-Amiriyya bi-Bulaq, 1898), 1:28, 70, 95; Egypt, Ministry of Finance, *The Census of Egypt Taken in 1907* (Cairo: National Printing Department, 1909), 97.

9. *Anis al-Jalis* 1, no. 1 (1898): 15. The exact figure for literate females in Egypt in the 1897 census, including foreigners, was 35,199 (*Census of 1907*, 97).

10. *Census of 1907*, 97.

11. Egypt, Ministry of Finance, *The Census of Egypt Taken in 1917* (Cairo: Government Press, 1920), 2:566–67.

12. *Census of 1897*, 1:70, 95; *Census of 1907*, 99; *Census of 1917*, 1:19–21.

13. See Daniel Panzac, "The Population of Egypt in the Nineteenth Century," *Asian and African Studies* 21 (1987): 11–32, esp. 30.

14. *Census of 1907*, 99–113.

15. *Census of 1907*, 114.

16. *Census of 1907*, 99, 97.

17. Zakiya al-Kafrawiyya, "Ma wara'a al-Khudur," *al-'Afaf* 1, no. 19 (17 Mar. 1911).

18. Elizabeth Cooper, *The Women of Egypt* (New York: F. A. Stokes, 1914), 167.

19. Hind Nawfal, "al-Marhuma Rahil al-Bustani," *al-Fatah* 1, no. 11 (1894): 519.

20. E. L. Butcher, *Things Seen in Egypt* (London: Seeley, 1910), 63.

21. Cooper, *Women of Egypt*, 345.

22. Labiba Hashim, "Nisa' al-Sharq wa'l-Lugha al-'Arabiyya," *Fatat al-Sharq* 2, no. 1 (1907): 19.

23. Al-Qalamawi, *Ahadith Jaddati*, 62, quoted in Abdel Kader, *Egyptian Women*, 101.

24. Labiba Hashim, *al-Ta'awun* (Cairo: Matba'at al-Ma'arif, 1912), 12.

25. Malaka Sa'd, *Rabbat al-Dar* (Cairo: Matba'at al-Tawfiq, 1915), 21.

26. Cooper, *Women of Egypt*, 241.

27. Zaynab Mursi, *al-Ayat al-Bayyinat fi Tarbiyat al-Banat* (Cairo: Matba'at Karara, 1912), 35.

28. Abdel-Rahman Rouchdy, *Rapport sur la Bibliothèque Khédiviale du Caire pour l'anneé 1887* (Cairo: Imprimerie Nationale, 1888), 10–20.

29. Donald Malcolm Reid, *Cairo University and the Making of Modern Egypt* (Cambridge: Cambridge University Press, 1990), 39–40.

30. Al-Qalamawi, *Ahadith Jaddati,* 62, quoted in Abdel Kader, *Egyptian Women,* 101. Virginia Woolf protested against being denied entry into an Oxbridge library in an essay written in the late 1920s (Virginia Woolf, *A Room of One's Own* [1929; rpt., New York: Harcourt Brace Jovanovich, 1957], 5–8).

31. Huda Shaarawi, *Harem Years: The Memoirs of an Egyptian Feminist,* trans. and intro. Margot Badran (London: Virago, 1986), 41–42.

32. 'Anbara Salam al-Khalidi, *Jawla fi'l-Dhikrayat bayna Lubnan wa-Filastin* (Beirut: Dar al-Nahar li'l-Nashr, 1978), 39–40.

33. Al-Khalidi, *Dhikrayat,* 31. 'Izz al-Din Abu al-Hasan 'Ali Ibn al-Athir (d. 1234) was a famous historian who lived in Mosul; Muhammad Ibn Musa al-Damiri (d. 1405) was born in Cairo and taught at al-Azhar (*Al-Munjid fi'l-'Alam,* 9th ed. [Beirut: Dar al-Mashriq, 1976], 8, 288).

34. Al-Khalidi, *Dhikrayat,* 31, 39, 64, 68.

35. Khadija al-Mihiyya, "al-Sawt," *al-'Afaf* 1, no. 30 (16 June 1911): 10–11.

36. Religious endowment (*waqf*) records provide an excellent source of data on private libraries when titles were catalogued as part of the trust. See Daniel Crecelius, "The Waqf of Muhammad Bey Abu al-Dhahab in Historical Perspective," *International Journal of Middle East Studies* 23 (1991): 57–81.

37. *Census of 1907,* 117, 97; B. L. Carter, *The Copts in Egyptian Politics* (London: Croom Helm, 1986), 5. The following discussion is based on Sa'd, *Rabbat al-Dar,* 23–26.

38. *Encyclopaedia of Islam,* 2d ed. (Leiden: E. J. Brill, 1978), s.v. "Kalila wa-Dimna"; Malaka inadvertently inverted the title of the work *Adab al-Din wa'l-Dunya* by al-Mawardi (d. 1058) (*Al-Munjid,* 29, 631).

39. See, e.g., Salima, *Harems et musulmanes,* 44–46.

40. See "I'lan," *al-Jins al-Latif* 3, no. 10 (1911): 288; *al-Jins al-Latif* 5, no. 8 (1913): 285; *al-Jins al-Latif* 8, no. 9 (1916): 234.

41. Rashid Rida, *al-Manar wa'l-Azhar* (Cairo, 1934–5), 179, cited in Albert Hourani, *Arabic Thought in the Liberal Age, 1798–1939,* 2d ed. (Cambridge: Cambridge University Press, 1983), 226.

42. Cooper, *Women of Egypt,* 241.

43. Rashid Rida, "Tarbiyat Sihhat al-Hamil," *al-Manar* 13, no. 4 (1910): 292.

44. Labiba Hashim, "Hadiyat al-'Id," *Fatat al-Sharq* 3, no. 4 (1909): 123.

45. Mursi, *al-Ayat al-Bayyinat,* 35.

46. Sa'd, *Rabbat al-Dar,* 24.

47. Hashim, "Hadiyat al-'Id," 128.
48. Butcher, *Things Seen in Egypt,* 63.
49. Firdaus Kamil, "Athar Qasim fi Wadi al-Qamar," *al-'Afaf* 2, no. 54 (11 Mar. 1914): 7.
50. "Hawadith Mahalliyya," *al-'Afaf* 1, no. 14 (10 Feb. 1911): 4.
51. Arthur Goldschmidt, Jr., "The Egyptian Nationalist Party: 1892–1919," in *Political and Social Change in Modern Egypt,* ed. P. M. Holt (London: Oxford University Press, 1968), 318 n.5.
52. FO 371/249/33861, Graham to Grey, Cairo, 4 Oct. 1907.
53. Walid Kazziha, "The Jaridah-Ummah Group and Egyptian Politics," *Middle Eastern Studies* 13 (1977): 379.
54. FO 371/3721/156659, G. S. Symes, "Note on Egyptian Press," Cairo, 5 Nov. 1919, p. 1.
55. John A. Haywood, *Modern Arabic Literature, 1800–1970* (London: Lund Humphries, 1971), 120.
56. Rae W. Fraser, "The Egyptian Newspaper Press," *The Nineteenth Century* 32 (1892): 222.
57. Charles C. Adams, *Islam and Modernism in Egypt: A Study of the Modern Reform Movement Inaugurated by Muhammad 'Abduh* (London: Oxford University Press, 1933), 180–81.
58. *Census of 1907,* 97.
59. *Al-Sayyidat wa'l-Banat* 1, no. 12 (1904): 374.
60. Fatima Rashid, "Khutba Khitamiyya," *Tarqiyat al-Mar'a* 1, no. 12 (1327/ 1909), 178.
61. Zakiya al-Kafrawiyya, "Muhadatha Tilifuniyya," *al-'Afaf* 1, no. 25 (5 May 1911): 6.
62. Labiba Hashim, "Ahamm Hawadith al-Shahr," *Fatat al-Sharq* 8, no. 5 (1914): 192.
63. Rida, *al-Manar wa'l-Azhar,* 179, cited in Hourani, *Arabic Thought,* 226.
64. *Al-Hilal* (Oct. 1897): 131, quoted by Ami Ayalon in *Language and Change in the Arab Middle East: The Evolution of Modern Political Discourse* (New York: Oxford University Press, 1987), 135.
65. FO 371/451/31779, Gorst, "The Press in Egypt," Cairo, 16 Sept. 1908.
66. Cooper, *Women of Egypt,* 241.
67. Rosa Antun, "al-Majalla bayna Ukhtayn," *al-Sayyidat wa'l-Banat* 1, no. 3 (1903): 68.
68. *Al-Hilal* (Oct. 1897): 131, quoted by Ayalon, *Language and Change.*
69. Martin Hartmann, *The Arabic Press of Egypt* (London: Luzac, 1899), 7.

70. On the wages of factory workers, see FO 371/450/16798, Gorst to Grey, Cairo, 8 May 1908.

71. Since one Egyptian pound, or one hundred piasters, was roughly equivalent to five dollars at exchange rates in the early 1900s, one issue of a women's journal would have been approximately twenty-five to thirty cents. See Charles Issawi, "Asymmetrical Development and Transport in Egypt, 1800–1914," in *Beginnings of Modernization in the Middle East: The Nineteenth Century,* ed. William R. Polk and Richard L. Chambers (Chicago: University of Chicago Press, 1968), 383.

72. *Fatat al-Nil* 1, no. 3 (1332/1914): 119.

73. *Al-Sayyidat wa'l-Banat* 1, no. 12 (1904): back page.

74. See *al-Jins al-Latif* 8, no. 6 (1915): 223; *al-'Afaf* 2, no. 63 (9 June 1914): 7.

75. See, e.g., *Anis al-Jalis* 4, no. 6 (1901): back pages.

76. *Fatat al-Nil* 1, no. 3 (1332/1914): 120.

77. *Al-Sayyidat wa'l-Banat* 1, no. 9 (1903): 259; *al-'Afaf* 1, no. 15 (17 Feb. 1911): 4.

78. Philippe de Tarrazi, *Ta'rikh al-Sihafa al-'Arabiyya* (Beirut: al-Matba'a al-Amirikaniyya, 1933), 4:326–27.

79. Wahida Minkunna, "Fi Sabil al-Ruqiyy," *al-Jins al-Latif* 4, no. 4 (1911): 100–105; Wahida Ukhra, "Nahnu wa'l-Ruqiyy," *al-Jins al-Latif* 4, no. 5 (1911): 133–36.

80. Sulayman al-Salimi, "Ila Mudir al-Busta al-'Amm," *al-'Afaf* 1, no. 29 (29 June 1911): 15.

81. See, e.g., Malaka Sa'd, "Kalimat Shukr wa-'Itab," *al-Jins al-Latif* 3, no. 4 (1910): 109.

82. Sulayman al-Salimi, "Madame Bustani," *al-'Afaf* 1, no. 3 (18 Nov. 1910): 4.

83. Bahiya Faraghli, "al-Madrasa al-Wataniyya," *Anis al-Jalis* 4, no. 7 (1901): 739–40.

84. *Revue du Monde Musulmane* 1, no. 2 (1906): 296.

85. *Al-Sayyidat wa'l-Banat* 1, no. 8 (1903): 254; vol. 1, no. 9 (1903): 279; vol. 2, no. 7 (1906): 183; vol. 2, no. 8 (1906): 223; vol. 2, no. 9 (1906): 263.

86. Sarah al-Mihiyya, "al-Tadbir al-Manzili," *Fatat al-Nil* 2, no. 3 (1333/1915): 98.

87. Sulayman al-Salimi, "al-Tazwir al-Barid," *al-'Afaf* 1, no. 27 (19 May 1911): 15; Alexandra Avierino, "Huquq al-Mar'a al-Muslima," *Anis al-Jalis* 1, no. 6 (1898): 161.

88. *Anis al-Jalis* 5, no. 2 (1902) through vol. 6, no. 2 (1903).

89. "Al-Mar'a Didduha wa-La-ha," *al-'Afaf* 1, no. 31 (25 June 1911): 2; Malak Amin, "Ila al-Katib Didd al-Mar'a," *al-'Afaf* 1, no. 34 (4 Aug. 1911): 8–9.
90. *Al-Sa'ada* 3, no. 2 (1904): 36.
91. Ibnat al-Nil, "al-Zawaj," *al-'Afaf* 1, no. 4 (2 Dec. 1910): 2–3.
92. See, e.g., Warda al-Yaziji, "Shukr wa-I'tidhar," *Fatat al-Sharq* 1, no. 3 (1906): 84–85; "I'lan," *al-Fatah* 1, no. 10 (1894): 434.
93. *Al-Sayyidat wa'l-Banat* 2, no. 1 (1904): 22; *al-Sayyidat wa'l-Banat* 1, no. 11 (1904): 336–38.

Chapter 5. The Rights of Woman

1. See, e.g., Muhja Suqi, "Huquq al-Mar'a," *al-Fatah* 1, no. 6 (1893): 251.
2. Huda Lutfi, "Manners and Customs of Fourteenth-Century Cairene Women: Female Anarchy versus Male Shar'i Order in Muslim Prescriptive Treatises," in *Women in Middle Eastern History: Shifting Boundaries in Sex and Gender,* ed. Nikki R. Keddie and Beth Baron (New Haven: Yale University Press, 1991), 99–121.
3. For examples of different typologies used to categorize the intellectual trends of this period, see Jamal Mohammed Ahmed, *The Intellectual Origins of Egyptian Nationalism* (London: Oxford University Press, 1960); M. A. Zaki Badawi, *The Reformers of Egypt* (London: Croom Helm, 1976); Hisham Sharabi, *Arab Intellectuals and the West: The Formative Years, 1875–1914* (Baltimore: Johns Hopkins University Press, 1970).
4. Jacob Landau, *Studies in the Arab Theater and Cinema* (Philadelphia: University of Pennsylvania Press, 1958), 74; Albert Hourani, *The Emergence of the Modern Middle East* (London: Macmillan, 1981), 117–18 nn.75–76; J. Heyworth-Dunne, *An Introduction to the History of Education in Modern Egypt* (London: Luzac, 1938), 375.
5. Byron D. Cannon, "Nineteenth-Century Arabic Writings on Women and Society: The Interim Role of the Masonic Press in Cairo—(al-Lata'if, 1885–1895)," *International Journal of Middle East Studies* 17 (1985): 463–84; Nadia Farag, "al-Muqtataf, 1876–1900: A Study of the Influence of Victorian Thought on Modern Arabic Thought" (D.Phil. diss., Oxford University, 1969), 186; Labiba Hashim, "Anisa Salima Rashid," *Fatat al-Sharq* 6, no. 9 (1912): 349.
6. Thomas Philipp, *The Syrians in Egypt, 1725–1975* (Stuttgart: Franz Steiner Verlag, 1985), 84.

7. Daniel Panzac, "The Population of Egypt in the Nineteenth Century," *Asian and African Studies* 21 (1987): 31.
8. Rosa Antun, " 'Awa'iduna al-Dhamima," *al-Sayyidat wa'l-Banat* 1, no. 7 (1903): 195.
9. Rosa Antun, " 'Awa'iduna al-Dhamima," *al-Sayyidat wa'l-Banat* 2, no. 3 (1905): 80; Labiba Hashim, "Sayyida badalan min 'Aqila," *Fatat al-Sharq* 6, no. 1 (1911): 14–16.
10. Hind Nawfal, "Idah wa-Iltimas wa-Istismah," *al-Fatah* 1, no. 1 (1892): 3, 6; see also idem, "Misr," *al-Fatah* 1, no. 5 (1893): 194–98.
11. Thomas Philipp, "Women in the Historical Perspective of an Early Arab Modernist (Gurgi Zaidan)," *Die Welt des Islams* 18 (1977–1978): 65–83.
12. FO 407/100, no. 53, Baring to Salisbury, 8 June 1890, p. 61; see also FO 407/100, no. 26, Baring to Salisbury, Cairo, 25 Apr. 1890, pp. 31–35.
13. Zachary Lockman, "The Egyptian Nationalist Movement and the Syrians in Egypt," *Immigrants and Minorities* 3 (1984): 233–51.
14. Labiba Hashim, "al-Mar'atan," *Fatat al-Sharq* 8, no. 4 (1914): 144.
15. Jurji Niqula Baz, "Majallat al-Nisa'," *Fatat Lubnan* 1, no. 1 (1914): 8.
16. Zaynab Fawwaz, *al-Durr al-Manthur fi Tabaqat Rabbat al-Khudur* (Cairo: al-Matba'a al-Kubra al-Amiriyya bi-Bulaq, 1312/1894), title page.
17. 'Umar Rida Kahhala, *A'lam al-Nisa' fi 'Alamay al-'Arab wa'l-Islam* (Beirut: Mu'assasat al-Risala, 1977), 2:82; Khayr al-Din al-Zirikli, *al-A'lam: Qamus Tarajim li-Ashhar al-Rijal wa'l-Nisa' min al-'Arab wa'l-Musta'ribin wa'l-Mustashriqin* (Beirut: Dar al-'Ilm, 1980), 3:67; Anwar Jundi, *Adab al-Mar'a al-'Arabiyya* (Cairo: Matba'at al-Risala, n.d.), 75–77; Zaynab Fawwaz, *al-Rasa'il al-Zaynabiyya* (1906; rpt., Cairo: al-Matba'a al-Mutawassita, 1915).
18. Nawfal, "Idah," 3.
19. Martin Hartmann, "La Femme dans l'Islam," *Le Lotus* 1, no. 6 (1901): 316–17.
20. Alexandra Averino, "Kitab Tahrir al-Mar'a," *Anis al-Jalis* 2, no. 5 (1899): 192; idem, "Tahrir al-Mar'a," *Anis al-Jalis* 2, no. 11 (1899): 406–11; idem, "Qasim Bey Amin—al-Mar'a al-Jadida," *Anis al-Jalis* 4, no. 1 (1901): 501–6; idem, "La Femme nouvelle," *Le Lotus* 1, no. 1 (1901): 18; idem, "La Femme nouvelle," *Le Lotus* 1, no. 2 (1901): 88.
21. Labiba Hashim, "al-Nisa' al-Sharqiyyat," *Fatat al-Sharq* 1, no. 4 (1907): 113.
22. These included Jurji Niqula Baz's *al-Hasna'* (Beirut, 1909), Mary 'Abduh 'Ajami's *al-'Arus* (Damascus, 1910), and Salima Rashid's *Fatat Lubnan* (Beirut, 1914).

23. See *al-Mar'a* 1, no. 2 (1893); Hashim, "al-Mar'atan," 144; Widad 'Asani, "al-Nahda al-Nisa'iyya," *Fatat Lubnan* 1, no. 6 (1914): 125; 'Anbara Salam al-Khalidi, *Jawla fi'l-Dhikrayat bayna Lubnan wa-Filastin* (Beirut: Dar al-Nahar li'l-Nashr, 1978), 64.

24. Salama Musa, *The Education of Salamah Musa,* trans. L.O.S. Schuman (Leiden: E. J. Brill, 1961), 54–56, 66, 29; (in Arabic) idem, *Tarbiyat Salama Musa* (Cairo: Lajnat al-Ta'lif wa'l-Tarjama wa'l-Nashr, 1958); Marqus Fahmi, *al-Mar'a fi'l-Sharq* (Cairo: Matba'at al-Ta'lif, 1894). See also Ibrahim A. Ibrahim, "Salama Musa: An Essay on Cultural Alienation," *Middle Eastern Studies* 15 (1979): 346–57; Vernon Egger, *A Fabian in Egypt: Salamah Musa and the Professional Classes in Egypt, 1909–1939* (New York: University Press of America, 1986).

25. See Beth Baron, "The Making and Breaking of Marital Bonds in Modern Egypt," in *Women in Middle Eastern History,* ed. Keddie and Baron, 280; idem, "Unveiling in Early Twentieth Century Egypt: Practical and Symbolic Considerations," *Middle Eastern Studies* 25 (1989): 379.

26. Malaka Sa'd, "al-Mar'a fi Misr," *al-Jins al-Latif* 1, no. 2 (1908): 38–39.

27. Munira 'Atiya Suriyal, "al-Mar'a al-Misriyya," *al-Jins al-Latif* 3, no. 10 (1911): 279–80.

28. Malaka Sa'd, "Ya Fatat al-Yawm Qumi," *al-Jins al-Latif* 12, no. 1 (1919): 11–12.

29. Muhammad 'Imara ascribes several chapters in Amin's *Tahrir al- Mar'a* to 'Abduh. See Muhammad 'Abduh, *al-A'mal al-Kamila li'l-Imam Muhammad 'Abduh,* ed. Muhammad 'Imara (Cairo: al-Mu'assasa al-'Arabiyya li'l-Dirasa wa'l-Nashr, 1972), 2:84, 105, 107, 116; Afaf Lutfi al-Sayyid, *Egypt and Cromer: A Study in Anglo-Egyptian Relations* (New York: Praeger, 1969), 187.

30. On Muhammad 'Abduh, see Charles C. Adams, *Islam and Modernism in Egypt: A Study of the Modern Reform Movement Inaugurated by Muhammad 'Abduh* (London: Oxford University Press, 1933); Albert Hourani, *Arabic Thought in the Liberal Age, 1798–1939,* 2d ed. (Cambridge: Cambridge University Press, 1983), 130–60; Elie Kedourie, *Afghani and 'Abduh: An Essay on Religious Unbelief and Political Activism in Modern Islam* (London: Frank Cass, 1966); Malcolm H. Kerr, *Islamic Reform* (Berkeley: University of California Press, 1966).

31. Moustafa Abdel Razek, "L'Influence de la femme dans la vie du Cheikh Mohamed Abdou," *L'Egytienne* 4, no. 40 (1928): 2–5.

32. See, e.g., Firdaus Tawfiq, *Khawatir wa-Sawanih* (Cairo: Matba'at Misr, 1919).

33. Shajarat al-Durr, "al-Talaq wa-Ta'addud al-Zawjat," *Anis al-Jalis* 1, no. 7 (1898): 203–6; Shajarat al-Durr, "Mujmal Hayat al-Nisa'," *Anis al-Jalis* 1, no. 6 (1898): 176–79.

34. See, e.g., "Bahth ma'a Bahithat al-Badiya," *al-'Afaf* 1, no. 30 (16 June 1911): 14.

35. Bahithat al-Badiya [Malak Hifni Nasif], *al-Nisa'iyyat* (Cairo: Matba'at al-Jarida, 1910).

36. See, e.g., Ihsan Ahmad, "Hadiqat al-Ghawani," *al-'Afaf* 1, no. 31 (26 June 1911): 5.

37. Fatima Rashid, "al-Mar'a wa-Huququha fi'l-Islam," *Tarqiyat al-Mar'a* 1, no. 10 (1326/1908): 146.

38. Deniz Kandiyoti, "Islam and Patriarchy: A Comparative Perspective," in *Women in Middle Eastern History,* ed. Keddie and Baron, 23–42.

39. See Nikki R. Keddie, "Western Rule versus Western Values: Suggestions for Comparative Study of Asian Intellectual History," *Diogenes* 26 (1959): 71–96.

40. Fatima Rashid, "Khutba," *Tarqiyat al-Mar'a* 1, no. 2 (1326/1908): 19.

41. Ibid., 17–21.

42. Fatima Rashid, "Kalima 'an al-Hala al-Hadira," *Tarqiyat al-Mar'a* 1, no. 5 (1326/1908): 76; idem, "al-Hijab," *Tarqiyat al-Mar'a* 1, no. 6 (1326/1908): 84.

43. Sarah al-Mihiyya, "Qata'tu," *al-'Afaf* 1, no. 5 (2 Dec. 1910): 2; see also idem, "al-Mar'a wa'l-Zina," *al-'Afaf* 1, no. 30 (17 June 1911): 11.

44. See, e.g., Fatima Rashid, "Yaqzat al-Mar'a al-Sharqiyya," *Tarqiyat al-Mar'a* 1, no. 11 (1326/1909): 161–65.

45. See, e.g., Sundus 'Abd al-Rahman, "Khutba," *Tarqiyat al-Mar'a* 1, no. 8 (1326/1908): 118.

46. Firdaus Kamil, "Athar Qasim fi Wadi al-Qamar," *al-'Afaf* 2, no. 54 (11 Mar. 1914): 7.

47. See Leila Ahmed, "Early Feminist Movements in the Middle East," in *Muslim Women,* ed. Freda Hussain (New York: St. Martin's, 1984), 121–22.

48. Juan Ricardo Cole, "Feminism, Class, and Islam in Turn-of-the-Century Egypt," *International Journal of Middle East Studies* 13 (1981): 387–407.

49. Sa'd, *Rabbat al-Dar,* 113.

50. Charles Smith, *Islam and the Search for Social Order in Modern Egypt: A Biography of Muhammad Husayn Haykal* (Albany: State University of New York Press, 1983), 30.

51. Labiba Hashim, *Kitab fi'l-Tarbiya* (Cairo: Matba'at al-Ma'arif, 1911), 87; see also idem, *al-Hilal* (June 1895): 82.

52. Alexandra Avierino, "Mushkilat al-Zawaj," *Anis al-Jalis* 5, no. 12 (1902): 1252.

53. Fatima Rashid, "Muhadatha Jalila," *Tarqiyat al-Mar'a* 1, no. 4 (1326/ 1908): 49.

54. Alexandra Avierino, "La Femme nouvelle," *Le Lotus* 1, no. 2 (1901): 88.

55. Labiba Hashim, "al-Umm wa-Rijal al-Mustaqbal," *Fatat al-Sharq* 2, no. 6 (1908): 209–11.

56. See, e.g, Nabawiyya Musa, *al-Mar'a wa'l-'Amal* (Alexandria: al-Matba'a al-Wataniyya, 1920), 37; Hashim, "al-Mar'atan," 143; Malaka Sa'd, "Madame Curie," *al-Jins al-Latif* 4, no. 8 (1912); idem, "Maria Mitchell," *al-Jins al-Latif* 12, no. 2 (1919); *al-Sa'ada* 1, no. 1 (1902): 12.

57. Nasif, *al-Nisa'iyyat,* 101–2.

58. Sarah al-Mihiyya, "al-Muqaddima," *Fatat al-Nil* 1, no. 1 (1332/1913): 5; Alexandra Avierino, "al-Sihafa al-Misriyya," *Anis al-Jalis* 6, no. 4 (1903): 1387; Labiba Hashim in Philippe de Tarrazi, *Ta'rikh al-Sihafa al-'Arabiyya* (Beirut: al-Matba'a al-Adabiyya, 1913), 1:17.

59. Fatima al-Kafrawiyya, "al-Rajul wa'l-Mar'a," *al-'Afaf* 1, no. 19 (17 Mar. 1911): 2–3; Nasif, *al-Nisa'iyyat,* 96; see also Salma Muhammad al-Ridawiyya, "al-'Adat al-Sayyi'a," *Fatat al-Nil* 1, no. 6 (1332/1914): 240–45; idem, "Ta'lim al-Banat," *Fatat al-Nil* 1, no. 2 (1332/1913): 66–68.

60. Amina Z., "Bab al-Ibar," *al-Sufur* 1, no. 44 (31 Mar. 1916): 5.

61. Earl of Cromer, *Modern Egypt* (London: Macmillan, 1908), 134. Similar remarks were made upon his leaving Egypt in 1907.

62. Alexandra Avierino, "al-Mar'a al-Misriyya wa-Istiqlal Misr," *Anis al-Jalis* 10, nos. 11–12 (1907): 351–56.

63. Fatima 'Aliya, "Shahirat al-Nisa'," *Fatat al-Sharq* 1, no. 6 (1907): 161–63.

64. Labiba Hashim, "Shahirat al-Nisa'," *Fatat al-Sharq* 2, no. 3 (1907): 81–82.

65. *Fatat al-Sharq* 2, no. 4 (1908): 145.

66. 'Abd al-Hamid Hamdi, "al-Mar'a al-Muslima," *al-Rayhana* 1, no. 1 (20 Mar. 1908): 2–5.

Chapter 6. Campaigning for Education

1. On Egyptian education under the British, see P. J. Vatikiotis, *The History of Egypt,* 3d ed. (London: Weidenfeld and Nicolson, 1985), chap. 18; Robert

Tignor, *Modernization and the British Rule in Egypt, 1882–1914* (Princeton: Princeton University Press, 1966), 319–48; Judith E. Tucker, *Women in Nineteenth-Century Egypt* (Cambridge: Cambridge University Press, 1985), 122–30; Donald M. Reid, "Educational and Career Choices of Egyptian Students, 1882–1922," *International Journal of Middle East Studies* 8 (1977): 349–77; Muhammad Abu As'ad, *Siyasat al-Ta'lim fi Misr taht al-Ihtilal al-Baritani, 1882–1922* (Cairo: Dar al-Nahda al-'Arabi, 1983).

2. Egypt, Dar al-Watha'iq al-Qawmiyya (National Archives, DW), Majlis al-Wuzara' (MW), Nizarat al-Ma'arif, A4, Yacoub Artin Pasha, 10 June 1892, "L'Enseignement des Jeunes Filles," 2, 5–6. The part of the government that dealt with education was alternatively the Ministry of Public Instruction, part of the Ministry of Public Works, and the Ministry of Education. The latter term is used here for consistency.

3. DW/MW, Artin, "L'Enseignement," 6–12.

4. DW/MW, Artin, "L'Enseignement," 8–9.

5. 'Anbara Salam al-Khalidi, *Jawla fi'l-Dhikrayat bayna Lubnan wa-Filastin* (Beirut: Dar al-Nahar li'l-Nashr, 1978), 26; Doria Shafiq, *al-Mar'a al-Misriyya* (Cairo: Matba'at al-Tawakkul, 1955), 91–92; Labiba Hashim, "Shahirat al-Nisa'," *Fatat al-Sharq* 1, no. 3 (1906): 65–67. On female education in an earlier period, see Jonathan P. Berkey, "Women and Islamic Education in the Mamluk Period," in *Women in Middle Eastern History: Shifting Boundaries in Sex and Gender,* ed. Nikki R. Keddie and Beth Baron (New Haven: Yale University Press, 1991), 143–57.

6. DW/MW, Artin, "L'Enseignement," 7; J. Heyworth-Dunne, *An Introduction to the History of Education in Modern Egypt* (London: Luzac, 1939), 14–15.

7. Salma Muhammad Ridawiyya, "Ta'lim al-Banat," *Fatat al-Nil* 1, no. 2 (1332/ 1913): 66–68.

8. See Beth Baron, "Mothers, Morality, and Nationalism in Pre-1919 Egypt," in *The Origins of Arab Nationalism,* ed. Rashid Khalidi et al. (New York: Columbia University Press, 1991), 282–83.

9. Regina 'Awwad, " 'Allimu al-Banat," *al-Sa'ada* 1, no. 4 (1902): 73; see also Alexandra Avierino, "al-Mar'a wa'l-Sharq," *Anis al-Jalis* 1, no. 1 (1898): 12–14; idem, "Ta'lim al-Fatah," *Anis al-Jalis* 1, no. 7 (1898): 193–97; idem, "Ta'lim al-Banat," *Anis al-Jalis* 1, no. 8 (1898): 245–47.

10. F. J. of Alexandria, "Kalima 'an Khutbat al-Anisa Victoria Sa'd," *al-Jins al-Latif* 9, no. 4 (1916): 139.

11. Najiya Mahmud, "al-Mar'a wa-Wujub Ta'limiha," *Tarqiyat al-Mar'a* 1, no. 5 (1326/1908): 73–75.

12. FO 407/150, no. 142, Cromer to Salisbury, Cairo, 26 Feb. 1899, "Annual Report of 1898," p. 130.

13. FO 407/157, no. 9, Cromer to Lansdowne, Cairo, 1 Mar. 1901, "Annual Report of 1900," pp. 58–59.

14. FO 407/164, no. 82, Cromer to Lansdowne, Cairo, 15 Mar. 1905, "Annual Report of 1904," p. 135.

15. FO 371/450/12686, Gorst to Grey, Cairo, 7 Mar. 1908, "Annual Report of 1907," p. 34.

16. FO 371/661/12738, Gorst to Grey, Cairo, 27 Mar. 1909, "Annual Report of 1908," p. 44.

17. FO 371/1362/15421, Kitchener to Grey, Cairo, 6 Apr. 1912, "Annual Report of 1911," pp. 25–26.

18. FO 371/1967/14817, Kitchener to Grey, Cairo, 28 Mar. 1914, "Annual Report of 1913," pp. 37–38.

19. See *Anis al-Jalis* 1, no. 10 (1898): 325–27; Tucker, *Women in Nineteenth-Century Egypt,* 129–30.

20. Timothy Mitchell cautions against seeing the kuttab, or "so-called Quran school," as a school, for "it was not the purpose of any distinct individual or institution to give organised instruction" (Timothy Mitchell, *Colonising Egypt* [Cambridge: Cambridge University Press, 1988], 87).

21. FO 407/150, no. 142, Cromer, "Annual Report of 1898," p. 130; FO 407/159, no. 32, Cromer to Lansdowne, Cairo, 21 Feb. 1902, "Annual Report of 1901," p. 70.

22. For more on this school, which essentially trained midwives in this period, see Laverne Kunkhe, "The 'Doctoress' on a Donkey: Women Health Officers in Nineteenth Century Egypt," *Clio Medica* 9 (1974): 193–205.

23. FO 371/ 1112/ 11940, Gorst to Grey, Cairo, 25 Mar. 1911, "Annual Report of 1910," pp. 54–55; FO 371/450/12686, Gorst, "Annual Report of 1907," pp. 32–34.

24. FO 371/661/12738, Gorst, "Annual Report of 1908," p. 44.

25. DW/MW, Artin, "L'Enseignement"; Heyworth-Dunne, *History of Education,* 374–75; James Williams, *Education in Egypt before British Control* (pamphlet) (Birmingham: n.p., 1939), 83.

26. DW/MW, Artin, "L'Enseignement," 1–2.

27. Hind Nawfal, "al-Madrasa al-Suyufiyya," *al-Fatah* 1, no. 2 (1893): 80.

28. FO 371/450/12686, Gorst, "Annual Report of 1907," pp. 31–32.

29. FO 407/157, no. 9, Cromer, "Annual Report of 1900," p. 58; DW/MW, Nizarat al-Ma'arif, al-Ta'lim al-Ibtida'i, A24, Ministère de L'Instruction

Publique, "Réglement de L'Examen du Certificat D'Etudes Primaires, 1905," p. 4.

30. DW/MW, Nizarat al-Ma'arif, 4A, Adly Yeghen to the Council of Ministers, Note on the "Creation des Ecoles Elémentaires Supérieres de Filles," 1; same series, Adly Yeghen, "Law Number 14," 14 June 1916.

31. FO 371/112/11940, Gorst, "Annual Report of 1910," p. 55.

32. Salama Musa, *The Education of Salamah Musa*, trans. L. O. S. Schuman (Leiden: E. J. Brill, 1961), 27. Salama and Nabawiyya Musa were not related.

33. DW, Muhafiz 'Abdin, Ta'lim 230, Ministry of Education, "Secondary Education Certification Examination," Cairo, 1907; FO 371/450/12686, Gorst, "Annual Report of 1907," p. 34.

34. Shafiq, *al-Mar'a al-Misriyya*, 92; Khayr al-Din al-Zirikli, *al-A'lam: Qamus Tarajim li-Ashhar al-Rijal wa'l-Nisa' min al-'Arab wa'l-Musta'ribin wa'l-Mustashriqin* (Beirut: Dar al-'Ilm, 1980), 8:7–8; Anwar Jundi, *Adab al-Mar'a al-'Arabiyya* (Cairo: Matba'at al-Risala, n.d.), 69–71; Nabawiyya Musa, *al-Mar'a wa'l-'Amal* (Alexandria: al-Matba'a al-Wataniyya, 1920).

35. DW/MW, Artin, "L'Enseignement," 12.

36. Heyworth-Dunn, *History of Education*, 375; DW/MW, Artin, "L'Enseignement," 4.

37. See, e.g., Mahmud Ibrahim, "Qism al-Mu'allimat al-Jadid," *Anis al-Jalis* 3, no. 10 (1900): 378–80.

38. FO 371/1638/14764, Kitchener to Grey, 22 Mar. 1913, "Annual Report of 1912," p. 30.

39. Elizabeth Cooper, *The Women of Egypt* (New York: F. A. Stokes, 1914), 201.

40. Malak Hifni Nasif, *Athar Bahithat al-Badiya*, ed. Majid al-Din Hifni Nasif and intro. Suhayr al-Qalamawi (Cairo: al-Mu'assasa al-Misriyya al-'Amma, 1962), intro.; Egypt, Wizarat al-Tarbiya wa'l-Ta'lim, Mathaf al-Tarbiya (MT), display giving a complete listing of the graduates of al-Saniyya Teachers' Training College from 1900 to 1910.

41. See MT display on education missions.

42. DW/MW, Nizarat al-Ma'arif, al-Irsaliyyat al-Misriyya, 7B4, Ahmed Mazloum to the Minister of Finance, 18 Aug. 1908; same series: 7B4, A. Hechmat to the Council of Ministers, 4 Sept. 1909; 7B4, A. Hechmat to the Council of Ministers, 24 July 1911; 7B4, J. Saba to the Council of Ministers, 23 July 1910; FO 371/1112/11940, Gorst, "Annual Report of 1910," p. 54; Cooper, *Women of Egypt*, 166.

43. *Al-Jarida* (4 Aug. 1907), cited in Mahmoud Bikheet al-Rabie, "Women

Writers and Critics in Modern Egypt, 1888–1963" (Ph.D..diss., University of London, School of Oriental and African Studies, 1965), 33; FO 371/895/47191, Cromer to Tyrell, 28 Oct. 1910.

44. M. F. H. "Irsaliyyat al-Banat li-Uruba," *al-'Afaf* 1, no. 32 (4 July 1911): 14.

45. Sulayman al-Salimi, "Ba'tha Nisa'iyya," *al-'Afaf* 2, no. 39 (3 Nov. 1911): 8.

46. Donald Malcolm Reid, *Cairo University and the Making of Modern Egypt* (Cambridge: Cambridge University Press, 1990), 51–56; 'Abd al-Mun'im al-Dusuqi al-Jami'i, *al-Jami'a al-Misriyya al-Qadima, Nash'atuha wa-Dawruha fi'l-Mujtama'*, 1908–1925 (Cairo: Dar al-Kitab al-Jami'a, 1908), 47–48. For more on this controversy, see chap. 8.

47. FO 371/1362/15421, Kitchener, "Annual Report of 1911," p. 28; FO 371/1966/16929, Kitchener to Grey, Cairo, 12 Apr. 1914, "Note on the Progress and Condition of Public Instruction in Egypt, 1913," pp. 111–16. According to the MT display on education missions, 116 girls attended foreign schools at government expense between 1901 and 1929.

48. Joel Beinin and Zachary Lockman, *Workers on the Nile* (Princeton: Princeton University Press, 1987), 167.

49. On the teaching profession, see Reid, "Educational and Career Choices"; idem, "The Rise of the Professional Organizations in Modern Egypt," *Comparative Studies in Society and History* 16 (1974): 24–57.

50. Heyworth-Dunne, *History of Education,* 310. There is some dispute on this chronology. See Samir Seikaly, "Coptic Communal Reform, 1860–1914," *Middle Eastern Studies* 6 (1970): 249. For background, see Riyad Suriyal, *al-Mujtama' al-Qibti fi Misr fi'l-Qarn al-Tasi' 'Ashara* (Cairo: Maktabat al-Muhibba, n.d.).

51. Hind Nawfal, "al-Aqbat," *al-Fatah* 1, no. 9 (1893): 359; Malaka Sa'd, "Jami'at al-Mahabba," *al-Jins al-Latif* 9, no. 2 (1916): 68–70.

52. Egypt, Ministry of Finance, *The Census of Egypt Taken in 1907* (Cairo: National Printing Dept., 1909), 98.

53. Jacob M. Landau, *Jews in Nineteenth-Century Egypt* (New York: New York University Press, 1969), 71–91; idem, "The Beginnings of Modernization in Education: The Jewish Community in Egypt as a Case Study," in *Beginnings of Modernization in the Middle East: The Nineteenth Century,* ed. William R. Polk and Richard L. Chambers (Chicago: University of Chicago Press, 1968), 299–312.

54. Ibrahim Ramzi, "Jam'iyyat Ta'lim al-Banat al-Islamiyya," *al-Mar'a fi'l-Islam* 1, no. 11 (1901): 176.

55. FO 407/150, no. 142, Cromer, "Annual Report of 1898," p. 130; Alexan-

dra Avierino, "Madrasat Husn al-Masarrat," *Anis al-Jalis* 7, no. 1 (1904): 1695; Sulayman al-Salimi, "Madaris al-Banat bi'l-Minya," *al-'Afaf* 1, no. 19 (17 Mar. 1911): 4.

56. DW/MW, Nizarat al-Ma'arif, A4, Zohra to Fakhry, 30 June 1894; see notice for a private school in *Anis al-Jalis* 2, no. 6 (1899): 244.

57. Charles Watson, *In the Valley of the Nile: A Survey of the Missionary Movement in Egypt* (New York: Fleming H. Revell, 1908), 188; Cooper, *Women of Egypt*, 361.

58. Watson, *Valley of the Nile*, 233. Watson was later instrumental in founding the American University in Cairo (Lawrence R. Murphy, *The American University in Cairo, 1919–1987* [Cairo: The American University in Cairo Press, 1987], 1–18).

59. Ibrahim Ramzi, "Ta'lim," *al-Mar'a fi'l-Islam* 1, no. 4 (1901): 63.

60. Cooper, *Women of Egypt*, 165–66; Watson, *Valley of the Nile*, 185.

61. Cooper, *Women of Egypt*, 169.

62. FO 141/817/4110, Dunlop to High Commissioner, Cairo, 27 Nov. 1916, "Note on the Desirability of Encouraging British Educational Institutions in Egypt."

63. FO 141/460/1102, Dunlop, "Principal Religious Orders of Women in Egypt"; FO 371/248/42303, J. L. Lynch, 27 Dec. 1907, "The Position of the Catholic Church, Latin and Coptic, in Egypt"; FO 141/817/4110, no. 6, "Statistics of Foreign Schools in Egypt."

64. DW/MW, al-Tawa'if wa'l-Jaliyat al-Ajnabiyya, 1B, no. 290, Rev. Andrew Watson to the minister of justice, 15 Mar. 1904; same series, no. 321, 28 May 1904.

65. Earl Elder, *Vindicating a Vision: The Story of the American Mission in Egypt, 1854–1954* (Philadelphia: United Presbyterian Church of North America, 1958), 133; Malaka Sa'd, "Kulliyyat al-Banat," *al-Jins al-Latif* 2, no. 9 (1910): 250–51; and under similar titles, vol. 6, no. 2 (1913): 63; vol. 9, no. 2 (1916): 51–54; vol. 10, no. 5 (1917): 163–64.

66. Regina 'Awwad, "Ta'lim al-Banat," *al-Sa'ada* 1, no. 10 (1902): 212.

67. Najiya Rashid, "Khatir al-Madaris al-Ajnabiyya," *Tarqiyat al-Mar'a* 1, no. 6 (1326/1908): 91–92.

68. Rosa Antun, "al-Lugha," *al-Sayyidat wa'l-Banat* 1, no. 7 (1903): 195.

69. See, e.g., Labiba Hashim, "al-Mar'a al-Sharqiyya," *Anis al-Jalis* 1, no. 5 (1898): 146–50; Regina 'Awwad, "al-Mar'a al-Mustaqbala," *al-Sa'ada* 2, nos. 7–8 (1904): 569.

70. FO 371/249/28247, Parliamentary Question, London, 15 Aug. 1907; FO 371/249/29116, Parliamentary Question, London, 22 Aug. 1907.

71. FO 371/247/8788, Dunlop, Cairo, 10 Feb. 1907, "Note with Reference to the Linguistic Basis of Instruction in the Egyptian Government Schools," annexed to the "Annual Report of 1906," pp. 113–15; FO 371/247/17626, Gorst to Grey, Cairo, 18 May 1907, Private Note; FO 371/450/12686, Gorst, "Annual Report of 1907," pp. 31–33; DW/MW, Nizarat al-Ma'arif, al-Irsaliyyat al-Misriyya, 7B4, Note from the Committee on Finances to the Council of Ministers, Cairo, 12 Aug. 1914.

72. Fatima 'Asim, "Jam'iyyat al-Nahda al-Nisa'iyya," *Fatat al-Sharq* 11, no. 5 (1916): 220; see also Rashid, "Khatir al-Madaris al-Ajnabiyya," 89.

73. DW/MW, Nizarat al-Ma'arif, al-Ta'lim al-Ibtida'i, A23, Saad Zagloul, Cairo, 2 Apr. 1907.

74. Cooper, *Women of Egypt,* 168.

75. FO 371/ 893/ 23124, Petition sent to Grey, Cairo, 20 June 1910, "The Unrest in Egypt and the Copts."

76. Cooper, *Women of Egypt,* 346.

77. FO 371/ 893/ 23124, "The Unrest in Egypt and the Copts"; DW/MW, Nizarat al-Ma'arif, al-Ta'lim al-Ibtida'i, A23, 1 Dec. 1906, table.

78. Rashid, "Khatir al-Madaris al-Ajnabiyya," 88–93, quotes p. 89.

79. 'Awwad, " 'Allimu al-Banat," 73–75; idem, "Ta'lim al-Banat," 214–16.

80. Malak Hifni Nasif, *al-Nisa'iyyat* (Cairo: Matba'at al-Jarida, 1910), 117.

81. Najib Hajj, "Madaris al-Banat wa-Ta'limuhunna," *Anis al-Jalis* 4, no. 6 (1901): 695, 691–97.

82. Regina 'Awwad, "al-Mar'a wa'l-Zawaj," *al-Sa'ada* 1, no. 5 (1902): 101.

83. FO 371/1112/11940, Gorst, "Annual Report of 1910," p. 55.

84. FO 371/1638/14764, Kitchener, "Annual Report of 1912," p. 30.

85. FO 371/1967/14817, Kitchener, "Annual Report of 1913," p. 37.

86. FO 371/1112/11940, Gorst, "Annual Report of 1910," p. 55.

87. FO 371/1638/14764, Kitchener, "Annual Report of 1912," p. 30.

88. Tucker, *Women in Nineteenth-Century Egypt,* 126.

89. See Ibid., 129–30.

Chapter 7. Rethinking Work and the Family

1. Nadia Hijab, *Womanpower: The Arab Debate on Women at Work* (Cambridge: Cambridge University Press, 1988), 10.

2. See Deniz Kandiyoti, "Islam and Patriarchy: A Comparative Perspective," *Women in Middle Eastern History: Shifting Boundaries in Sex and Gender*, ed. Nikki R. Keddie and Beth Baron (New Haven: Yale University Press, 1991), 23–42.

3. Robert L. Tignor, *State, Private Enterprise, and Economic Change in Egypt, 1918–1952* (Princeton: Princeton University Press, 1984), chap. 1; Joel Beinin and Zachary Lockman, *Workers on the Nile* (Princeton: Princeton University Press, 1987), chap. 2.

4. Judith E. Tucker, *Women in Nineteenth-Century Egypt* (Cambridge: Cambridge University Press, 1985), chap. 2.

5. Donald Quataert, "Ottoman Women, Households, and Textile Manufacturing, 1800–1914," in *Women in Middle Eastern History*, ed. Keddie and Baron, 161–76.

6. Gabriel Baer, *Studies in the Social History of Modern Egypt* (Chicago: University of Chicago Press, 1969), 161–89; Ehud R. Toledano, *The Ottoman Slave Trade and Its Suppression, 1840–1890* (Princeton: Princeton University Press, 1982), 224–27; Tucker, *Women in Nineteenth-Century Egypt*, chap. 5.

7. Fatima Rashid, "Muhadatha Jalila," *Tarqiyat al-Mar'a* 1, no. 4 (1326/1908): 49–53.

8. Fatima Rashid, "Bahth Ijtima'i," *Tarqiyat al-Mar'a* 1, no. 4 (1326/1908): 58–61; idem, "al-Mar'a wa-Huququha fi'l-Islam," *Tarqiyat al-Mar'a* 1, no. 10 (1326/1908): 146–51; idem, "Yaqzat al-Mar'a al-Sharqiyya," *Tarqiyat al-Mar'a* 1, no. 11 (1326/1909): 161–65.

9. Tucker, *Women in Nineteenth-Century Egypt*, 10–15.

10. Sarah al-Mihiyya, "al-Nisa' wa'l-'Amal," *Fatat al-Nil* 1, no. 6 (1332/1914): 245–47.

11. Ibid., 246.

12. Bahithat al-Badiya [Malak Hifni Nasif], *al-Nisa'iyyat* (Cairo: Matba'at al-Jarida, 1910), 99–100.

13. Egypt, Ministry of Finance, *The Census of Egypt Taken in 1907* (Cairo: National Printing Dept., 1909), ix, 92; idem, *The Census of Egypt Taken in 1917* (Cairo: Government Press, 1921), 2:xvii.

14. See Tucker, *Women in Nineteenth-Century Egypt*, 90. On underestimates of female labor in more recent census data and surveys, see James Toth, "Pride, Purdah, or Paychecks: What Maintains the Gender Division of Labor in Rural Egypt?" *International Journal of Middle East Studies* 23 (1991): 213–36. Interestingly, the 1917 census recognized many more female agricultural-

ists—40 percent of the total agricultural labor force—than the more recent studies cited by Toth (*Census of 1917* 2:364).

15. Egypt, Nizarat al-Maliyya, *Ta'dad Sukkan al-Qutr al-Misri 1897* (hereafter *Census of 1897*) (Cairo: al-Matba'a al-Kubra al-Amiriyya bi-Bulaq, 1898), 1:34–36. The 1897 census is generally considered the first reliable one taken in Egypt (Daniel Panzac, "The Population of Egypt in the Nineteenth Century," *Asian and African Studies* 21 [1987]: 12).

16. *Census of 1907*, 10, 163, 279–83.

17. *Census of 1917*, 2:x; FO 371/3727/98452, Lloyd, Cairo, 4 July 1919, "Native Administration in Minia." The number of conscripts in 1918 reached 106,850 (Nathan J. Brown, *Peasant Politics in Modern Egypt: The Struggle Against the State* [New Haven: Yale University Press, 1990], 198).

18. *Census of 1917*, 2:364–79.

19. See, e.g., Elizabeth Cooper, *The Women of Egypt* (New York: F. A. Stokes, 1914), 109, 192–93.

20. *Census of 1917*, 2:378.

21. Gabriel Baer, *Egyptian Guilds in Modern Times* (Jerusalem: Israel Oriental Society, 1964), 33.

22. Baer, *Egyptian Guilds*; for a different perspective on the decline of guilds, see Beinin and Lockman, *Workers on the Nile*, 32.

23. St. Antony's Private Papers, Oxford University, Nina Baird Correspondence, letter from Hilda Ridler, n.d.; FO 371/10060/6663, Egypt, "Annual Report of 1923," p. 48.

24. FO 371/450/13819, Brailsford, "The New Egypt," *Daily News* (8 Apr. 1908); FO 371/450/16798, Gorst to Grey, Cairo, 8 May 1908; FO 371/450/22948, Knight to Grey, London, 1 July 1908.

25. FO 371/450/44336, Graham to Mallet, Cairo, 12 Dec. 1908; FO 371/659/19193, Gorst to Grey, Cairo, 14 May 1909; FO 371/659/43318, Gorst to Grey, Cairo, 15 Nov. 1909; FO 371/892/11188, Gorst to Grey, Cairo, 26 Mar. 1910, "Annual Report of 1909," p. 30; Beinin and Lockman, *Workers on the Nile*, 45 n.31.

26. FO 141/466/1415, To the President of the International Association for the Repression of the White Slave Trade from Sub-Committee No. 4, Cairo, 11 Dec. 1918, pp.12–22.

27. Beinin and Lockman, *Workers on the Nile*, 205, 341, 345.

28. Baer, *Social History*, 187.

29. *Census of 1897*, 1:35; *Census of 1917*, 2:378.

30. Najib Mahfuz, *Bayn al-Qasrayn* (1956; rpt., Cairo: Dar Misr, 1979), 386, 355–64, 263–67; Naguib Mahfouz, *Palace Walk,* trans. William Maynard Hutchins and Olive E. Kenny (New York: Doubleday, 1990), 408, 375–84, 275–79. On the use of this novel as a source for the study of Egyptian history, see Israel Gershoni, "Between Ottomanism and Egyptianism: The Evolution of 'National Sentiment' in the Cairene Middle Class as Reflected in Najib Mahfuz's 'Bayn al-Qasrayn,'" in *Studies in Islamic Society,* ed. Gabriel R. Warburg and Gad G. Gilbar (Haifa: Haifa University Press, 1984), 233–36.

31. Tucker, *Women in Nineteenth-Century Egypt,* 92–93; Sulayman al-Salimi, "Safalat Ajzaji," *al-'Afaf* 2, no. 67 (7 Sept. 1914): 6; Zakiya al-Kafrawiyya, "Ma wara'a al-Khudur," *al-'Afaf* 1, no. 19 (17 Mar. 1911): 2.

32. Cooper, *Women of Egypt,* 192–93.

33. Malaka Sa'd, *Rabbat al-Dar* (Cairo: Matba'at al-Tawfiq, 1915), 97–99.

34. FO 141/466/1415, Sub-Committee No. 4, Cairo, 11 Dec. 1918, pp. 18, 14–15.

35. Sarah al-Mihiyya, "al-Tadbir al-Manzili," *Fatat al-Nil* 2, no. 3 (1333/1915): 98. On the pay of female factory workers, see n.24.

36. Alexandra Avierino, "Istilfat Nazar," *Anis al-Jalis* 1, no. 4 (1898): 118–19; see also idem, "Tadbir al-Manzil," *Anis al-Jalis* 2, no. 7 (1899): 277–80.

37. Rosa Antun, "al-Khadimat," *al-Sayyidat wa'l-Banat* 1, no. 8 (1903): 232.

38. *Al-Sa'ada* 1, no. 8 (1902): 169.

39. Sulayman al-Salimi, "al-Sayyidat wa'l-Khadimat," *al-'Afaf* 2, no. 52 (9 Feb. 1914): 7; *al-'Afaf* 2, no. 64 (19 June 1914): 6.

40. See, e.g., Hind Nawfal, "Bab Tadbir al-Manzil," *al-Fatah* 1, no. 4 (1893): 166–67.

41. Kathryn Shevelow described the feminizing mission of the early English women's journals in this way in her *Women and Print Culture: The Construction of Femininity in the Early Periodical* (London: Routledge, 1989), 190. Some of the themes that emerged during this period echoed the cult of domesticity of mid-nineteenth-century America. See Kathryn Kish Sklar, *Catharine Beecher: A Study in American Domesticity* (New Haven: Yale University Press, 1973); Mary Ryan, "The Empire of the Mother: American Writing About Domesticity, 1830–1860," *Women and History* 2 (1982).

42. "Tadbir al-Manzil," *al-Manar* 1, no. 13 (1316/1898): 235; "Tadbir al-Manzil al-Hadith," *Fatat al-Sharq* 5, no. 4 (1911): 149; Malaka Sa'd, *Rabbat al-Dar.* Home economics was translated literally as *iqtisad al-manzil* in an Arabic

women's journal produced in the United States by 'Afifa Karam, who was obviously influenced by the American home economics movement ('Afifa Karam, "Iqtisad al-Manzil," *al-'Alam al-Jadid al-Nisa'i* 3, no. 10 [1912]).

43. Labiba Hashim, "Ta'lim al-Banat," *Fatat al-Sharq* 5, no. 2 (1910): 45.
44. Sa'd, *Rabbat al-Dar,* 159, 151–279.
45. Ibid., 17.
46. A. F. of Cairo, "Ma Arjuhu," *al-Sufur* 6, no. 262 (28 Jan. 1921): 2–3.
47. Labiba Hashim, *Kitab fi'l-Tarbiya* (Cairo: Matba'at al-Ma'arif), 91; Alexandra Avierino, "Tadbir al-Manzil," *Anis al-Jalis* 3, no. 1 (1900): 33–35.
48. Sa'd, *Rabbat al-Dar,* 92–94; al-Mihiyya, "al-Tadbir al-Manzili."
49. Sa'd, *Rabbat al-Dar,* 15–16.
50. Huda Shaarawi, *Harem Years: The Memoirs of an Egyptian Feminist, 1879–1924,* trans. and intro. Margot Badran (London: Virago, 1986), 69.
51. Cooper, *Women of Egypt,* 121, 123.
52. Sa'd, *Rabbat al-Dar,* 113, 104–50.
53. Al-Mihiyya, "al-Tadbir al-Manzili," 98; Esther Moyal, "Mamlakat al-Mar'a," *al-Hasna'* 1, no. 2 (1909): 52–55.
54. See Avner Gil'adi, *Children of Islam: Concepts of Childhood in Medieval Muslim Society* (London: Macmillan, 1992).
55. Najiya Mahmud, "Huquq al-Mar'a wa'l-Ta'lim," *Tarqiyat al-Mar'a* 1, no. 3 (1326/1908): 40.
56. "Tadbir Sihhat al-Hamil wa'l-Nafsa' wa'l-Tifl," *al-Jins al-Latif* 1, no. 6 (1908): 194; "Tadbir Sihhat," *Fatat al-Sharq* 3, no. 4 (1909): 145–46; "Tadbir Sihhat," *al-Manar* 13, no. 4 (1910): 291; "Nasa'ih li'l-Ummahat," *al-Jins al-Latif* 3, no. 4 (1910): 107.
57. Qasim Amin, *al-Mar'a al-Jadida* (Cairo: Matba'at al-Sha'b, 1900), 158.
58. Al-Sayyid Qasim, "Nasiha li'l-'A'ilat," *al-Rayhana* 1, no. 3 (1325/1907): 81.
59. FO 371/3203/177595, Appendix 11, Elgood, Cairo, 2 July 1918, "Medical Aid for Women and Children"; see "I'yadat al-Duktur Wadi' Saydanawi," *al-Sa'ada* 3, no. 1 (1904), back cover.
60. FO 371/3203/177595, Appendix 17, Goodman, 27 Jan. 1913, "Note on Midwives"; FO 371/3728/114805, Mohamed Ali to Balfour, London, 9 Aug. 1919; *Census of 1907,* 282; Laverne Kuhnke, "The 'Doctoress' on a Donkey: Women Health Officers in Nineteenth Century Egypt," *Clio Medica* 9 (1974): 193–205.
61. See "al-Sihha fi'l-Jins al-Latif," *al-Fatah* 1, no. 5 (1893): 216–18; *al-'Afaf* 1, no. 2 (11 Nov. 1910): 3; Malak Hifni Nasif, *Athar Bahithat al-Badiya,* ed.

Majid al-Din Hifni Nasif (Cairo: al-Mu'assasa al-Misriyya al-'Amma, 1962), 162; 'Aliya Muhammad, "Talibat Madrasat al-Tibb," *al-'Afaf* 2, no. 65 (10 July 1914).

62. Cooper, *Women of Egypt*, 110.

63. FO 371/3203/177595, Appendix 11, Elgood, Cairo, 2 July 1918.

64. FO 371/892/11188, Gorst, "Annual Report of 1909," p. 34; FO 371/1112/11940, Gorst to Grey, Cairo, 25 Mar. 1911, "Annual Report of 1910," p. 43.

65. Rosa Antun, "'Awa'iduna al-Dhamima," *al-Sayyidat wa'l-Banat* 1, no. 6 (1903): 161–66; idem, "Akhbar al-Sayyidat," *al-Sayyidat wa'l-Banat* 2, no. 6 (1905): 172; Alexandra Avierino, "Mudawat al-Atfal," *Anis al-Jalis* 1, no. 5 (1898): 134–37.

66. Afaf Lutfi al-Sayyid Marsot, "The Revolutionary Gentlewomen in Egypt," in *Women in the Muslim World*, ed. Lois Beck and Nikki Keddie (Cambridge: Harvard University Press, 1978), 265.

67. Quoted in Soha Abdel Kader, *Egyptian Women in a Changing Society, 1899–1987* (Boulder: Lynne Rienner, 1988), 26.

68. Rosa Antun, "al-Murdi'," *al-Sayyidat wa'l-Banat* 1, no. 8 (1903): 234.

69. Regina 'Awwad, "al-Rada'a wa'l-Ta'rikh," *al-Sa'ada* 1, no. 2 (1902): 36–37; idem, "al-Rada'a wa-Afkar al-Kataba," *al-Sa'ada* 1, no. 2 (1902): 37–38; Esther Moyal, "Tabi' Mawani' al-Rada'a," *al-'A'ila* 1, no. 17 (26 Dec. 1899): 266–69.

70. Shaarawi, *Harem Years*, 86.

71. For legal background on this topic as well as information on premodern practices, see B. F. Musallam, *Sex and Society in Islam: Birth Control before the Nineteenth Century* (Cambridge: Cambridge University Press, 1983).

72. FO 371/3203/177595, Appendix 15, Oulton, "Note on the Hospital Section."

73. "Ghaflat al-Aba'," *al-'Afaf* 2, no. 41 (1 Dec. 1911): 8.

74. Shajarat al-Durr, "Mujmal Hayat al-Nisa'," *Anis al-Jalis* 1, no. 6 (1898): 177.

75. Sa'd, *Rabbat al-Dar*, 31.

76. *Census of 1917*, 2:675, 677.

77. Alan Duben argues that family size was exaggerated by contemporary observers in Istanbul. Using the original main rosters of the Ottoman census of 1907, he reconstructs a picture of household composition in the Ottoman capital, providing important observations on age at marriage, family size, and occurrence of multi-generational households. See Alan Duben, "Household Formation in Late Ottoman Istanbul," *International Journal of*

Middle East Studies 22 (1990): 419–35. For comparison with an Arab town in an earlier period, see Judith E. Tucker, "Ties that Bound: Women and Family in Eighteenth and Nineteenth Century Nablus," in *Women in Middle Eastern History*, ed. Keddie and Baron, 243.

78. Regina 'Awwad, "al-Nisa' fi'l-Sharq," *al-Sa'ada* 1, no. 4 (1902): 75–76.
79. Hashim, *Kitab fi'l-Tarbiya*.
80. Rosa Antun, "al-Ziyarat," *al-Sayyidat wa'l-Banat* 1, no. 7 (1903): 194; idem, "Taslim al-Awlad li'l-Khadam," *al-Sayyidat wa'l-Banat* 1, no. 8 (1903): 233–34.
81. Madame Ibrahim Yusuf, "al-Bab al-Tibbi," *al-Jins al-Latif* 3, no. 4 (1910): 102–3; "Une mère désolée," *Le Lotus* 1, no. 9 (1901): 536; "Jeune mère inquiète," *Le Lotus* 1, no. 10 (1902): 600.
82. Regina 'Awwad, "Ahamm Asbab al-'Adwa," *al-Sa'ada* 1, no. 9 (1902): 195; *al-Sa'ada* 1, no. 3 (1902): 56.
83. Khadija Rashad, "Laysat al-Tarbiya Qasira 'ala Nasa'ih," *al-Rayhana* 1, no. 3 (1325/1907): 77–80; Tifla Kabira (a big child), "La'b Baytiyya li'l-Atfal," *al-Jins al-Latif* 9, no. 9 (1917): 342–43.
84. Labiba Hashim, "al-Umm wa-Rijal al-Mustaqbal," *Fatat al-Sharq* 2, no. 6 (1908): 209–11; Rosa Antun, "Tafdil al-Ghulam 'ala al-Ibna," *al-Sayyidat wa'l-Banat* 1, no. 9 (1903): 265–67; Sarah al-Mihiyya, "al-Tamth," *Fatat al-Nil* 1, no. 3 (1332/1914): 101–3.
85. Edward William Lane, *An Account of the Manners and Customs of the Modern Egyptians* (3d ed. 1842; rpt., London: Ward and Lock, 1890), 143. Although Lane is generally considered reliable, Duben points out the potential pitfalls of this sort of evidence on age at marriage (Duben, "Household Formation," 420–21).
86. Nasif, *al-Nisa'iyyat*, 32.
87. Anna Y. Thompson, "The Woman Question in Egypt," *The Moslem World* 4, no. 3 (1914): 266; FO 141/466/1415, McBarnet, "The New Penal Code," from *L'Egypte Contemporaine*, no. 46 (1919): 382–86.
88. J. N. D. Anderson, "Recent Developments in Shari'a Law III," *The Muslim World* 41 (1951): 113–15; John L. Esposito, *Women in Muslim Family Law* (Syracuse, N.Y.: Syracuse University Press, 1982), 52.
89. *Census of 1907*, 92; *Census of 1917*, 2: diagram no. 4.
90. For a fuller discussion of this, see Beth Baron, "The Making and Breaking of Marital Bonds in Modern Egypt," in *Women in Middle Eastern History*, ed. Keddie and Baron, 275–91.

91. Shajarat al-Durr, "al-Talaq wa-Ta'addud al-Zawjat," *Anis al-Jalis* 1, no. 7 (1898): 206; see also, "al-Mar'a al-Muslima fi Misr," *Anis al-Jalis* 5, no. 2 (1902): 980–81.

92. Sulayman al-Salimi, "Rufaqa' bi'l-Qawarir," *al-'Afaf* 1, no. 36 (17 Oct. 1911): 7.

93. *Census of 1907*, 91.

94. Shajarat al-Durr, "al-Talaq," 203–6.

95. See, e.g., Sulayman al-Salimi, "Ittaqi Allah Ya Rajul," *al-'Afaf* 1, no. 29 (9 June 1911): 15; idem, "Rufaqa' bi'l-Qawarir"; idem, "La Tuharrijuha," *al-'Afaf* 2, no. 64 (19 June 1914): 6; "Qatil Zawjatihi," *al-Jins al-Latif* 12, no. 3 (1919): 99–104.

96. Anderson, "Recent Developments V," 271–88.

97. 'Aliya, "al-Mar'a al-Misriyya," *al-Sufur* 5, no. 205 (19 June 1919): 3.

98. Nabawiyya Musa, *al-Mar'a wa'l-'Amal* (Alexandria: al-Matba'a al-Watan-iyya, 1920). For a look at Nabawiyya Musa in the context of interwar intellectuals, see Giora Eliraz, "Egyptian Intellectuals and Women's Emancipation, 1919–1939," *Asian and African Studies* 16 (1982): 95–120.

Chapter 8. The Advent of Associations

1. See Gabriel Baer, *Egyptian Guilds in Modern Times* (Jerusalem: Israel Oriental Society, 1964); F. De Jong, *Turuq and Turuq-Linked Institutions in Nineteenth Century Egypt* (Leiden: E. J. Brill, 1978).

2. Judith E. Tucker, *Women in Nineteenth-Century Egypt* (Cambridge: Cambridge University Press, 1985), 104–15; Afaf Lutfi al-Sayyid Marsot, "The Revolutionary Gentlewomen in Egypt," in *Women in the Muslim World,* ed. Lois Beck and Nikki Keddie (Cambridge: Harvard University Press, 1978), 261–76.

3. For a broader conceptualization of politics, see Joan Wallach Scott, *Gender and the Politics of History* (New York: Columbia University Press, 1988).

4. Hind Nawfal, "Idah wa-Iltimas wa-Istismah," *al-Fatah* 1, no. 1 (1892): 2.

5. Jacob M. Landau, *Parties and Parliaments in Egypt* (Tel Aviv: Israel Press, 1953), 45, 50.

6. On female politics on the popular level, see Judith Tucker, "Women and State in Nineteenth-Century Egypt: Insurrectionary Women," *Middle East Report* (Jan.-Feb. 1986): 9–13.

7. Baer, *Social History,* chap. 5.

8. Thomas Philipp, *The Syrians in Egypt, 1725–1975* (Stuttgart: Franz Steiner Verlag, 1985), 123–35.

9. Samir Seikaly, "Coptic Communal Reform: 1860–1914," *Middle Eastern Studies* 6 (1970): 252; P. J. Vatikiotis, *The History of Egypt*, 3d ed. (London: Weidenfeld and Nicolson, 1985), 197.

10. Naguib Mahfouz, *The History of Medical Education in Egypt* (Cairo: Government Press of Bulaq, 1935), 106.

11. Huda Shaarawi, *Harem Years: The Memoirs of an Egyptian Feminist, 1879–1924*, trans. and intro. Margot Badran (London: Virago, 1986), 94.

12. On the use of nationalist rhetoric to legitimize charitable endeavors, see Beth Baron, "Mothers, Morality, and Nationalism in Pre-1919 Egypt," in *The Origins of Arab Nationalism*, ed. Rashid Khalidi et al. (New York: Columbia University Press, 1991), 271–88, esp. 280–81.

13. Ahmad 'Abd Ar-Raziq, *La femme au temps des mamlouks en Egypte* (Cairo: Institut Français d'Archéologie Orientale, 1973), 19–27; Carl F. Petry, "Class Solidarity versus Gender Gain: Women as Custodians of Property in Later Medieval Egypt," *Women in Middle Eastern History: Shifting Boundaries in Sex and Gender*, ed. Nikki R. Keddie and Beth Baron (New Haven: Yale University Press, 1991), 122–42.

14. FO 371/247/8788, Cromer to Grey, Cairo, 3 Mar. 1907, "Annual Report of 1906," p. 97; *al-'Afaf* 1, no. 13 (3 Feb. 1912): 4; on the grant to the university, see n.75 below.

15. There is some dispute on how often women managed waqfs. Judith Tucker reports for nineteenth-century Egypt, "Women not infrequently administered both charitable and family *waqfs* as official *nazirahs*," but gives no percentages (Tucker, *Women in Nineteenth-Century Egypt*, 96). In a study that focused on sixteenth-century Istanbul but drew examples from elsewhere, Gabriel Baer found for Palestine that "only 5% of the managers of waqfs established in the Ottoman period and mentioned in the Mandatory *sijill* of Jaffa were women." Baer concluded that women played a smaller role as managers of waqfs than as founders (Gabriel Baer, "Women and Waqf: An Analysis of the Istanbul *Tahrir* of 1546," *Asian and African Studies* 17 (1983): 14ff.).

16. *Anis al-Jalis* 6, no. 11 (1903): 1620–22; *Fatat al-Sharq* 1, no. 1 (1906): 24; *al-Sayyidat wa'l-Banat* 2, no. 8 (1906): 211–15; *Fatat al-Sharq* 6, no. 10 (1912): 366–68; *al-Jins al-Latif* 3, no. 10 (1911): 280–81.

17. Jacob M. Landau, *Jews in Nineteenth-Century Egypt* (New York: New York University Press, 1969), 64–68.

18. Zaynab Anis, "Jam'iyyat al-Shafaqa bi'l-Atfal," *al-Rayhana* 1, no. 1 (20 Mar. 1908): 6–7; M. M., "al-Nahda al-Nisa'iyya fi Misr," *Fatat al-Sharq* 2, no. 6 (1908): 220–23; Fatima Rashid, "Itmam 'Amal Jalil," *Tarqiyat al-Mar'a* 1, no. 5 (1326/1908): 76–77.

19. FO 371/892/11188, Gorst to Grey, Cairo, 26 Mar. 1910, "Annual Report of 1909," p. 34; FO 371/1112/11940, Gorst to Grey, Cairo, 25 Mar. 1911, "Annual Report of 1910," p. 43.

20. Huda Sha'rawi Association Papers (HSAP), American University in Cairo, file 3, Hawwa' Idris, "Hoda Chaaraoui," p. 5; *Fatat al-Sharq* 4, no. 7 (1910): 268; Labiba Hashim, "Jam'iyyat Mabarrat Muhammad 'Ali," *Fatat al-Sharq* 8, no. 5 (1914): 194; Shaarawi, *Harem Years,* 94–96; Emine Foat Tugay, *Three Centuries: Family Chronicles of Turkey and Egypt* (London: Oxford University Press, 1963), 105–9; Afaf Lutfi al-Sayyid Marsot discusses the history of this organization under the direction of Hidiya Barakat in "Revolutionary Gentlewomen."

21. Daisy Griggs Philips, "The Growth of the Egyptian Feminist Movement," *The Moslem World* 21 (1926): 278–79.

22. Grace Thompson Seton, *A Woman Tenderfoot in Egypt* (New York: Dodd and Mead, 1923), 46–49, 13; Marsot, "Revolutionary Gentlewomen," 272; Tugay, *Three Generations,* 105–9.

23. Elizabeth Cooper, *The Women of Egypt* (New York: F. A. Stokes, 1914), 330.

24. Malaka Sa'd, "al-Mashghal al-Butrusi," *al-Jins al-Latif* 4, no. 6 (1911): 163–71; idem, "Ma'rid al-Khayri," *al-Jins al-Latif* 9, no. 7 (1917): 295–96.

25. Cooper, *Women of Egypt,* 239.

26. 'Aziza Fawzi, "Lajnat Sayyidat bi'l-'Abbasiyya," *al-'Afaf* 1, no. 37 (21 Oct. 1911): 5–7.

27. Wataniyya bi'l-Rif (a patriot in the countryside), "Nahdat al-Sayyidat," *al-'Afaf* 1, no. 38 (27 Oct. 1911): 7.

28. Malak Hifni Nasif, *Athar Bahithat al-Badiya,* ed. Majid al-Din Hifni Nasif and intro. Suhayr al-Qalamawi (Cairo: al-Mu'assasa al-Misriyya al-'Amma, 1962), 289; 'Umar Rida Kahhala, *A'lam al-Nisa' fi 'Alamay al-'Arab wa'l-Islam* (Beirut: Mu'assasat al-Risala, 1977), 5:76; see also Ilyas Zakhura, *al-Suriyyun fi Misr* (Cairo: al-Matba'a al-'Arabiyya, 1927), 147.

29. See, e.g., *al-'Afaf* 1, no. 3 (18 Nov. 1910): 4; *al-Jins al-Latif* 10, no. 1 (1917): 25.

30. Tugay, *Three Centuries,* 108–9; Marsot, "Revolutionary Gentlewomen," 271–75.

31. Personal interview with Leila Doss, Cairo, 25 Dec. 1985.

32. Since the government has had difficulty in fulfilling its promise of providing welfare services, private groups have once again stepped into the void. The Muslim Brotherhood has been particularly active in setting up free clinics and other services in poor neighborhoods. See Robert Bianchi, *Unruly Corporatism: Associational Life in Twentieth Century Egypt* (New York: Oxford University Press, 1989), 187–93.

33. Earl L. Sullivan, *Women in Egyptian Public Life* (Syracuse, N.Y.: Syracuse University Press, 1986), 32.

34. On one chapter in this story, women's voluntary activities during the malarial epidemic of the mid-1940s, see Nancy Elizabeth Gallagher, *Egypt's Other Wars: Epidemics and the Politics of Public Health* (Syracuse, N.Y.: Syracuse University Press, 1990), 40–55.

35. Shaarawi, *Harem Years*, 78–80. Eugénie Le Brun wrote *Harem et musulmanes d'Egypte (lettres)* (Paris: Felix Juvens, n.d.) and *Les Repudiées* (Paris: Felix Juvens, 1908) under the pen name Riya Salima.

36. Afaf Lutfi al-Sayyid, *Egypt and Cromer: A Study in Anglo-Egyptian Relations* (New York: Praeger, 1969), 95; Mary Flounders Arnett, "Qasim Amin and the Beginnings of the Feminist Movement in Egypt" (D.Phil. diss., Dropsie College, 1965), 76–79; Yusuf As'ad Daghir, *Masadir al-Dirasat al-Adabiyya* (Beirut: l'Université Libanaise, 1972), 137; Aida Adib, "Mayy Ziyada and her Contribution to Arabic Literature" (M.A. thesis, American University in Cairo, 1966), 105–18.

37. S. S., "Zahrat Misr," *al-Muqtataf* 13, no. 9 (1889): 616–17.

38. Esther Azhari, "Murasalat al-Jihat," *al-Fatah* 1, no. 5 (1893): 233–34; Nadia Farag, "al-Muqtataf, 1876–1900: A Study of the Influence of Victorian Thought on Modern Arabic Thought" (D.Phil. diss., Oxford University, 1969), 49–50.

39. Fatima Rashid, "Jam'iyyat Tarqiyat al-Mar'a," *Tarqiyat al-Mar'a* 1, no. 1 (1326/1908): 3–6; idem, "Awwal Thamara," *Tarqiyat al-Mar'a* 1, no. 5 (1326/1908): 77; Yunan Labib Rizq, *Sihafat al-Hizb al-Watani, 1907–1912* (Cairo: al-Hay'a al-Misriyya al-'Amma li'l-Kitab, 1985), 98–109, 220–32.

40. See Deniz Kandiyoti, "Islam and Patriarchy: A Comparative Perspective," in *Women in Middle Eastern History*, ed. Keddie and Baron, 23–42, esp. 27.

41. Fatima Rashid, "Khutba Khitamiyya," *Tarqiyat al-Mar'a* 1, no. 12 (1327/1909): 177–79.

42. Fatima Rashid, "al-Mar'a al-Muslima," *al-Rayhana* 1, no. 1 (20 Mar. 1908): 4.

43. Lists of the names of members appeared scattered throughout vol. 1 of *Tarqiyat al-Mar'a* (1326–27/1908–9); Rashid, "Khutba Khitamiyya," 178; Rizq, *Sihafat al-Hizb al-Watani,* 224–25.
44. *Al-'Afaf* 1, no. 26 (12 May 1911): 14.
45. *Al-'Afaf* 1, no. 27 (19 May 1911): 14.
46. Sulayman al-Salimi, "Didd al-'Afaf," *al-'Afaf* 1, no. 28 (29 May 1911): 14; compare frontispieces from *al-'Afaf* 1, no. 26 (12 May 1911) and *al-'Afaf* 1, no. 29 (9 June 1911).
47. Cooper, *Women of Egypt,* 239.
48. Zakiya al-Kafrawiyya, "Jam'iyya li-Tahsin al-Azya'," *al-'Afaf* 1, no. 26 (12 May 1911): 13–14.
49. Labiba Hashim, "al-Nahda al-Nisa'iyya fi Misr," *Fatat al-Sharq* 8, no. 5 (1914): 183–88. Henriette Devonshire wrote on Islamic architecture in Egypt among other topics. See, e.g., Mme R. L. Devonshire, *L'Egypte Musulmane et les fondateurs de ses monuments* (Paris: Librairie Orientale et Americaine, 1926); for a portrait, see *L'Egyptienne* 7, no. 66 (1931).
50. Hashim, "al-Nahda al-Nisa'iyya," 183–88; Haram 'Abd al-Sattar Bey al-Basil [Malak Hifni Nasif], "Jam'iyyat Ittihad al-Sayyidat," *al-'Afaf* 2, no. 52 (9 Feb. 1914): 7; Bahithat al-Badiya [Malak Hifni Nasif], *al-'Afaf* 2, no. 53 (27 Feb. 1914): 7; "Jam'iyyat Ittihad al-Nisa' al-Tahdhibi," *al-'Afaf* 2, no. 54 (11 Mar. 1914); Bahithat al-Badiya, "Ta'thir al-Mar'a fi'l-'Alam," *Fatat al-Sharq* 8, no. 6 (1914): 221–31; idem, "Ta'thir al-Mar'a fi'l-'Alam," *al-Jins al-Latif* 6, no. 10 (1914): 272.
51. Hashim, "al-Nahda al-Nisa'iyya," 185.
52. HSAP, file 3, Hawwa' Idris, "Huda Sha'rawi, Ibnat 'Ammati," p. 1; Sarah al-Mihiyya, "Jam'iyyat al-Ruqiyy al-Adabi li'l-Sayyidat al-Misriyyat," *Fatat al-Nil* 1, no. 6 (1332/1914): 215–16; Labiba Hashim, "Jam'iyyat al-Ruqiyy al-Adabi li'l-Sayyidat al-Misriyyat," *Fatat al-Sharq* 8, no. 8 (1914): 310–12; Widad Muhsani, "al-Nahda al-Nisa'iyya," *Fatat Lubnan* 1, no. 6 (1914): 125–27; Huda Sha'rawi, *Mudhakkirat Huda Sha'rawi* (Cairo: Dar al-Hilal, n.d.), 131–32; Shaarawi, *Harem Years,* 98–100.
53. On the passing of these societies, see al-Misriyya (the Egyptian), "Majalis al-Sayyidat," *al-Sufur* 1, no. 34 (21 Jan. 1916): 2–3; idem, "al-'Awda ila al-Qahira," *al-Sufur* 2, no. 79 (8 Dec. 1916): 3–4.
54. Fatima 'Asim, "Jam'iyyat al-Nahda al-Nisa'iyya," *Fatat al-Sharq* 11, no. 5 (1916): 219–20.
55. "Ama Hana la-ki al-Waqt," *al-Jins al-Latif* 10, no. 9 (1918): 228.

56. Dawlat Hanim 'Ismat Bey, "Khutba," *Tarqiyat al-Mar'a* 1, no. 1 (1326/ 1908): 13.

57. Bruce M. Borthwick, "The Islamic Sermon as a Channel of Political Communication," *The Middle East Journal* 21 (1967): 300, 303–4, 312; Patrick Daniel Gaffney, "The Islamic Preacher: His Role in the Mosque and the Community," *American Research Center in Egypt Newsletter*, no. 110 (1979): 3–13.

58. Malak Hifni Nasif asked that women be allowed to attend Friday prayers at the mosque when she submitted proposals to the Egyptian congress of 1911. *Minutes of the Proceedings of the First Egyptian Congress* (Alexandria: Imprimerie d'Alexandrie, 1911), 114. For more on this, see below.

59. See vol. 1 of *Tarqiyat al-Mar'a* (1326–27/1908–9).

60. See, e.g., Labiba Hashim, "Ta'thir al-'Ilm al-Sahih," *Fatat al-Sharq* 2, no. 2 (1907): 44–48; idem, "Ta'lim al-Banat," *Fatat al-Sharq* 5, no. 2 (1910): 44–52; idem, "Muhammad Pasha Muhibb," and "Ta'awun," *Fatat al-Sharq* 6, no. 10 (1912): 366–84; idem, *al-Ta'awun* (Cairo: Matba'at al-Ma'arif, 1912).

61. See, e.g., Malaka Sa'd, "al-Mashghal al-Butrusi"; Olivia 'Abd al-Shahid, "Khutba," *al-Jins al-Latif* 5, no. 8 (1913): 275–80; idem, "al-Mar'a al-Misriyya," *Fatat al-Sharq* 8, no. 5 (1914): 173–82; idem, "al-Mar'a al-Misriyya," *al-Jins al-Latif* 6, no. 9 (1914): 256–62.

62. See, e.g., "Khutbat Amina Hanim Namazi," *al-'Afaf* 1, no. 38 (27 Oct. 1911): 5–6.

63. Malaka Sa'd, "Bad' al-Hayah," *al-Jins al-Latif* 2, no. 2 (1909): 33–53; Rashid Rida, "Khutbat Khatiba Misriyya 'ala al-Nisa'," *al-Manar* 12, no. 5 (1909): 353–71; Bahithat al-Badiya [Malak Hifni Nasif], *al-Nisa'iyyat* (Cairo: Matba'at al-Jarida, 1910), 95; *Athar Bahithat al-Badiya*, 20; Charlotte Cameron, *A Woman's Winter in Africa* (London: Stanley Paul, 1913), 42.

64. *First Egyptian Congress*, 113–18; FO 371/1113/18097, Cheetham to Grey, Cairo, 6 May 1911; Charles C. Adams, *Islam and Modernism in Egypt: A Study of the Modern Reform Movement Inaugurated by Muhammad 'Abduh* (London: Oxford University Press, 1933), 235–39; *Encyclopaedia of Islam*, 2d ed. (Leiden: E. J. Brill, 1991), s.v. "Malak Hifni Nasif"; Soha Abdel Kader, *Egyptian Women in a Changing Society, 1899–1987* (Boulder, Colo.: Lynne Rienner, 1988), 67.

65. *First Egyptian Congress*, 292–95; FO 371/1113/18097, Cheetham to Grey, Cairo, 6 May 1911.

66. *First Egyptian Congress*, 288–91.

67. *Al-'Afaf* 1, no. 26 (12 May 1911): 14.

68. M. Y. Hanim Sabri, "Muhadatha," *al-Rayhana* 1, no. 3 (1325/1907): 76.

69. Haggai Erlich, *Students and University in Twentieth Century Egyptian Politics* (London: Frank Cass, 1989), 9–45; Donald M. Reid, "Educational and Career Choices of Egyptian Students, 1882–1922," *International Journal of Middle East Studies* 8 (1977): 379–404.

70. Egypt, Dar al-Watha'iq al-Qawmiyya (National Archives, DW), Muhafiz 'Abdin, Ta'lim 237, Poster, "Université Egyptienne," Cairo, 1911–1912; Donald Malcolm Reid, *Cairo University and the Making of Modern Egypt* (Cambridge: Cambridge University Press, 1990), 51–56.

71. Zakiya al-Kafrawiyya, "Taj al-Mar'a," *al-'Afaf* 1, no. 22 (7 Apr. 1911): 1; idem, "Muhadatha Tilifuniyya," *al-'Afaf* 1, no. 25 (5 May 1911): 6; Malaka Sa'd, "al-Jami'a al-Misriyya," *al-Jins al-Latif* 3, no. 10 (1911): 281–82; "Khutab al-Sayyidat fi'l-Jami'a," *al-Muqtataf* 38, no. 3 (1911): 287.

72. Jurji Niqula Baz, "Sahibat Fatat al-Sharq fi'l-Jami'a al-Misriyya," *al-Hasna'* 2, no. 7 (1911): 330; Labiba Hashim, "al-Tarbiya," *Fatat al-Sharq* 5, no. 5 (1911): 169–84, and throughout vol. 5; idem, *Kitab fi'l-Tarbiya* (Cairo: Matba'at al-Ma'arif, 1911); *Fatat al-Sharq* 8, no. 2 (1913): 69.

73. FO 371/661/12738, Gorst to Grey, Cairo, 27 Mar. 1909, "Annual Report of 1908," p. 44; FO 371/1112/11940, Gorst, "Annual Report of 1910," p. 58.

74. 'Abd al-Mun'im al-Dissuqi al-Jami'i, *al-Jami'a al-Misriyya al-Qadima, Nash'atuha wa-Dawruha fi'l-Mujtama', 1908–1925* (Cairo: Dar al-Kitab al-Jami'a, 1908), 47–48; Erlich, *Students and University,* 38–39; Reid, *Cairo University,* 55–56.

75. FO 141/745/8900, Office of the Public Custodian to War, Trade and Licensing Office, re: "Daira Princess Fatma Hanem Ismail," Cairo, 22 Mar. 1919; FO 141/745/8900, Mohamed Djemaleddin to Allenby, Cairo, 26 Nov. 1920; Erlich, *Students and University,* 29.

76. Malaka Sa'd, "Haflat Ta'bin Bahithat al-Badiya," *al-Jins al-Latif* 12, no. 2 (1919): 53–54.

77. See chap. 1, n.100.

78. See Bahija Sidqi Rashid et al., *al-Ittihad al-Nisa'i al-Misri* (Cairo: Dar Ma'mun, n.d.).

79. Cynthia Nelson, "Biography and Women's History: On Interpreting Doria Shafik," in *Women in Middle Eastern History,* ed. Keddie and Baron, 310–33; Selma Botman, "The Experience of Women in the Egyptian Communist

Movement, 1939–1954," *Women's Studies International Forum* 11 (1988): 117–26; Valerie J. Hoffman, "An Islamic Activist: Zaynab al-Ghazali," in *Women and the Family in the Middle East: New Voices of Change,* ed. Elizabeth Warnock Fernea (Austin: University of Texas Press, 1985): 233–54.

80. Sullivan, *Women in Public Life,* 45.

INDEX

Index

Index
❧❧❧

Index

Index

Women's journals, 1–9, 13–14, 55–57, 99–100, 188–93; advertising in, 69, 94; agents for, 69–70, 72, 94; and associations, 169; attrition rate of, 78; audience of, 66; back issues of, 71–72, 88; banners of, 63; bilingual, 22, 23, 24; birth of, 14–16; camaraderie between, 75–78; on childraising, 163; circulation of, 91; competition between, 75–78; consumption of, 8; contents of, 64–67; cost of producing, 67–68; covers of, 62; distribution of, 93; domestic ideology in, 166–67; drawings for, 62; editors of, 64–65, 67, 96–97; foreign influences and borrowings in, 60–61, 65; funding of, 67–71; genres in, 54; on girls' education, 124–25, 137–43; on health care, 159–60; interconnectedness of, 37; longevity of, 78; male contributors to, 95; medical advice in, 163; monthly, 63; new journals, 75–76; offices of, 71; opponents of, 48–49; photographs in, 66; pricing of, 74, 93–94, 220n71; prizes by, 64; production of, 8, 58–59, 79; pseudonyms in, 43, 45–48, 56, 96; publishing on schedule by, 96; readers of, 65, 93–99; running operation of, 71–74; self-images of writers, 119–20; on servants, 154–55; on sewing, 158; social contexts of, 9; solicitation of contributions to, 64–65; subscriptions to, 68, 69–70, 93–94, 96; titles of, 62–63, 76; Turkish, 61; on wage work, 146–

49, 166–67; on wet nurses, 161. *See also specific titles*
Women's periodicals, 60–61, 76–77. *See also* Women's journals
Women writers. *See specific writers;* Womens' journals
Working conditions, 151–55
Working women. *See* Wage work
World Columbian Exposition, 20
World War I, 34, 70, 78
Writers' associations, 44
Writing, 39–43, 41, 43–44, 56–57, 75

al-Yaziji, Warda, 51, 77, 98
Yaziji clan, 26
Young Turk revolution of *1908,* 21, 61, 108
Youth, literacy among, 82–83
Youth, theme of, 62, 63
Yusuf, Shaykh 'Ali, 25, 44

Zaghlul, Sa'd, 19, 20, 33, 35, 138, 139, 170
al-Zahawi, Jamil Sidqi, 77
al-Zahra. *See* 'Abd al-Shahid, Olivia
al-Zahra (The flower), 22
"Zahra," girls' school of, 134
Zahrat Misr (Flower of Egypt), 176
Zar, 34, 112
Zaydan, Jurji, 16, 73, 77, 86, 87, 106, 206n38
Zaynab (Haykal), 44–45, 52
Ziyada, Mayy, 176, 179, 185
Zola, Emile, 21, 200n37
al-Zuhur, 86